Dead

Dead Man Running

From Alcohol to Atacama

Billy Isherwood

Dead Man Running

Spiderwize
Mews Cottage
The Causeway, Kennoway
Kingdom of Fife
KY8 5JU
Scotland UK

www.spiderwize.com

ISBN: 978-1-907294-34-1

This book is dedicated to my children
Hayley, Billy and Bethany Isherwood.

Who I wish I could have given more too,
but gave all I had.

My love for you all is forever in my heart
Dad xxx

CONTENTS

ACKNOWLEDGMENTS

How does one say thank you and acknowledge the special people and friends who helped me, not only in the writing of this book but also by encouraging me along the journey that one day I hope will lead to full recovery.

If I had to name them all it would warrant another book. However in the preparation of this book a special thank you goes out to Gill Dalliday, Alex Fredman (Whitby Gazette), Heather Metcalfe, plus Bridget and Beth Wilkinson who gave up their time and offered their advice on how to proceed in the writing of this book

There are now those who helped me to prepare for the Atacama desert marathon and not only helped me to train but also showed concern and gave encouragement whenever I went back on the bottle to gain sobriety again.

My journey began at the Fitness Machine Gym (Whitby) with Harry the proprietor who was always there with a cup of coffee and an ear when I needed it.

The training team, which are Claire Fowler who pushed me and trusted in my abilities to prepare for the Atacama Desert Marathon.

Ian Carr who supported and treated any of my sports injuries and Denise Taylor who ran along side me in a sponsored full marathon around Whitby whilst in training for the Atacama.

There are those who would not thank me if I mentioned their names on helping me financially to make this dream come true

Thank you!

A special thank you to those who I can name who helped me financially who are Pastor David Nellist and the congregation of the Maranatha Church.

Jack & Megan Barber a young couple saving up for their future together who gave me a sum of money that went beyond my wildest expectations.

Last but by no means least my partner Bridget who believed in me when other didn't, her love, dedication and support without which, my dream could not have been possible.

This is a true story of a boy born in the Lancashire mill town of Farnworth near Bolton in 1951. Who from day one had to survive a childhood that knew only extreme poverty, violence and the mental torture of being kept a prisoner in his own home, which eventually led him into a world of alcohol and drug abuse

That boy was me

and this is my story

INTRODUCTION

If you are looking for a book that's grammatically correct, full of wonderful descriptive scenes and William Wordsworth jargon, then put this back on shelf. On the other hand, if you are wanting to read 'summat bout bloody life' with all its ups and downs, told in layman's terms. Then look no further cos it doesn't get any simpler than this book.

I was born in the same area as the great Bolton steeplejack, Fred Dibnah, so, to pinch one of his phrases "Aye, they had it bloody hard in them days".

Whilst writing this book, I have made every effort to tell my story like I would to any person sat opposite me in a bar. Having had only the basic education, I left school with no certificates or qualifications to my name; in fact I was in the lowest stream possible at my secondary school, George Tomlinson in Kearsley, Lancashire. My dad would remark that if I got any lower I would be under the floorboards. I received all kind of well meaning advice about how I should present my book in a literature readable story, which I chose to ignore and make no apologies for this.

To quote Del Boy from the TV sitcom 'Only Fools and Horses': "They don't speak proper English like what we do".

I was born in the mill town of Farnworth, near Bolton in 1951. I was one of nine children. I made my entrance into a home that knew only poverty, and violence. We had no choice but to wear clothes that sometimes my mother would beg from the rag and bone man's cart. Our feet were often covered with socks that were nothing more than sewn up holes. Also, come winter and summer, we wore wellies.

There used to be a joke going around when I was a kid, it went like this:

'Them buggers are that poor that when they come outside the house, the pigeons throw bread at them.'

Well, that just about summed our family up.

We were never allowed out to play but would have to sit in silence for hours upon hours listening to other kids playing outside instead. Often we would get beaten by our dad, for no apparent reason except the fact that we should 'never have been born' and told we were just 'Saturday night piss ups'. There was never enough for us all to eat and it was hard trying to keep warm in the winter when we had no coal to burn. Added together, all this made life unbearable.

For thirty years and more, I struggled with my alcoholism and drug abuse, written off eventually by the medical profession with the words that I would either be dead in a few years before I reached the age of 50 or would end up committing suicide. Not that I took any notice of them or their advice.

To quote Del Boy again, "There is no-one more deaf than them that won't listen"

Well that just about sums me up; even today I have a problem with listening and prefer the Lancashire saying, "It'll be reet"

Life for me began when I discovered booze; I say that because I learned so much from the people I met in the bars of my home town in Farnworth: The Saddle, Rose and Crown, Smokey Joe's (Three Crowns), The Queen's, The Post Office, The Wellington, The Freemason's, The Black Horse, The Bridgewater, and the Market Inn. I learned how to handle being wound up, 'cos that's what the lads did to one another in the pubs. For instance if your girlfriend split up with you, then you had to get used to the ribbing about which one of your mates was gonna set about 'screwing' her next. Always a hard one that, but you had to learn to take it on the chin and laugh along with them 'cos if you bit they would make your life hell, but all done with a sense of camaraderie.

I also learnt how to stick up for myself, that was hard 'cos I spent my childhood and school years being beaten and bullied. I wanted to run with the gang and we all relied on each other in fights, so just knowing I could dish it out as well as take it was a big buzz for me. I also learnt that some of my mates had also had a hard violent upbringing, and we just had to 'Get on wi' it'.

If we weren't getting 'pissed' in the bars around Farnworth, then we would meet at the bus station, gather a gang together and go to Little Hulton to fight with the local Crombie boys down there. The Farnworth boys had, and always will have, a reputation for being hard around the Bolton area. If we weren't scrapping down there, we would be 'tooling up' for the home game football matches at Bolton Wanderers. We had our own little section in the Lever End amongst the Bolton fans where we were ready to exchange punches with the visiting fans. We would be really psyched up if we had the big names coming down, especially Manchester United, that's when you earned your colors. I knocked about with the Crombie boys of

Farnworth who wore ice blue sweaters or socks, the little Hultoners wore red. After a game we would make our way back to Farnworth, getting 'pissed' along the way, all the time laughing and sharing stories of the punch-ups we'd had.

The booze was a great life, was fun. I didn't think it could get any better, that is until the day I was introduced to drugs, then it became a new ball game, but enough said. It's all in the book, so read on.

He who dares wins and he who doesn't don't, Del Boy

CHAPTER 1

On your marks get set
Hang on a minute I'm not ready yet
I know I'm geared up and should be ready to run
But I'm trapped in my past and it wasn't much fun
Yet this is the place to confront my demons face to face
So on your marks get set, let's start the race.

The Desert

It was getting difficult for me to focus in the distance and differentiate between the glow-sticks that enabled us to follow the desert course and the stars in the sky. Though it was only 6pm the night fell quickly onto the bleak desert, followed as quickly by the rapid drop in temperature. I was completely taken by surprise. One minute I was jogging along in the sun, listening to the music on my I Pod, the next I was frantically searching in my backpack for the equipment I needed to keep me safe and warm in this hostile environment. Never have I experienced such a dramatic climate change from day to night.

We had been warned at the course briefing, held each morning, that this would happen and that we should make sure we knew exactly where we had placed things in our backpacks. I have a problem with listening! Even though I heard what was said my attitude has always *been 'Yeah, it'll be reet'* a Lancashire answer to everything and one I may add, that has stood me in good stead. But at that moment I could have kicked myself!

After finding and putting on my jacket, hat, and thermal gloves, and switching on my night light worn like a miner's lamp over the top of your head, I tried to settle back into my pace and keep on course, running for a few minutes and then walking. This was proving difficult as I had to keep the light pointing down towards my feet in case I fell over something. The ground had some nasty rocks just waiting to do some damage to my already mashed-up feet. When I pointed the light down to protect my footing then I was unable to see where I was going it was a no win situation.

This desert terrain was, to say the least, unpredictable; one minute rocky then next mountainous sand dunes. You could find yourself crossing a river, or maybe climbing over sharp rocky ridges, or negotiating your way through the freezing slot canyons, or - the worst of the worst - the dreaded salt flats that resembled white coral, parts crunchy with each step and parts unresisting to your feet.

Each morning found me, along with some of the other early risers, fighting to get near the camp fire to get at least a fragment of heat on my tired body. I put that down to the sleepless night I experienced due to the freezing conditions huddled up in my sleeping bag trying to seek warmth.

Each night found me running along on my own. The feeling of being alone in the desert with only my thoughts and music for company is one I cannot describe except it was lonely and became heightened more as the night wore on. Out there in the desert, surrounded by the orange snow-tipped Andes mountains and high-rising sand dunes, that feeling of being the only person on the planet, made me feel vulnerable and gave me all kinds of paranoid thoughts. What if I injure myself? Have I enough water to last me to the next checkpoint? What if my night-light packs in out here, in the totally black, below-freezing desert? Or, the biggest one of all, what if I get lost? Which I did, several times!

The first time I got lost was after I had just passed through an open air patio of a little restaurant. I remember thinking how strange it was to see a restaurant here. I was to find out later that a lot of tourists came out here to camp and experience the sights and environment of living in a desert. It's obvious really for the locals to jump on the tourist trade and build a restaurant. I'd been following the red markers which marked our route. They had led me along a fast-flowing river which I had to cross several times in order to get passed some obstruction or other. The next minute found me running up a steep rocky path and on reaching the top I found I was passing through the outside of a restaurant surrounded by tables and chairs. These were shaded by a bamboo roof and the place was totally empty. I ran on following the course, when suddenly I lost sight of the red flags. We had been warned that if we could not see any then we were off the course and to retrace our steps back to the last marker and to look around "cos they were there, somewhere". But I'd been running along listening to the sounds coming from my headphones when it dawned on me that I couldn't see any flags, I'd been lost in my thoughts and music. I didn't know how long I'd been running off course. I remember stopping and thinking what do I do? Just imagine it if you can, I didn't know how far I had drifted off course, there was no-one around to ask, nor did I know if the markers were further ahead or behind me I pulled up and took off my headphones and just stood there in awe, staring at the mountains and the desert that surrounded me. I had to make a decision; either to press on or retrace my steps which could mean going back a couple of miles. I just didn't know. The enormity of what to do was agonizing. If I go back only to find out I was going in the right direction all along then that would be a 'ball-breaker', but on the other hand, if I continued and found out I was going in the wrong direction, then I'd be further off the course. Added to this was the fact that we had to make a certain check point (CP) in a given time and failing to do this would result in a DNF (did not finish). Getting a DNF meant no medal even if you continued on to complete the course, which some poor sods did. Eventually I decided to go back.

My mind was racing. Here I was running back across ground I had already covered and what if the markers where further behind me *"What a load of bollocks"* I thought, and then suddenly, in the distance, I saw a load of dust heading my way. It turned out to be a search and rescue jeep, driven by the American marshals who were responsible for the well-being of the competitors. I was greeted by a *"You're off the fuckin' course"*, said in a nice manner. I replied in a not so nice manner, *"Where's the fuckin' markers then?"*

"Get in the back of the truck and we'll take you back to where you strayed from the markers", said my rescuer. I was running in the wrong direction after all. It had to be my fault, I do have a selective brain that only sees what it wants to see, but if I thought that little episode was bad, it was nothing compared to really getting lost - that lay ahead of me and had I known this at the time I may have packed it all in.

Being out there, alone at night in the desert, suffering from fatigue and mental stress, it's funny how your mind can play tricks on you, with all kinds of paranoid thoughts running through your head, and ever-increasing tiredness. Every so often, I thought there were other runners in front of me, and I could see shadows. I would remove my headphones to call out to them, only to be greeted by deafening, black, freezing silence, scary. Desperately I would look ahead again at the glow-sticks (which replaced the red markers used during the day) and then put my head down and make what I thought was a bee-line for them, only to find I had run off the course. This, we were told, was a definite no-no. Under no circumstances must you wander off the course for the desert hides many snares. Obvious advice but, like I've already said, sometimes my eyes played tricks on me, and I was following the night stars instead of the glow-sticks, talk about chasing rainbows!, Eventually, I got into the habit of going up to some of the glow-sticks and touching them, just to make sure they were real and I was indeed on the right track.

This was my first night alone in the desert. What I didn't know was, it would not be my last. In fact, I was to experience four more nights running/walking with only myself and my iPod for company.

Welcome to the Atacama Desert Marathon!

CHAPTER 2

All my bags are packed I'm ready to go
The adrenalin pumping and I'm smoking more
I feel like an astronaut getting ready to take off
I'm scared inside but all you see is my laugh

Journey's End

Look, you can see the desert I heard someone say, as the plane started its descent to land at Calama Airport in Chile. I turned my head wearily towards the plane's window to take a look, and what my eyes focused on looked quite daunting. Mile after mile of dark, brown-colored sand, as far as the eye could see, surrounded by the jagged, orange-colored snow-tipped mountainous Andes invaded my tired brain. It was difficult to take it all in. The plane that was flying me to my final destination was also carrying other fellow competitors. The whole scenario became too much for me; I was both physically and mentally drained. It must have been well over 36 hours since I had kissed Bridget goodbye at York Railway Station and I was all in.

"Here's your passport, and all your currency and I've written out an itinerary for you." I smiled inwardly at my partner Bridget. What would I do without her? She had put down all the information I needed whilst I was away, even down to how much I had to pay the cab driver once I landed in Calama, Chile.

"His name is Franco." He will be waiting for you at the airport, holding a card with your name on it. You are to pay him 14,000 pesos." Marvels of the internet eh!!!

Even while she was telling me, I was already reading the itinerary she had typed for me the night before. Yes, it was all there. The next day, I read, is a rest day. Take it easy! Relax! You know you can do it! The last piece she put in was, The Eagle Has Landed! Bless her! Remember, keep these flight tickets safe, as well as your passport. *"It'll be reet"* I told her, reverting back to my Lancashire accent and one that the great Bolton comedian, Peter Kay, has immortalized.

The order came over the tannoy on the plane to fasten your seat belts. At last, I thought I've made it. Finally we touched down and the 36 hour long journey was over, but the big one was waiting. Grabbing my backpack, I descended down the plane's steps. Walking towards a small building with an Arrivals sign over it, I looked back at the plane and was surprised to see it had pulled up just off the runway and the tarmac was free of sand. I wondered how they managed to keep the sand off it considering that we were in the middle of a desert. All around me that's all I could see, an airport built in the middle of a sea/sand and mountains.

The Arrivals Lounge at Calama Airport was a hive of activity. All around me were other competitors picking up their luggage and (like me, I suspect) eyeing each other up. My backpack looked the biggest and the heaviest, and once again - not for the first time - a feeling of panic and doubt on my ability to run and complete a desert marathon attacked my innermost being.

It's funny how the mind conjures up things. I thought I'd have a taxi all by myself to drive me to San Pedro but I could not have been more wrong! The taxi driver squeezed as many runners into his taxi as possible. I suddenly realized this tiny airport was, of course, in the middle of the desert so he was hardly likely to just take me.

The drive to San Pedro was very scenic. In the distance we could see the snow-tipped mountains of the Andes. On the journey I thought that we would be passing through towns and villages but I was to be disappointed. Pity really, as I so much wanted to see the local people and their culture on this drive. But we were in a desert so there were mountainous sand dunes on either side of the road, and every now and then the driver would point out some volcano, or an archaeological place of interest but it was all wasted on me. I was beginning to hallucinate (and not on L.S.D.) and everything around me seemed unreal and distorted. I was definitely wasted.

It was getting dark as we approached the town of San Pedro. The taxi driver began to drop the others off at their located hotels and I was one of the last to be dropped off at mine. I was so tired I just wanted my room key, and throw my backpack down and myself onto a bed.

Things didn't go smoothly at the hotel that Bridget had booked for me on the internet. Apparently I wasn't expected; in fact they had not even heard of me. I stood waiting for over an hour as a Chilean man made some desperate phone calls in Spanish before he eventually smiled and, nodding his head at me in a 'yes' gesture, grabbed my bag and arm and literally took me to my room.

Once inside, the room consisted of two beds, and a separate bathroom/shower and toilet. It was bloody freezing in there. I threw my bag down on the bed. The taxi had passed through the main centre of the town on arrival and it was about 9pm. I realized that I was hungry so I decided to go out, have a look around and buy some food. No matter what, whenever I go to somewhere new I want to explore so, even though I was all in, like a little boy full of adventure, I went out.

I noticed as I walked through the main street that there were no street lamps, so the town was lit only up by the local shops. There were also a lot of dogs freely roaming around popping in and out of shops and, even though the shops were open, the town seemed deserted except for a group of men leaning against a wall, smoking and chatting noisily away. I remember thinking as I passed them, "its suddenly gone quiet". It was all so surreal to me. I didn't wander far; tomorrow would be a day to explore but right now I wanted something to eat. I eventually went into a small dusty shop to be greeted by a large Mexican-looking man wearing a poncho. I expected to be greeted by a *"Hey Gringo, you want tequila?"* But he smiled and said in *English "Hallo, what would you like to buy?"* Looking around, I saw two other large poncho-wearing men picking their teeth, and yes, as they smiled at me; one man was missing his front teeth. I smiled inwardly and resisted the urge to throw my poncho (had I been wearing one) over my shoulder to reveal my gun. It was a typical grocer shop, so I bought two very large tomatoes, some meaty looking sausage, two large packets of crisps and a coke, paid, said *"Chow"* and left.

Once back at the hotel room, I unpacked the food out of the bag to realize, to my horror; I had left the sausage on the counter. The reason for this was that the man who served me had taken me over to another counter to show me his sausage (know what I mean?). There, on display hanging from hooks, were a variety of all different sizes and flavors but, not understanding what the flavors were, I just chose the biggest meatiest-looking one - and I had left the bloody thing behind. I was really hungry by now; only one thing for it, I had to go back to the saloon. I pictured myself strapping on my gun and holster, rolling a cigarette and moseying on down there.

I was greeted once back at the shop with the big Mexican looking shopkeeper holding my sausages with a huge smile on his face shaking his head at me in a friendly gesture which stripped me of my Clint Eastwood image.

Having eventually got back to the room and eaten, I crawled thankfully into my bed. The night was very cold but I already knew that over here, even though the days were very hot, the temperature dropped dramatically as night-time fell. Also, the heaters that were in the room were turned off. Thankfully, there were two very thick blankets on my bed. Usually it takes a while for me to drop off but, after traveling for over 36 hours, I went off like a light.

San Pedro is about 8,000ft above sea level and the race was to begin at 14,000ft. Having never been more than three floors above sea level, I had no experience of altitude sickness before coming here. I had read everything about what to expect regarding altitude sickness but that morning it was lost somewhere at the back of my mind.

I could hear the cocks crowing as I stirred in my bed, stretching out and giving a big yawn. I was greeted with a "Good morning!" Looking up, I saw another competitor laid in the single bed next to mine - and forgive me, room mate, if you are reading this, but I have forgotten your name! I knew before I arrived that I would have to share a room with someone, which disappointed me. I snore, so I'm told, quite loudly and I would have preferred to have been on my own, and not felt guilty at keeping someone awake with my Pavarotti snoring opera. If I had kept him awake, he didn't say anything. He turned out to be very helpful. He had already taken part in one of the desert runs, so I considered him to be a veteran and questioned him relentlessly on what to expect. He also helped me downsize my backpack by discarding some of my food and electrolytes. "You won't be needing all this", he told me, "remember you have six days humping this across the desert and it doesn't get any lighter. Even as you eat the food each day, you still feel the weight". After he had finished, my pack weighed in at 30 pounds and was reported as one of the heaviest.

Having arrived the night before in San Pedro, I would only have today to look around before we were all taken out to start the race the next day. So, after eating my breakfast in the hotel, I was keen to take a look at this little desert town.

Whilst sorting out my backpack, I became aware that I was breathing faster than normal and also feeling a bit light-headed. I went into the shower and switched on the cold water tap. I love having cold showers. For me, it's better than coffee as it certainly wakes me up and kicks my brain into gear. Waking up somewhat under the cold water treatment, I turned on the hot water to soap myself. Suddenly the room was spinning and I felt myself falling backward. I reached out and grabbed the shower curtain as I fell. The next minute found me laid flat on my back, clutching the shower curtain rail in one hand and the shower head in the other. My new-found room mate shouted through the bathroom door asking, "What's happened?" I replied, "I fell over because I went all dizzy and have ended up falling flat on my back and have pulled all the shower curtains/rail and taps down with me as I tried to brake my fall." I was afraid to move, wondering whether I had done any damage to my back and whether for me the Marathon would be over before it had begun. My room mate then said, "Does that mean I won't be able to take a shower?" Through the pain in my back and gritted teeth, I sarcastically replied, "Wait a minute and I'll give you one".

As I walked around it, the town of San Pedro reminded me like one out of them old cowboy films - you know the kind? A dusty main road with ram shackled buildings on either side. I had an image of Clint Eastwood walking down with one of those Mexican ponchos slung across his shoulders and I noticed that several locals were wearing them. The town itself was quite pleasant as was the locals. I walked into a little old café and met a fellow competitor; he was an American, very friendly and helpful. I told him about my experience that morning in the shower, and that I was still feeling disorientated and that my heart and breathing was quite heavy. He smiled and suggested I drink some local coke tea (cocaine) he explained that it would help me with my breathing, he also warned me not to drink to much though or I would be running like Steve McQueen in the film Papillion, you know were he escapes in Papa New Guiana with a fellow prisoner and they start munching on the coco leaves to give them energy. I took his advice and had a couple of cups and it seemed to help for a short while. I remember after leaving the café and my new found friend I found myself walking around the town completely spaced out. Everything reminded me of what its like when your tripping out on acid completely disorientated, and not real its like I was inside myself looking out, I was used to being outta my head thru past experience so I just rode it until it became the norm, I knew it would pass.

CHAPTER 3

A HAUNTED CHILDHOOD

Take me back to the years that still haunt me
Like the cuckoo in a clock
Forever springing out
Until no more

To Number 4 Paxton Place, that old terraced house
Sat miserable in a cobbled cul-de-sac street
Whose four walls became the prisoner of children
Inside it's spirit wept filthy and bleeding
Until no more

Let me look once again into its backyard
With the outside toilet, smelly, decorated by cut squared
newspaper, stuck onto a nail
Without a light, dark cold and bleak
Except for the rays that found their way in
Through the old rotten door along with the rats
Until no more

Let me walk around its empty yard
And touch the tin bath hanging there on the wall
Waiting for Sunday the weekly scrub
And smell the green carbolic soap
Applied to our skin with a scrubbing brush and a smack for
being dirty
Until no more

I want to walk up to the backyard door
Like inside painted black and remove the bolt that was forever on
To look outside so I can see what I can hear
Barking dogs, the gossipy women as they hang out the washing
Or walk up to the rag and bone man's horse
And stroke it so I can get rid of that feeling of fear
Until no more
Let me stand inside the bedroom with its two beds
One for my parents the other for me and my brother
Huddled under an old army coat to keep warm
Listening fascinated by the moans and springs of the bed
Along with the alcoholic fumes and urine from the potty Day in
day out
Until no more

Let me walk once again into my sisters' bedroom
And look at the brown damp colored circles on the walls
And make faces out of them like we used to as if gazing at
clouds
And listen to the stories they would tell one another in whispers
Under their worn out blankets and once again wonder
How six of them managed to sleep in that bed
Until no more

Take me back once again inside its walls
I want to stand in the living room with its worn out sofa
And rocking chair and the old wooden kitchen chair
Where we sat in silence listening to the ticking clock
Staring at the black hearth fireplace starved of coal
I want to look at the threadbare carpet that has lost its pattern
Like us kids, worn out
Until no more

Let me hold once again the belt that would have us dancing
around the room
Holding our backs and legs and burn it
Or maybe keep it along with the memories that have made me
who I am
I see that terraced house weeping for playing a part
Of torture yet happy as its walls are torn down
Forever no more

I want to be able to comfort my mam as she packs clothes into a bag
For us kids to take to the rag man to get weighed for money
As she weepily hands us a note to take to the shop
Saying "Get what you can of this list but make sure you get
bread and jam
Forget those bloody cigs"
I want to catch up to those kids taking clothes they needed
And give them some money as they walk down the road
Wearing wellies, fear of the bullies waiting for them
Near the rag yard and say
Enough no more

I want to go back to the beginning
And hold my brothers and sisters in comfort
Take them out to play buy them an ice cream
I want to see their little faces light up as I read them a bedtime story
I want to see them laugh as I tickle them and play games with them
But I can't those days have gone
We are just left with scars and memories
And a past open door
Until no more

The Beginning

First came the banging on the ceiling from the bedroom above, followed by my dad's angry voice threatening what he would do to us kids "if he had to come down those bloody stairs". He didn't have to tell us twice because he always carried out his threats which resulted in us kids - all nine of us - screaming, crying and rubbing our legs and backs.

Welcome to life in Lancashire in the 1950s. Lowry tried to capture it painted on canvas. Towering mills, thin stooped figures, grime and poverty and no bloody hope. But there is only so much you can paint. The rest is left to the imagination of the observer and, as the saying goes, "every picture tells a story". I could have been one of those figures so this is my story.

I was born in 1951 in a two-up two-down terraced house in a cobbled cul-de-sac street surrounded by mills in the town of Farnworth, just outside Bolton in Lancashire. I was one of nine kids. Our Barbara was the eldest, then came Bernice, Eileen, Me, Roy, Jean, Brenda, Mavis and last, but not least, our Michael. I believe that when we were all walking out together there wasn't much (except for age difference) to tell us apart. We were all undernourished, all wore rags and wellingtons and not a bloody smile on any of our faces. We really didn't get a chance to discover ourselves or life in general cos we were kept, as my dad used to say, in place and "under control", which meant being beaten and kept prisoners in our sad, starved, terraced house.

I was fourth in line to the throne and our house was typical of most of the houses around that time. We had two rooms downstairs, the front room and in the back the kitchen, upstairs were two bedrooms and outside in the back yard was the toilet. To describe these rooms won't take long; starved of furniture, drawers, sofa, pictures, ornaments, books, comics, toys, LOVE and, not 'till very much later in life, a television. We had the bare basics one needed to live. The wallpaper was brown and stained through the damp, and the little carpet we had was threadbare with holes.

The front room had, as its centerpiece, a big black hearth fireplace; not only did it keep me warm but also this was to be my comforter and entertainer, but only when we had money to put coal on it. It was the place where we all sat in silence staring into the flames. Heaven knows what world of fantasies or imagination my brothers and sisters entered into but, for me, when the fire was blazing it took me off into a strange comforting world of adventure; I became a knight fighting the dragon, the Lone Ranger killing the baddies, and a wizard casting my spells. But on most occasions it wasn't lit and the front room was dark and cold, while we sat there - all nine of us - listening to the clock ticking away on the mantelpiece. In the kitchen was a white stone sink with a bowl in it and inside the tiny larder we kept our food and plates. We never used things like knives and forks; always our fingers or perhaps take it in turn to use a spoon.

There was little furniture, little money, food or clothes. We had an outside toilet; a tin bath hung on a nail in the backyard and nearby was a bloody great mill that had tried to break the spirit of the community. At the back of our house was some spare land that was known locally as *the Bonk*. This was a place where the local kids played and also where the men used to meet to play 'pitch a penny'; it was also used for the bonfire on bonfire night. It was patrolled by the stray, thin, mangy cats and dogs, and also rats and mice. It was a world all to itself and me and my brothers and sisters viewed it from my sisters' bedroom window in our terraced house: the reason for this was we were not allowed outside to play.

My dad had always been ill, for as long as I can remember. He suffered from rheumatoid arthritis, a condition that struck him at an early age and over the years only got worse. Work for him was difficult, which resulted in our lives getting worse as time moved on. The pills and steroids they gave him, fuelled with the ever-present booze, resulted in unpredictable mood swings. I cannot write really about my dad or how he felt or his upbringing because I don't know. I can only write about how I felt and how my life was, which was scared most of the time,.

My mam was a small good looking women she was one of three children and left school at the age of 14yr to go and work in the mill. She was born in 1925 and my dad In 1921 he was one of four so I'm told, I never met his side of the family except for one of his sisters, my aunty Florrie.

I remember the first time I felt real fear. My dad had just knocked my mum and eldest sister Barbara unconscious and was dragging them outside into the backyard. I would have been about four at the time and I just stood there, frozen to the spot in fear, watching and screaming. I wet myself. This was my first real experience of violence but one of many I came to expect.

Over the years I was to witness beatings delivered insanely on me and my brothers and sisters that was hard to bear but witnessing my mother getting beat up was unbearable.

The beatings became more severe as time past. My dad would thrash us with the buckle end of his belt until you couldn't breathe, and then he would continue until you stopped the screaming and crying. Every Sunday he would get the tin bath down that was hung onto a nail on the wall in the backyard. Sunday was the bath day and he would place the tin bath next to the fire and one by one (sometimes two) he would stand us up in the tin bath then with a large hard bar of green carbolic soap plus a scrubbing brush he would set about bathing us.

We all hated bath nights because we would get a good hiding for being dirty and the brush would be applied harshly to our skin in an attempt to clean us up. After the bath we would be sent straight upstairs to bed and in the winter it was bloody freezing and still early in the afternoon.

Inside the main bedroom of our house were two beds, one for my mam and dad, and one for me and my brother Roy. We slept in mam and dad's room and there was one bed in the other room for my six sisters. Our Michael who came much later, eventually joined me and our Roy in mi mam and dads room.

Me and my brother slept under an old khaki army coat and so did my sisters. There was no carpet on the stairs and just a little rug downstairs. My mam didn't have much cleaning up to do or clothes to wash because we didn't have 'much of owt'. But she was kept busy trying to make ends meet. Scratching and scraping, begging and borrowing for whatever it took to put some form of food in our bellies and ale down my dad's throat. Without the ale, it was a nightmare.

We were sent to various shops with a note in our hands asking for credit. There wasn't much on the list; usually a loaf of bread, a pot of jam and anything else they could let us have until national assistance pay day. It was very embarrassing to be refused, especially if there was anyone was in the shop that you knew.

What was even harder was going back home empty-handed. I hated walking through the front door, seeing my brothers and sisters looking up anxiously with anticipation on their faces hoping I had brought something home to eat, and the despair on my mam's face when she realized she could not feed us. It was heartbreaking. My dad would usually get his coat on and shout to me and our Roy to get 'us coats on' and then he would take us for long walks, one on each side of him, and this was done in silence as well. Sometimes he would walk through the park. This could be torture, for inside the park were the swings and, more often than not, he would walk past them. Even when he did allow us to play on the swings it would not be for long. We spent most of the times in the park sat down watching people bowling. We used to pray that a bowl would come our way and roll into the little ditch that was there to catch the balls that rolled off the green, then we would take it in turns to pick it up and put it back on the grass; we weren't allowed to roll it. Still, it was something to do.

We hated them walks. Whatever season it was, come rain or shine, winter or summer, we went out and walked in silence with our dad.

I can never remember a day without rows between my mam and dad. Each day one (if not all) of us kids would get the belt for no other reason than being born. My dad liked complete control and the only way he was going to get this was through violence. As my mam would say "lashing out or mental cruelty, that's all you're good for". It's hard for me, as I sit here writing this, to bring to mind any one particular incident for I can only remember violence in our household. I remember the teachers at my junior school asking me "Where did you get these bruises from?", but our dad would instruct us what we had to say if we were ever asked these questions. We would have to say that we had been fighting with our sisters and brothers. Whenever we heard our dad getting up outta bed we would all shake with fear as he came downstairs, his moods were always unpredictable; by that I mean from being in a bad temper to being totally, insanely, out of control.

I do believe at some point in my dad's life he was a fairly good person. Sometimes we would get a glimpse of his gentler side but as he got older and his arthritis ate away at his joints the pain became unbearable for him and so would us kids. We would sometimes come home from school to hear him singing or whistling or larking about with me mam, but any attempts to join in this happy bonding would be met with hostility, and we would all end up sitting on the sofa in silence. I hated it whenever he dragged one of my brothers or sisters into the other room to dish out his temper and all for no fuckin' reason except just being there. The helplessness I felt listening to their screams would reduce me to tears. I would have sooner took the beatings myself than to listen to their pleas begging him to stop. If my mam made any attempt to try and stop him, it would result in her getting thrown to the floor, kicked and then dragged around the room by her hair. He would take particular pleasure in doing this whenever she took time to do her hair. It was heartbreaking listening to my mam cry as she tried to tidy her hair up after his violent episode.

How does one describe those feeling that you have when someone is thrashing the life out of you and all you have for them is love. When I was being thrashed I so much wanted my dad to pick me up in his arms and love me, he was my hero. Whenever he beat me all that I saw on his face and eyes was pure evil not that I knew what evil looked liked but I sensed when I saw the sadistic smile on his face that he was enjoying it and I knew this couldn't be right.

Whoever my dad was beating on, the rest of the kids would scream and cry for him to stop but this always ended up with some, if not all of us getting the same treatment. When he lay in bed sleeping off the booze, sometimes we could be lucky enough to talk in whispers and if we got really daring we would silently play hide and seek. Just one false move, say if one of us accidentally knocked a chair over and woke him up he would be down those bloody stairs. We could hear the bed creak and his footsteps on the bare floor boards as he came down. Everyone of us would huddle up together on the sofa for protection not that it worked but it bought some time as he grabbed us one by one and led us into the kitchen as he "taught us a bloody lesson we will never forget". Whilst all this was going on my mam would try and protect us from which he would repeatedly knock her to the floor.

Even though we were all sent to bed around 6pm come winter or summer that didn't stop him dishing out the violence. If he heard us talking or getting out of bed to sneak a look at each other he would be up and in both rooms beating the crap out of us.

Eventually as time moved on and we where worn out through the fear of beatings we withdrew and receded to the fact of trying to be as good and well behaved as possible, but that was hard to do when none of us had even reached our 10th birthday.

One of our usual meals for breakfast back in the 50s was 'pobs'. For those who don't know what this delicate dish was it consisted of bread broke up into a saucer and then sprinkled with sugar (if we had any), then milk poured over. Cheap and not too hard on the purse.

We were allowed to read if my mam could get any books or comics from the rag and bone man when he came down our street, but we had to turn the pages quietly or my dad would take them off us. I don't know why he insisted on this silence, maybe if he couldn't hear us then we weren't there. You'd think he would let us out to play just so that he could have the peace and quiet that he always went on about. but then I suppose he wouldn't have the control he liked and, in our house, he had complete control over everything.

The worst moment in our house was if my dad didn't have his beer money, then it was hell. There would be no reading comics if my mam had been lucky to beg some from the rag man's cart, no fidgeting, coughing, no lights on, curtains drawn: all we had to look at - if we where fortunate to have it lit was the fire and that became our TV accompanied by the clock ticking away on the mantelpiece.

The winter was always hardest to endure. Having little coal to burn or even clothes to wear, trying to keep warm in our house was a near impossibility. All the walls where covered in dark damp patches and in some parts you could wipe the wet condensation of them. Even though we went to bed early, it took ages to get warm huddled under an old army coat. As the dark nights quickly drew in, having to go outside to the toilet for a six-year-old was a frightening experience. With no lights coming from inside the house to light up the backyard, you had to feel your way to the toilet and then once you got to it, there was no light inside there either. So when I had to go, I would ask if our Roy or perhaps one of my sisters could come with me. Sometimes my dad would say yes, but more often than not it was a no with the words "Tha's frightened of tha own shadow thee".

My dad had a potty under the bed for him to use and he didn't really like anyone using it but himself. He would make us all go to the toilet before we went to bed standing there making sure you managed to force a trickle of pee out so that we wouldn't have an excuse to use the potty. Well you can imagine not being able to use the potty, scared of going the outside toilet and the ever increasing fear growing in us, that if we wet the beds we would get another beating in the morning. We also slept in the clothes that we went to school in. This would cause great distress for me mam if we had wet them during the night

CHAPTER 4

THE RACE
Day 1

Sunday July 23 rd 2006
Camp Bartello.
Stage 1, The Inca Trail
Distance 36km/22.5m
Elevation 4,288m down to 2,700m (14,065ft to 8,856ft)

The night before the race was to begin, all competitors including myself, were taken out into the desert and shown to the tents that we would sleep in and share for the next six days and nights of the race.

In the tent that I shared with seven other fellow-competitors I tossed and turned in my sleeping bag. I am not the best of sleepers at most times this was not only because I was bloody freezing but also because I was wrestling with all kinds of thoughts going through my brain. Will I get lost? I don't have a good sense of direction at the best of times, so how would I fare in a desert? What about climbing up through those rugged ravines? I hate heights. What if I get injured? And the big one, what if I don't finish the race? I quickly pushed that one to the back of my mind and remembered my brother Roy's last words. He had said to me, "Remember, Billy. No fuckin' surrender!"

On the morning of day one, we gathered around the camp fire early in order to get close to the fire. A briefing was to be held before we set off on the buses to take us to the start line. We were to have these briefings every day to familiarize us with the terrain, distance, expected temperature/weather and the cut-off times we had to make at certain check points (CP's). Failure to make these times resulted in disqualification without exception. I'm afraid to say, several competitors didn't make these times even though some of them went on to finish the course.

The Atacama Desert Crossing 2006 commenced at 9.45am. We were informed that the start camp had been moved due to bad weather. The distance for the first day was supposed to have been 36km. (about 22.5miles). The organizers had decided to move the start line 100ft below the official 14,000ft due to below-freezing temperatures and heavy winds.

This first day found me full of excitement. Here I was at last standing in the line with my fellow competitors, inside an old churchyard high up in the Chilean Andes, 13,500ft above sea level. The mayor of San Pedro and his wife were to start the race. This would be done by the ringing of the church bells and on the third ring the Atacama Desert Marathon 2006 would officially begin. 150 miles to be run over six days through some of the most grueling terrain.

I remember standing there with my backpack on weighing thirty pounds thinking, "Have I trained enough?" I believed I had.

Week in, week out I would wake up each morning at around 4.30am and run thirteen miles, carrying a backpack weighing about seventeen pounds. Then in the afternoon, and because I live next to the seaside, I would run another eight miles over the sand, still wearing the back-pack. In some places it was very rocky. This I needed in order to harden my feet against blisters, at least that was the theory. It didn't work because I got blisters, loads of them. I would also go along to my local gym where Claire one of the fitness trainers and great friend, would greet me.

Claire was there with ever present smile along with the other trainers Denise and Ian who were always ready to assist and give advice in any way. It felt good for me to be a part of their friendship. I would then do some work on the treadmill, cross trainer, and weights.

The church bell rang and we were off. My heart was pounding so much - not just through adrenalin but also the high altitude - I thought it would burst out of my chest. I was suffering from altitude sickness, feeling dizzy and 'spaced out'.

The day before the race we had to get all our equipment checked out to make sure we took the obligatory equipment, and we had to sign over our waiver rights should anything serious happen to us on the marathon. After we had gone through this we had to have a medical check-up. It was whilst I was undergoing my check that an official Racing The Planet American doctor diagnosed me as suffering from altitude sickness. My breathing was erratic as well as my heart which I could feel pounding in my chest. Added to this I was becoming disorientated. He handed me some pills and informed me that he would check me over again before the start of the race. If I still showed signs of these symptoms then I would not be able to take part. I said to him "Are you mad? I've not come all this way for nothing," and then added, "It'll be reet". Unfortunately though I was still suffering but he knew I meant business cos I told him I would run it with or without his permission. He smiled and said, "Take it easy out there, Billy", and passed me fit. My symptoms lasted several hours, but got easier the more we descended. My head ached, I was dizzy and disorientated, but I fought against all that as I set off running with my fellow competitors.

At the first morning's briefing for the day ahead, we were told that today's course would involve some river crossings, maybe a dozen or so. Now that turned out a laugh. These are not your average floating-on-a-river-on-a-sunny-day rivers. No! These are fast-moving, freezing, rocky, up-to-your-knees, let's-push-you-off-balance, rivers, and the kind one crosses with great trepidation. Imagine it, not once, not twice, but at least fifty times we crossed these rivers - with a shaking of my head and "Don't fancy crossing these!" again, and again, and again!

The rivers would sometimes run through freezing slot canyons and the views were spectacular. These were lost on me just like the water the temperature dropped below freezing when you entered these slot-canyons. One minute the sun was burning down on your back, then as soon as you entered these canyons the temperature dropped dramatically...

Two miles into the race and I got my first sight of a river which curved its way down the mountain we were running on. On crossing these rivers, every move I made was taken with carefully chosen steps as I negotiated where I should place my feet on the various rocks protruding from it. In some parts, the water covered your knees and I was aware that it was very important not to get my backpack wet for it carried not only my food but also my sleeping bag, nightlights, and also a change of clothes. I was later to find out that some poor sods fell into it 'head over arse'.

All my thoughts about how I should approach this marathon from day one went outta the window on that first day. I was well charged up for it and like anything in my life I went for it like a horny bull loose in a field of cows - you know, full charge!

From the moment I entered this event, my main thought and I reckon, everyone else's - was to finish the event, get the medal and go home to a hero's welcome. There was a 150 runners lined up to take part in the Atacama Desert Marathon and sadly 25 did not finish it.

Each day we had to pass through three CP's before we got to camp. These were strategically positioned over each 26 mile course. At each CP you would collect water if you had run out. It is important to remember that on these extreme marathons you have to carry everything you need for the full six days, hence the backpack. Also whilst running/walking each stage you had to carry your own water. It became difficult to gauge just how much water to take between each CP. You didn't want to take too much to add more weight to what you were already carrying, or again, too little. You could end up having to do maybe three miles without water and in this desert heat to run out of water causes great hardship.

Back to the CPs. Once you arrived at one of these, the marshals would take down your number, which was worn at the front of your T-shirt and had to be shown at all times. Then they would mark your passport. This was a card with your name and number on it placed into a plastic case worn around your neck. Failing to have this on you at each CP would mean instant disqualification.

It was good to reach a CP! Time to rest for a short while and, if you needed any medical attention, a doctor was always there. These were American doctors and I found them to be very helpful, friendly, and extremely professional. One would get a chance to catch up on any gossip which always involved the race, and to see how your fellow-competitors were doing in the race.

It was hard to take in that I was actually here in the Atacama Desert taking part in an extreme 150 mile marathon. With Tamla Motown music blasting in my ears from the iPod I was wearing, I just kept my head down as I navigated my way around the changing terrain. I felt strong both physically and mentally and was enjoying the run. Although it was hot and the ground rocky and unpredictable, I plodded on at a slow trot. I wore a small bag around my waist in which I had packed energy bars, peanuts, and my blister kit. I needed these within easy reach. I also carried two water bottles, one in each hand. At the start of the race I put them in my backpack but it was a pain in the arse having to stop and take off my pack to retrieve them. I knew I was in a good position in the field of runners for I had passed many during the course of the day, mostly through the rivers. I was also aware that this marathon was gonna get worse over the next six days and I didn't want to risk being burnt out or even injuring myself. As hard as it was for me to slow my pace down I had to do it. Good thing too 'cos 26 miles to cover in a desert is a lot harder than 26 miles on a normal marathon.

I felt all my preparation running over the rocks on the beaches of Whitby was paying off, for the course on this first day (except for the rivers) was rocky and rough. I so much wanted to stop and take pictures of the ever-changing scenery -

the volcano sat high in between the spectacular mountainous Andes, the wild roaming Llamas, or the little orange colored shacks that were home to some shepherd or other - but I couldn't be 'arsed' to stop and take the camera from my waist pouch. My only focus was to complete this first day in the time required.

I noticed that the more I descended down the course my breathing wasn't quite as erratic, and my senses were coming back. I didn't feel as 'spaced out' as I had been at the start, so the doc was right when he told me the more I descended, the easier it would get.

Having reached the second CP, it felt good to be able to take of my pack and eat an energy bar. The people who manned the CPs were angels. They really took good care of you and made you feel special. If you wanted to eat some of your dried food, hot water was at hand. I have to say I never bothered; instead I would munch on the salted peanuts and energy bars I had brought with me and to be honest I had no desire to eat 'owt', which is unusual for me 'cos by gum I can eat. The stuff I had fetched with me and everyone was required to take dried food, was about as appetizing as a battered Mars bar - not that I've tried one but the thought makes me want to 'honk up'. I never stayed longer than about 15 minutes at any of the CPs. I knew after the briefings,that it would get dark by 6pm and I didn't fancy being out in a desert after dark... little did I know.

It was at CP3 on this first day that I was told I was lying in position 52 in the race. Now, out of 150 runners, this made me feel very good. During that first day's run, I was feeling fit both physically and mentally apart from the altitude sickness I was experiencing at the beginning. I did not want to lose this position, so after replenishing my water and eating an energy bar I was off again.

The last four miles into camp seemed to go on for ever. With just two miles left to go, I was told by one of the marshals on the course that there were no more river crossings left, and that it was a straight run in. I found this not to be the case and, over the next six days, we all learnt not to believe what they told us. I don't think that they deliberately lied to us. No-one was fully sure what lay ahead. The course was planned by a Frenchman called Pierre, who I wanted to strangle each day!

Anyway, to get back to the race, two miles in and no more river crossings, and yet I crossed two more and the miles seemed to go on and on! For me it felt very hot, except of course in the water and going through the slot canyons. The temperatures were reaching 32°C (100°F). Bad enough to walk the course with just a T-shirt and shorts on, but when you're carrying a 30-pound backpack and running/walking 26 miles against a clock it became unbearable at times.

For those amateur runners like myself the last mile or so of a marathon is a ball-breaker, and mine, on these last two miles, were being broken. My back was aching with carrying the back-pack, the backs of my legs were aching, my throat felt very dry despite the little sips of water I was constantly taking, and I just wanted it to finish. But it's like that illusion of running down a long corridor; you can see the door at the end, but it doesn't seem to get any nearer. I could see the international flags in the distance being flown around the camp to represent the competitors' countries, but the corridor just seemed to go on and on! At last I ran under the banner announcing 'The Atacama Crossing'! I had done it! I had completed stage1!

I did finish holding the same position - 52 - on my first day. Now, anyone who has finished a marathon will tell you of that feeling of exhilaration. To do it through a desert increases that feeling.

I got my passport stamped and walked along to find my tent. Picture it! about forty tents all pitched up in rows in the desert. These were taken down each day by the Chilean workers and then transported another 26 miles to the end of the next day's event, and so on until the 150 miles of the race were finished. The race was organized to finish in the village of San Pedro where we had stayed in our designated hotels on arrival for the race. The distance we had covered in stage 1 turned out to be eighteen miles. Only another 132 miles and six more days left to run! Would I, or for that matter, could I make it?

CHAPTER 5

The Salvation Army band is playing in our street
Its Sunday morning the church bells ringing a treat
There's calmness and serenity
You can feel it in the air
But all that's outside our house
Inside it's nothing but despair.

We're rummaging through our cast off clothes
Trying on this and that
My mam is busy with a darning needle
It's a hopeless case at that
Me dad's got a bad head on
Saturday night supped him dry
I remembered last night as I got into bed
I could hear my mother cry.
Just another bloody day!!

Walking Day

On Sunday mornings my mother would get us kids ready to go to the Methodist church. Not, I believe for any Christian upbringing but so that my dad could sleep off Saturday night's booze. Looking back it really was a joke. My poor mam having to find Sunday best clothes for us to wear when we hardly had any, if you could call them clothes at all. Try to imagine it, nine kids holding each other's hands, dressed in clothes either too big or too small, all of them smelly and with holes that had been darned once too often. On our feet we usually wore wellies or shoes with cardboard tucked inside the soles to stop our feet getting wet. This wasn't much help because if it did rain the cardboard got soggy which then stuck out of our shoes followed by our socks. What a sight we must have looked. I sometimes wonder if Lowry was about taking sketches of this sorrowful sight.

The good thing about walking to church was that it got us out of the house. We could play, laugh, sing, and shout if we wanted, but we had nothing but unhappiness inside our hearts. Still just to be outside and away from our dad was a blessing. Once inside the church the people would say what good children we were, "they always sit quietly and do as they are told". We'd been trained well. As you can imagine our house was not a happy household. We would have to sit quietly in silence sometimes for hours. The only sound to be heard, apart from listening to the other kids playing outside, was the ticking of the clock on the mantelpiece. That sound was to haunt me all my life and, even up to this present day, I still get flashbacks from the past whenever I hear a clock ticking.

I used to love the walking days that occurred once a year. All the churches around the area would hold a parade where the older and bigger kids would carry the banners in the front, while the rest of us kids would walk behind our represented church. It was a big affair and the whole town would turn out. Everyone would be dressed up in their Sunday best and march behind the bands. What would happen was, that the people who lined the streets to watch this procession would be on the look out for the kids they knew and would run out into the road to give then some money, usually a penny or two. After walking around the town, we would all go back to church to eat sandwiches and cake. It was a very special day for us, a real treat.

Once it was over, we would go back home and put the money on the table for me dad to count out how much each of us had got. He would sometimes let us keep a penny or two but we were poor so it was usually divided out for food and I suspect beer money for him. The temptation to hide some of the pennies was strong, but my dad's belt was stronger should he ever find out.

CHAPTER 6

Holding his food bowl Oliver begged for more
Such was his hunger it overcome friend or foe
His skinny little frame screamed out for a bite
He risked all for a morsel such was his plight

Hunger

The lad stood on his stool in the school dining hall, of George Tomlinson secondary modern In Kearsley with his hands on his head while more than 100 pupils ate their lunch.

That day at home had started as always with my dad rowing with my mum, while us kids looked on in fear hoping it would not end in violence. But it ended with my mam swallowing a load of pills. She had done this before. I didn't know it at the time but it was a cry for help. We were all screaming and crying for my dad to take the pills off her as she stuffed handfuls into her mouth. I could see my dad was visibly shaken as he struggled and fought with her to grab them from her clutch. This was something he had no control of and his way of handling this was to laugh and taunt her as he fought with her. He shouted to us all to "get out of the bloody house and get to school" and that "you won't have a mam when you get back home". We all walked up the road trying to hide our tears. If the neighbours had seen us crying and told me dad we would get beaten again.

I felt physically sick and scared as to what would happen to 'me mam' and if she would be there when we got home. I remember at school registration my form teacher sensed there was something up with me. He took me outside and asked me what the matter was. I could never tell him. We could never tell anyone what was going on in our house. We had been warned over and over again from my dad what we would get if we mentioned what went on inside our house. We had also been sent to school that morning without breakfast. We may have only got toast but it eased the hunger pains till lunchtime at school where we got a school dinner. These episodes with my mam swallowing pills as a cry for help, though not frequent, happened every now and then. The fear that she would die was unbearable, not only because we loved her but, without my mam, it didn't bear thinking about what life would be like with just me dad. It was already a living nightmare with him but at least we drew some form of love and comfort from me mam when she had the time. Anyroad, my dad would not have survived without me mam, she was the rock in the family.

I was one of those poor unfortunate kids who qualified for free school meals. How embarrassing it was every Friday when the teacher took dinner money off those who could pay then shouted out the names of the others who couldn't as if we were scum. When lunchtime came I struggled in the queue with all the other kids, hoping to get a place in the first sitting which, on this occasion I did. As we filed into the dining hall, you could see all the tables lined up one behind the other in a neat row with the servers sat at the end.

These servers consisted of pupils elected by the teachers to bring the meals up from the serving hatch and then dish the food out equally. Well, that was the plan and in some cases it happened. However a lot of the servers were school bullies and it still baffles me as to how they got those jobs. I can only assume that if they were given responsibility, they may respond with some respect towards their teachers but this idea never worked. Just like the queue outside - and despite the fact the teachers tried in vain to seat everyone orderly - the kids fought for the best servers. Because I was only small and scared of any form of aggression, I always ended up with the worst server you could get.

Five servers at a time went to the serving hatch and as ours went up us kids looked at each other nervously. We must have looked a pathetic sight. Just like me, this lot were the runt of life's litter - thin, poorly dressed, nervous and smelly. I remember our server. We'd been to junior school together. He'd bullied me there and carried on his duty into secondary school. However, I would like to point out that, five years after leaving school, we became good friends. The bully came back to the table with a big grin on his face. He was going to eat well today; he'd got a full house! The tiny portions he put on our plates we eagerly rammed into our mouths and this procedure was repeated when it was time for dessert.

So how did I end up stood on my table with my hands on my head? Quite simple really - I sneaked into the second sitting. The second sitting was always the best as most of the pupils who went to the second sitting had well off parents, so I figured they'd had a good breakfast and probably weren't as hungry as most of the poor sods in the first one. They would sneak off to smoke a fag at the back of the gym and then queue quite orderly. I remember feeling very scared as I walked into the dining hall. I had never done anything wrong or against the rules for fear of my dad's belt if he ever found out.

My fears were soon calmed, as the server was actually talking friendly to the other pupils on his table as I gingerly sat down. I could smell the food being dished up and once again felt the hunger pains in my stomach.

Soon it was time for our server to go up to the hatch. He returned with silver trays then asked us all to pass our plates down one at a time. Mine was the last but I was getting excited as I saw the generous portions he was dishing out and soon my plate was placed in front of me. I heard the server ask, "Did anyone want any more?. I resisted the desire to say "yes" because my plate was full.

I picked up my knife and fork and for the second time resisted the urge to quickly gorge myself. I was on my third forkful when I heard the sound of a whistle being loudly blown in the hall. A teacher stood up and instructed everyone to put down their knives and forks. When he had got everyone's attention, he informed us that, "a certain greedy pupil, not satisfied at having eaten in the first sitting, was now joining everyone to help himself once again in the second sitting". If that wasn't enough he also announced that my parents weren't even paying for this privilege because this certain pupil also received free school meals. He then turned his eyes to me. "Isherwood" he shouted, "stand on your stool so everyone can get a good look at you, you greedy little parasite".

I didn't know what a parasite was. I nervously stood on the chair resisting once again the urge to cry. I managed this quite well as my dad had trained me. I was sent to the vice headmaster's classroom after lunch as he was the one who dished out the punishment. I remember standing outside his classroom shaking with fear. You would think by now I would have got used to punishment but I never did. It wasn't the violence but the mental torture of being weak and not being able to stop it that caused me anxiety day in day out.

As I knocked on his door, I heard him bark for whomever it was to come in. I approached his table, shaking with fear. He was sitting calmly on his chair and his eyes never once left mine. He had red hair and a thin moustache that matched the color of his hair. His face resembled someone who was choking, bright red. The room was silent unlike most of the other teachers who struggled to try and keep order in a room full of deprived, working class, Lancashire kids. As I entered, all the class had their heads down busy getting on with whatever it was they were doing. I then got thrashed in front of them for being hungry.

At my senior school life was worse just for the simple fact I was getting older and becoming more aware of my poverty and the smelly clothes that I wore. I formed a friendship with two lads Colin Shaw and Jimmy Murphy who stuck with me through thick and thin. We were the class clowns and always getting up to some mischief or other. Both Colin and Jimmy had a natural talent for making people laugh. The bullies would jump onto this fact and try to force them to do something against school rules in order for them to get a laugh out off it. Unlike me, both Colin and Jimmy could stick up for themselves, Jimmy was only a small kid but a tough one, Colin was above average size and even if he got picked on he never once lost face.

Believe it or not but my memories of my school days apart from the bullying are lost somewhere at the back of my drink and drug fuelled mind.

I was a skinny little smelly undernourished kid at school who was constantly bullied so it didn't matter whether i was at home or in school, life was just the same always. I was getting a beating one way or another. My dad was not interested in our education. We were just work fodder to him and he couldn't wait till we left school so we could bring a wage home. We were not allowed to bring homework home and he told the teachers so. He would say "you've got em for eight bloody hours, when they come home they've got bloody work to do so don't give em owt else to do". The teachers I believe couldn't care less, I was always getting told of for smelling looking dirty and for the scruffy rags I wore. I didn't have any gym kit for when we did P.E or football kit and even when we were taken to the local swimming baths I had no swimwear. One of the female teachers once made me put on some girls knickers she had found in the changing rooms to go swimming in. We were a mixed class, so both boys and girls went to the swimming baths together. I lived my school days in shame. I was not involved in any of the sport activities I was the one who carried things onto the field and was a runner for the teacher.

I was in the lowest stream at my senior school and was known as one of the thick ones. I did love reading books though I suppose because we had none at home unless we were lucky enough for my mam to beg any, books were my escape. The books I read for someone of the age of 12 would seem strange cos they were kids books, fairy tale, or Enid Blyton. I loved them and would dream that I lived in them.

Whenever we came home from school as soon as I entered the street where I lived, fear would kick in. I would say bye to my mates wishing I could go home with them, then I would nervously open our back door to the atmosphere of evil and silence. I would walk in and look at my mam I could always tell if things where wrong cos she'd be sat rocking on her chair in the back room, and my dad in the front. I would sit down joining my brothers and sisters in the silent cell listening for my dad to move in the other room and when he did we all held our breath.

He seemed to find any excuse to beat us and sometimes he would walk in clutching 'The Belt in his hand wrapped tightly around his fist. We would look at each other curl up in a ball for protection then the beatings would start. The buckle end of the belt is very painful when it's wrapped around your neck from a high swing and would take your breath away. The screaming would reach full pitch and my mam would be up fighting with my dad to no avail, it just made things worse. After the onslaught he would send us scurrying upstairs to bed with nothing to eat. For a while we had the safety of lying under the bed coats licking our wounds listening to the fight still going on down stairs with mi mam and dad.

My dad was a big man who liked to dress well and always took time over his appearance constantly combing his hair, and I suspect a ladies man. He certainly talked to a few when he took me and our Roy out on his walks but threatened us to keep our mouths shut.

We always ended up with in lice in our hair and it was terrible to get sent home from school because of this, my dad would go mental calling us dirty bastards and lashing us until he exhausted himself. I mean what the fuck were we supposed to do, we could only have a bath once a week which supervised with fists for being dirty. Though he didn't like to use his fists cos it made his arthritis hurt more he could still loose it and smash one of us in the face. Once the pain hit him he would go downstairs for the belt to finish the job off.

CHAPTER 7

Slap bang wallop what a picture what a photograph
Still inside my mind, run but can't hide
Wounded scars buried deep inside
Hard hands, kicking feet, huddled up underneath a chair
What a picture what a picture fear can be seen behind your eyes
All your letters and those promises were lies

Bogey Man

I could write chapter upon chapter about the violence me and my brothers and sisters endured. I believe they will have their own recollections of what went on inside our house. Indeed I'm sure there are plenty of poor unfortunate sods out there who probably have far worse tales to tell than me, but I want to write about how this cruel upbringing affected me as I was growing up especially being kept in silence and a prisoner. There will, however, be parts of my story that will touch on the abuse we all endured. Then again, on reflection, this is about me so I think from now on I'll stick with me and my life. This is my story.

As I was the eldest boy and named after 'me dad Billy', I was the one who had to be kept in place, whatever that meant. My dad would beat me just so if I did anything wrong he'd say "you'll know what to expect". I remember how he accused me of being the trouble maker, now that's a laugh in itself cos having never been allowed outside to play there wasn't much

44

trouble you could get up to. I do recall once sneaking into the larder to pinch a slice of bread. The bread had to be kept counted so me mam knew how many slices she had left before we went out to tick some more from the shops. I was inside the larder and had just taken a slice when from nowhere my dad walked in. I turned around sharply putting my hand that held the bread behind my back. I was shaking all over with fear and guilt must have been written all over my face. He quickly sensed this and asked me what I was up to and what I had in my hand behind my back. Funny innit how even though we get found out when we have wronged, the urge to lie is strong. I did just that and lied. My dad grabbed me spun me round twisting my arm up my back and pulling the bread from my hand all with one hand whilst the other undid the buckle on his belt. He took me in the other room screaming what a thieving little bastard I was. He forced the bread into my mouth and down my throat and thrashed me with the buckle end of the belt. I thought I would choke to death trying to swallow and scream in pain at the same time. The buckle end of the belt was used on me for serious things he considered really bad.

I'm there in your dreams
I'm under the bed
I'm behind the curtains
And inside your head
I play with your shadows
Find me if you can
I'm going to get you
Boo I'm the Bogey Man

My dad would tell me about the bogey man that lived under his bed and, if I didn't do as I was told, he was going to lock me in there so the bogey man would take me away. Wanting to play when you're three years old, was that wrong? Talking, laughing, was that wrong? No, but as the saying goes 'you can't do right, for doing wrong'.

Because my dad had arthritis, he couldn't use his hands. It hurt him too much. He used to say, "I won't use my hands. I'll use the belt". Okay, a slap or two was to be expected by kids then but my dad would beat me while holding my little hands up above my head until I couldn't breathe. The sobs that raked through my body were uncontrollable. Then he would shout for me to stop crying and he would use the belt until I nearly choked trying not to cry. Then he would drag me upstairs and put me into the bedroom for the bogey man to take me away. The bedroom was always dark. The curtains were black. My dad had told me about how an old man who lived there before had died in this room. I was pushed into the room bruised and shaking with fear. He would say, "make a noise and you'll get more of this", waving the belt in front of me. Then he would shut the door with a bang.

I remember on one occasion inside the bedroom I was frozen to the spot, I wet myself and still stifling the sobs with my eyes closed I waited for the bogey man to come and get me. Overcome with fear, I screamed and screamed. I didn't care. My fear of the bogey man far outweighed my fear of the belt. I could hear footsteps coming upstairs. We had no carpet on the stairs, just bare floorboards, and as the steps got nearer, I moved away from the door and curled up in a ball on the floor for the next onslaught. The door opened. I put my hands over my head to ward of the blows when suddenly hands lifted me gently off the floor. It was my mam. I could see she had been crying and also her hair was all in disarray. My dad had a habit of dragging my mother around the house by her hair. She carried me downstairs. My dad had gone out for one of his walks. We had an old rocking chair in the front room and she sat me on her knee stroking my hair. She rocked all the pain away until I fell asleep. My dad came back later and acted as though nothing had happened. That was the most confusing bit for me. Mam called it 'mental cruelty'.

Our house was pure evil. You could feel it. The insanity was all around, just waiting to come out to play. We all sat around gingerly looking at each other for comfort. Sometimes, after my dad had been for one of his walks, he would taunt my mam about a certain woman he had been seeing then he would get up close to her and say this woman's name as he held up his middle finger...saying "Finger up dick". This taunting would upset me mam and she would go at my dad claws drawn all to no avail cos he always won. After he had finished beating her up he would turn and look around insanely at us kids cowering on the sofa already pleading with him to "please don't hurt us" but one by one he would lash us until his thirst for violence had been quenched. We would be covered in marks and bruises from the onslaught and the screaming must have sounded like a slaughter house from the people passing by the window. Even though the police where sometimes called nothing was done about it, but this was the 1950s. Whenever anyone called at our house, my dad would go into the kitchen until they left. Not that many people ever called he would see or speak to no one. There were times when he would go into hospital. It was called Prestwich Hospital and was known locally at the time, as the 'nut house'.

My mam once ended up there, not surprisingly. Whenever my dad went into the hospital, we could be normal. Not that we knew what 'normal' was. I thought life must be like this for everyone. But life was different when our dad was in hospital. My mam would tell us stories and let us play games. But there were still nine mouths to feed and she was only young herself. Sometimes she could have a short fuse but compared to me dad, life was a piece of cake with me mam.

My mam couldn't always afford to visit dad as we had no money for the bus fare. Not long after dad had been in hospital, the letters would arrive. Mam would sit us down and read them to us. "Your dad's getting better. He says he doesn't mean to hurt you, he's been ill and he promises us all that when he comes home this time things are going to be different".

She really believed him or perhaps, like us, she wanted to believe and when he did finally come home, things would be different for a short time.

"Why don't you kids go into the backyard and play," my dad would say. We would look at him hesitantly, "Go on, it's okay". "Oh, thanks dad" we would say in unison. Then we would go up to him to give him a kiss. "Thanks dad. We'll be good, honest" we would say.

Have you ever seen those old German films where they torture a prisoner then come into his cell with a meal and a cigarette saying there's been a mistake and they are sorry? For a couple of days they feed him up and treat him well until, one day, the cell door opens and they once again drag him back to the torture cell and it starts all over again.

Well, that's what it was like for us. A couple of days playing, then the back door would open and there would stand my dad with his belt in his hand. "Get inside this bloody house" he'd shouted and it would start all over again.

> Scrimping and scraping borrowing this and that
> Get it of peter to pay Paul back
> Buy a bit of food for the hungry mouths to feed
> Nowt left in't kitty, but still there's other needs.

Rent day would find us kids all crouched down and hiding behind the sofa. The rent man had come round for the rent. I can clearly remember how this man looked 'cos he was always calling round to collect the arrears. He was a tall lanky man with a Roman nose. He had a deformed right arm. It just didn't hang right and, in his other hand, he carried a black bag for the rent money.

"I know you're in there, Mrs. Isherwood", he would shout through the letter box. "You're getting too far behind. You must come into the office to see me at the town hall or we will have to evict you." And then he would skulk away.

Me mam played a neat trick with his request, which was meant to pull at his heart-strings. She had learnt how to survive; it was a mother's instinct. She would get all us kids dressed and, the next day at the council office, we would all pile into the rent man's office. He was a nice man and I'm sure we owe it to him that we weren't evicted.

He would always get out of his chair, smile and greet my mam like a gentleman. Then he would smile at all us kids. He would listen sympathetically at my mam's pleas for more time to settle the arrears. He'd heard it all before. We weren't the only poor sods in Farnworth that had no money but we were there at the top because of my dad's disability. After my mam had sobbed out promises she couldn't keep and he knew it too. He would say "I'll see what I can do but you must try to pay something even if it's only a shilling a week". A shilling. Was he mad? My mam could feed us all for two days on a shilling. When I say 'feed', I mean jam butties. My mam promised she would and we all left his office. More time was bought again.

> The ups and downs whys and buts
> In and outs never enough
> Tears cried in silence suffering alone
> Emptiness, numbness, an ill wind blown.

I remember one winter there was a coal shortage and we had to go down to the coal yard and join the long slow-moving queue in order to get a bag of coal. We had no money but this hadn't been a problem before as my mam would pay the coal bill when she got my dad's sick money. But that day, it was cash on the nose. We had queued most of the day in the freezing snow to be told we couldn't have any without paying up front first. The worst thing was, having to walk home back to a freezing house with no heating and little food. The only thing to do was to go to bed and try and get warm under the army coat that covered our bed. It took ages for me and our Roy, snuggling up to each other, before we finally felt warm, and sleep rescued us from our living nightmare.

My dad was a good snooker player and had it not been for the arthritis in his hands, he would have been up there with the best of them. He once had a job at Melling's Bakery in Farnworth. One day, he came home and told my mam he had been challenged to a game by one of his workmates. The bet was his wages against this man's. Now my mam, who was level-headed, also knew my dad was good, so she agreed for him to take on the bet. On the night of the match she got ready to go with him to the club where the game was to be held. My eldest sister Barbara babysat us all. With the ringing in her ears about "how we'd better bloody behave ourselves," off they went to the club. My dad won. The next morning for breakfast we all had a boiled egg each and for a short time things were pretty relaxed. My dad was on a high and so was my mam. She told all the neighbors how her man had taken on a bet of a whole week's wages, played on a game of snooker, and won.

Then there was the time when my dad got a job as a postman over Christmas. I hated this 'cos I would have to get up early in the mornings to go with him. I'd have to wait outside the sorting office, hiding so nobody could see he was taking his little son with him. It would be cold and dark and my dad had told us this was when the Bogey Man came out. All those stories about the Bogey Man left me feeling scared all the time and my dad would taunt me by saying, as he pointed to me, "That one's afraid of his own shadow". Well, not quite true, just the shadows I couldn't see which he told me were there.

When my dad collected the mail for delivery, he would come and get me from where I would be hiding behind a corner at the end of the street. We would walk down the streets where mail had to be delivered and he would give me letters to deliver on the opposite side of the road. I hated the long dark paths of some of the Victorian houses where I had to post mail. I would run as fast as I could up those paths with their overgrown trees and hedges that seemed to want to grab you on either side. I would be aware of the noises in the dark: a bird flying out of a tree would set my heart racing fast or a cat jumping out in front of me all added to my anxiety. Was the Bogey Man hiding, waiting to grab me?

But the worst of the worst was when we had to cut through St John's churchyard with its long winding path and gravestones on either side. My dad had a sadistic streak in him and got pleasure out of saying, "Is that a hand sticking up from that grave? Maybe someone's trying to get out," and when I tried to hold him, he'd laugh and say "Get off stop being soft, you girl".

> Be respectful to your elders and do has your told
> Children should be seen not heard and never left alone
> Never let your left hand know what the right is doing
> Keep your ears close to the ground
> Cos there's no one you are a foolin

One morning the next door neighbor, an elderly lady, knocked on the door. The night before, me mam and dad had gone to the pub and my eldest sister Barbara, had baby-sat us all. Our Barbara would wait 15 minutes 'cos our dad would always say he may sneak back to see what was going on. After a while we got used to this lie, it would take a fire to get him out of pub. Barbara would bring us all down to play nothing much just games like 'I spy' or mimicking 'me dad' for a laugh, or 'tig you're on'. This would last for about an hour, then we were put back to bed, as far as we were concerned we had been playing quietly.

My dad answered the knock on the door to be met by our next door neighbor. "I don't like to complain," she said, "and I don't want to get anyone into trouble but last night I thought there was a murder going on, what with all the screaming and commotion." My dad apologized to her and said he would sort it out. We all froze to the spot. We knew what his 'sorting out' was and so did our next door neighbor; she must have heard the screams coming from our house when he dished his 'sorting out'. One by one my sisters were beaten starting with our poor

Barbara, and then moving down the line. Even our poor mam got it that day. He saved me and our Roy 'till last. After he had exhausted himself on 'teaching them a lesson they shall never forget', me and our Roy were told to put your bloody coats on. We were 'gonna get it' outside.

Where we lived, there was a back lane that must have been about a quarter of a mile long. First, he knocked me to the floor, then our Roy. Talk about 'marching them up to the hill and back again'. We walked there and back, being repeatedly floored to the ground by his blows 'till we got back home black and blue - and for just doing what comes natural – playing!

CHAPTER 8

The wheels on the bus go round and round
Round and round, round and round
And sometimes they were up but mostly down
All day long.

Poverty & Cameraderie

The shopkeeper opened the note I had just handed her. We'd been down this path before. I waited, hoping she would get the items my mam had asked for on credit. This is how it always went: she would read the note and if we were to get something, she would get them and put them on the counter. It was always the same things my mam needed to feed us: two loaves of bread, a pot of jam and 'a pat of marg', and, if possible, five woodbines for my dad. Then she would bring out a red book from under the counter and write down what we'd just had on credit. She would then write something on the note I'd just handed her, fold it and give it back to me. No words were spoken.

Now if on the other hand she read the note, took out her pen and wrote something on the note, folded it and handed it back to me, there would be no food that day. Well, not until my mam had managed to sort something else out if she was lucky, and many a time she wasn't. The next thing she would do was to try another shop where they knew her and felt some sympathy for her dilemma; and whenever she could, she did pay them back. Mam would sometimes send us on the Rag run taking some of our clothes to weigh in for money which she would then spend on food. I would keep my fingers crossed that it wasn't the rag run cos of the bullies which could sometimes be much worse than the hunger. It could be one of those days when, no matter what we tried, we'd go to bed that night having 'eaten nowt'.

There was of course, always my grandma Martha, my mum's mum. This would only be a last resort 'cos, as you can imagine, my grandma hated my dad. "He ought to go out and get some bloody work, lazy, good-for-nothing sod", she'd tell mam. She lived at the other side of town and if we did go there, you can bet your life she'd come back with us to have a word with my dad. Grandma wasn't scared of dad and once belted him with her walking stick. I suspect he was scared of her.

I really loved my grandma. Sometimes my mam would run away back to her and take us kids with her. As we got older mam would go and leave us with my dad but not for long. He would send us down with notes pleading for her to come back and she always did.

My grandmother was a really old-looking Victorian woman. She always had a shawl wrapped around her shoulders, wore clogs on her feet and she smoked a pipe. She would sit in her rocking chair telling us stories about my grandad who had fought in the First World War, as she looked deep into the coal fire. One of her habits, when she wanted to spit into the fire, was to make an extra *rock* in her chair. It was like someone getting ready to jump up then, as she neared the fire, she would spit and stay in the same position watching the spittle sizzle in the fire until it went out. Then she would settle back to her rhythmic rocking.

One of her favorite stories, and one I loved the most, was of my grandad, Jack, who was in charge of the horses in the trenches in the First World War. She would say, "He loved them bloody horses and would have brought one home if I let him". His job was to feed them and when the shelling started, try to keep them calm. One particular day, as the shelling started heavily, the horses were rearing up nervously. He was doing his best trying to keep them calm by stroking and talking to them. He had names for all of them, my grandma told us. He was only a young man and it must have been pretty scary for him too. My grandad would go round each one of them stroking them. Suddenly a sergeant appeared carrying a stick under his arm. He looked at the horses rearing in the air and took his stick from underneath his arm and started to hit them in an attempt to bring order into the situation. On seeing this, my grandad saw red and took the stick off him and started hitting the sergeant with it. "How do you bloody like it?" he shouted. Grandad was put on a charge for assaulting a non-commissioned officer in wartime, a charge that could have had him facing the firing squad. My grandma had the official charge sheet and court report.

When my grandad appeared in front of the military court, he said, in his defense, that his job was to keep the horses as calm as possible when the shelling started. He truly loved those horses. Under heavy shelling from the enemy, tension was high so to see the sergeant whipping the horses made him see red. Those horses, he said, were vital in pulling the big guns forward. They would not have been good for owt if that sergeant had kept on whipping em. The court agreed with him but this was the First World War and you don't go round 'belting NCOs'. Under the circumstances, he was locked up for a short time in a military prison.

My grandma was a strong woman. She took no nonsense off anyone. She would tell my mam. "I know he beats those kids and you, and that they aren't allowed out to play. He wants bloody sortin' out, that man of yours, and if you won't do it, I bloody well will".

"It would have been no good, it would have made thing worse. He's ill", my mam would say. "He's in a lot of pain."

"He's sick alright," said my grandma, "sick in t'head".

My mam would plead for my grandma to stay away and reluctantly she would, but sometimes she would turn up unexpectedly. The visit would always result in my dad getting his coat on pretty sharpish and disappearing.

I used to love it at school when it was Christmas and we had our Christmas party. I went to St John's School in Church Road in Farnworth. On these special occasions we had to take a plate with us with our name on it. I suppose the reason for this was that most families around that time had little of anything so to lose a plate was a big deal - well, certainly in our family. Oh what joy, as the song goes, 'food, glorious food'!

Cakes, trifles, jelly and custard I rammed them down my neck. I always ended up feeling sick afterwards, as I'm sure most kids do. It just wasn't the food that was tempting; it was the amount I could see. Long rows of tables piled high with all these goodies and the teachers telling us all to help ourselves. There was plenty of choice of everything and I wasn't the only poor deprived sod in that hall. It was like a scene from the Peter Pan film where the kids get together, all gorging themselves and chucking food at each other. Those were the best moments of my life as a little boy. But if you rewind the film a little, to the part where the kids are sat down pretending to eat food that wasn't there, that was what it was like in our house all the time, pretending to eat food that wasn't there.

> Rockets and cartwheels sparklers spun round wildly
> Ale supped with loud songs, fire burning madly
> Kids eating baked spuds, treacle toffee stuck to face
> I'm stood watching it quietly my dad's looking on, just in case.

There were some good moments in my little life but not many. Bonfire nights, was one of them moments with the magic of fireworks. At the back of our house and the surrounding houses in Elsmere Street was a spare bit of land known locally as *the Bonk*. This was a place where all the unemployed men hung out to play 'Pitch a Penny', a gambling game, and they would get a couple of local kids to keep an eye out for the bobbies (police) in case they came round. It was also the place where you could see men fast asleep, drunk on booze and crashed out on the ground.

In fact, that was where my dad was found one day. As far as I can remember he had been coming back from the pub but had collapsed because his ulcer had burst. One of the neighbors had spotted him and had gone over to see if he was alright. This act, believe it or not, probably saved his life. They had to pump a lot of blood into him. My mam would say afterwards this was the reason he was like he was "cos they'd pumped bad blood into him."

I remember us all being at the hospital. My mam was crying and the doctor was telling her it was 'touch and go' whether he would make it through the night because he'd been bleeding internally for a long time. When we all got back home we all piled into my mam's room. The girls got into bed with my mam, and me and my brother got into ours. My mam was still crying, as was everyone else. I think it was because my mam was. On the wall next to my mam's bed hung a crucifix and, as my mam was weeping and cuddling the girls, suddenly the room became brighter and next to the crucifix we saw a figure appear. It stood so majestically and was so serene and peaceful. We were all transfixed on this vision and not in the least bit afraid. Then its face, which I cannot describe, smiled, and it bowed its head and disappeared.

There was silence in the room, no one spoke and there was just a strange sense of peace. My mother got out of bed and went down on her knees, weeping this time, but with a smile on her face. She turned to us all as we looked on, hypnotized, and said, "Don't be afraid, everything's going to be alright now. Go to sleep, your dad's going to be fine." Those few words spoken by my mam brought back fear in me again. The next morning the doctors at the hospital said that they had been amazed at 'me dad's' quick recovery. My mam smiled and 'said nowt'.

Getting back to bonfire night, this spare waste ground called *the Bonk* was used by all the neighbors in the street for hanging out their washing, or just bringing out chairs so they could sit and gather for a gossip. Bonfire night was a neighborly event. Everyone got involved. We used to watch the local kids from our sisters' bedroom gathering the wood, our hearts aching to be a part of it. Each neighbor had discussed what each would do; this was a poor neighborhood and the community spirit to give us kids a good bonfire was something to behold. It's surprising, looking back, what those good folk managed to find for special events. Some would provide *spuds* for baking on the fire, some would bake Parkin (ginger) cake. Others would make treacle toffee and everyone would pitch in for fireworks, and the men, of course, would bring out crates of ale.

At 6pm all the back gates would open and the men would carry out sofas, chairs and tables, as us kids looked on excitedly. You could hear every now and then the phrase, "wait a bloody moment, it'll get lit when it gets lit."

Boards were put up for the spinning wheels to be hung on, milk bottles placed safely away for the rockets, 'Guy Fawkes' being placed gingerly on top of the bonfire, and the sofas and chairs being positioned safely around the fire. All the men seemed to have a fag or a pipe in their mouths, while the women were busy bringing out the *spuds*, Parkin and treacle toffee, plus the crates of ale. And as they busied themselves setting all this out on the tables, the other women would be trying to keep all the kids in order You could sometimes hear a kid get 'a clout round their ear hole' with the words, "I bloody well warned you, you'll go inside in a minute and you'll see no bloody bonfire. Now sit 'the sen' down and be quiet or I'll tell your bloody dad. Same every bloody year - you'd think he's never seen one before."

All of this commotion just added to the excitement of the forthcoming spectacle and was handed out and received in good humor. At last the petrol would come out. The men really took this part seriously, checking the coast was clear and I suppose showing off their *macho* side.

"Reet. Get them kids back. This bloody thing's goin' to go up like nobody's business."

"Aye like last year's, Jack. Thee cudn't leet a fag up."

"Ahh well. thee should know, like the year thee nearly set all't bloody street on fire."

All this, again, was part of the build-up to the evening.

And what an evening! Dad would take us to stand near our gate and watch the goings on from a distance still not allowing us to join in. After us kids stood in amazement and watched the fireworks go off, the real party would begin. Spuds were chucked on the fire. Treacle toffee was smashed into pieces. The Parkin was cut and dished out to all kids including us, followed by the baked spuds wrapped in newspaper with heaps of margarine over them.

When we had been fed, it was the grown-ups turn and this again was a real show. Someone would bring out a tin whistle, others' spoons to play, someone played a washing board that was strummed with some plastic bit and then the songs would begin. The old songs like 'On Mother Kelly's Doorstep' and 'Roll out the Barrel'. They would all join hands in a big circle around the fire and sing and dance around it. Occasionally we would be allowed to join in with this especially if my dad had had a few drinks. Everyone laughing, singing, joking, even the women would have a bottle of beer in their hand. Oh how we danced. We danced through the night. It was sheer community bliss. Some times the neighbours would come to our rescue by grabbing our little hands and saying to my dad, "Tha doesn't mind if they dance wi us dost thee". My dad being the coward that he was and also wanting everyone to believe he was a good dad. He would smile and nod his head, but we knew he was watching us so we tried to behave to his rules about 'not getting too carried away'.

Lancashire life in the early 50s seemed to be stuck in a time warp from the 20s. After all, in a matter of 30 years there had been two world wars that had robbed families of fathers, brothers, mothers, sisters. This had left a depression where the only hope of a livelihood was either the mills or down in the coal pits; not much choice and all for little money and prospects. Everything was still rationed and any chance of escape from this non-existence was to 'bugger off' but to where? You needed money for that and the mill and pit owners made sure you just had enough to live on. They owned you if you worked down in the pits. They provided you with a house and then you were expected to buy your food from their shops and if your spouse was unfortunate to be involved in an accident (which were frequent) and couldn't work or, even worse, was killed, then out you went - it was the workhouse for you.

It's funny what power and money can buy. Usually the mill owners had the best pews in the church and after the sermon the vicar could be found being wined and dined at the mill owners' houses. Funny how this type of brain-washing worked in families: 'know your place', 'after all, Mr. Arkwright is good enough to give us a job', don't forget to tip your cap should he pass you in the street'. Yes, this type of mentality was typical of the era I was born into. Heaven knows how bad it was back in the 20s, when my mam and dad were born; their time warp would be stuck somewhere in the 1890s.

I can still remember 'The Knocker Upper' who went around in the early morning armed with a long pole with some metal strands attached to the end of it. She was an old Victorian looking woman who wore a long black Victorian dress, shawl and on her feet clogs. Her job was to go round the houses to wake up the workers for the mills and pits. You could here her clogs scraping on the cobbled streets as she made her way around to each house. She would use the pole to reach the bedroom windows and with the metal strands on the end knock away until someone appeared at the window to show her they were up, she wouldn't leave and continued to knock until this happened for this she received a penny a week still she had a lot of houses to knock up so I reckon she earned a tidy amount.

CHAPTER 9

Day 2

Monday 24th July 2006
Stage 2 - Quebrada Pass (Small Canyon)
Distance: 42 kilometers/26 miles
Elevation: +193 meters, -558 meters

5.30am found me once again tossing and turning in my sleeping bag and bloody freezing. Being somewhat of an insomniac, I hardly slept this second night before stage 2 of the marathon. I wanted to get out of my sleeping bag and go to the camp fire, plus I needed the toilet, but I felt so tired, and anxious too, about how I would fare that day on another gruelling desert run.

This was only the second day and with still 132 miles in front of me, I couldn't help feeling a bit apprehensive. After all, I was a 55-year-old 'alkie' trying to recover. I pushed these thoughts out of my mind and remembered my brother Roy's departing words to me, "No Fuckin' Surrender". He also added, "4 - 4 - 2". When I asked him what it meant, he replied it was the playing formation that England played when they won the 1966 World Cup against Germany. So there we have it. I thought, "4 – 4 – 2. No Fuckin' Surrender."

Eventually I struggled out of my sleeping bag, grabbed a packet of dried breakfast porridge, and made my way towards the campfire, stopping off at the toilet. Well, I say 'toilet' - the Chileans who were in charge of erecting and pulling down the site each day, would dig three holes 100 meters away from the camp for everyone to use. So you can imagine with 200 people using these each day, the stench was terrible. At the campfire I found other fellow-insomniacs huddled around it. As usual we were to have a briefing at 8am about what to expect on that day's course. Pierre informed us we would be covering 42 kilometers (26 miles) with 11 kilometers (7 miles) of this to be run through slot canyons filled with knee-high icy water.

After several nervous visits to the toilet, I lined up with the other competitors. It's worth pointing out that they had put up outside the officials' tent, the results from yesterday's run and there I was - positioned 52nd. My time was 7 hours, 53 minutes and 59 seconds. As soon as I saw it, I got the my competitive head on. This was not my plan; I just wanted to complete each stage in the time allocated. So I had to bring myself back down to earth and stick to my plan.

The countdown began and we were off, running under the official Atacama banner as we passed all the international flags that were lined up around the camp. I had positioned myself at the back, stuck my I Pod on, and started off at a steady pace. Before I knew it I found myself indeed up to my knees in freezing rushing waters that ran through the slot canyons. Once you entered these canyons, you immediately felt the drop in temperature as the sun disappeared. I was holding two bottles of water, one in each hand, which I found far easier than trying to retrieve them from the sides of my back-pack. I had purchased just one walking pole, having been given sound advice that one would do the job just as well as two. However on the flight over here, this pole had been taken from me at Madrid airport.

Let me explain. During the run-up to this event, I had got in contact (via the official *Racing the Planet* website) with a competitor who had successfully completed the 2004 Atacama Desert Marathon. Her name was Liz and she lived in New Jersey in the USA. Liz had suggested only taking one walking pole as it could do just as good a job as two. Amongst other valuable information, she also advised me against checking in my backpack onto the plane, for if it were to go missing I would not be able to do the marathon. So I heeded her warning, hence the bag came with me onto the plane, minus the pole at Madrid airport. The security official said that the pole could be used as a weapon; I felt like 'sticking the nut' on him and saying "So, can this".

It was a hard slog, trudging through those river-infested canyons plus we all thought that, after yesterday, we had finished with "all this river shit'. The freezing water gushed rapidly around your feet and legs and in some parts it rose up to your knees and seemed determined to knock you over. Without a pole to steady me and also carrying two water bottles, one in each hand, it took careful steps to pass through this section. This was also where the runners began to get separated as each one went at their own pace.

Once through these canyons, the views were once again spectacular with the surrounding volcanoes and red peak valleys. The scene opened up to my first view of the desert, miles and miles of dirty brown sand together with lovely, white, high-rising sand dunes that resembled waterfalls as the sand flowed down them. The sun was beating down on me from the clear blue sky. I stood for a moment, just drinking it all in, whilst thinking to myself, "What have you let yourself in for?"

I was no veteran runner and, apart from the street marathons I had done, I feared this was way above my league.

Then our Roy's words came back to me:

"4 – 4 – 2! N – F – S!"

Taking a deep breath, I quoted a line from Shakespeare's Henry V:
>"He that out lives this day and comes safe home
>   Will stand on tiptoe when this day is named
>   And rouse him in the name of Crispin"

Here I substituted Atacama for Crispin

It was as hard for me going down the dunes as it was going up them. I had not brought with me any gaiters to stop the sand getting into my running shoes, so I was constantly stopping - which was 'a pain in the arse' having to empty the tons of sand that found their way into them. The sun was beating down heavily on me, which was a warm welcome after coming out of the canyon. I was so thirsty and dreaming of drinking (not for the first time) an ice cold coke but the only thing I had to quench my thirst was the water in the bottles I carried, and this was warm. I had to resist the urge to take a long swig, as this water had to last me to the next CP, and I knew that drinking loads would be fatal in this heat and would just cause me to throw up. I found that out whilst training in Crete. After running a couple of miles on the beach, I was so dry I drank all the water in my bottle and threw up straight away, so a lesson was learnt - it don't help though when you're 'gagging' for a drink.

Peter Kay, that famous Bolton comedian, tells a joke about middle-aged men getting lost, especially when they come out of a supermarket and cannot remember where they left their car. They run around panicking, pointing their finger, whilst saying, "Sierra's gone! Bloody Sierra's gone!" Well, that's me, short-term memory and no sense of direction. So you will not be surprised that I missed the red markers that outlined the course and ended up getting lost and going 3.5 kilometers off course! A land rover pulled up, with a couple of American marshals shouting to inform me that I was going the wrong way. I had already figured this out having seen no runners in front or behind me. I then had to go back to find a red marker and follow the course from there. This was also the advice Pierre had given us if we found ourselves lost.

A section that we passed through was known as The Valley of The Moon and it certainly was a spectacular sight as you looked up, and saw that you were surrounded by the rugged, red, peaked mountains of the Andes. I remember just standing there and removing my headphones to listen to the silence and how loud that is. Once again that feeling of being alone and vulnerable enveloped me. I knew I would not get to see anyone until I reached a CP. At times I did stop to take of my backpack and do some stretching exercises and have a good look around, but always at the back of my mind were the cut off times we had to reach the CP. Even though you had an idea how far away you were from them, it didn't help, for the terrain changed constantly and one thing I didn't fancy climbing was one of those bloody great sand mountains with just twenty minutes or so to do it in. I plodded on at a slow trot. The music helped, especially if The Rolling Stones came blasting through my ears. That would give me an energy boost and I would find myself running with a new spring in my step. I still had to keep it to a slow pace - this was only the second day and I needed all the fuel I had in my tank to complete the course.

I made it to the CP at the required time. There were some unfortunates who were getting treatment for blisters, or some other injuries on their feet incurred that day, and I silently thanked God that mine were fine. Apart from some anxious thoughts, I was feeling good and positive and, despite the freezing waters inside the slot canyons, I was enjoying myself.

But this was to be short-lived. Having reached the last CP, I set off to finish the last 10 kilometers (6 miles) and it was on this section that night fell. I had already put on my thermal jacket and night light. Darkness and the lonely silence overwhelmed me. I never got used to being on my own in that bloody desert with my paranoid thoughts. Sometimes to keep me sane I would stop and dance to a particular song that came on my i-pod. What the heck, no-one could see me, not that that bothered me much. I would have a bop mimicking Peter Kay and saying, "I've not lost it, put a bit of Tamla Motown on fer't lads", then I'd walk up to the imaginary bar and order a pint of Stella with the words, 'Ding dang do start ya engines', crazy eh? But then again 'nowt wrong wi' that'.

I made it into camp around 8pm. It starts to get dark around 5.30pm - 6pm, so I had spent a couple of hours out there on my own. My timing for that first full marathon on day 2 was 11 hours, 22 minutes, 20 seconds. I was elated.
Another day over! "4 – 4 – 2! No Fuckin' Surrender!"

CHAPTER 10

"Dressed in rags complete with wellies
Jam butty in hand for empty bellies
Body battered, mind confused
Toss the coin heads or tails you lose

You have to go out in order to get in
But just like the garbage I live in a bin
There's a cobbled street outside our door
That leads to the mill where poor folk go
Washing lines outside back yards
Not much on'em times are hard

The rag and bone man cries for scrap
He'll give you a stone for this and that
Bent figured Lowry's living in gloom
Poverty and violence now't else in't room
Sit down in silence or you'll get a clout
We're only kids but we can't play out

Rag and Bone Run

The days I dreaded the most were when my mam had to find some form of clothing to take to the ragman. In those days, the rag and bone men came round the streets crying out "rag bone" and the poor women, huddled under shawls on their shoulders, would take out anything they could lay their hands on to the man waiting next to his horse and cart. For this they would usually get a rubbing stone. A rubbing stone was a white stone used to clean the front step of their terraced houses. Lancashire women in them days, even though they had nowt, were very house proud and all the terraced houses had their doorsteps and outside window sills scrubbed white. Sometimes, perhaps they would exchange their cast off clothes for some other stuff on the rag man's cart which some poor sod had had to give up to exchange for summat else.

But if you wanted money (and you didn't get much), then you had to take the cast off clothes down to 'the yard'. The owner of the yard was called Tommy Taylor and his yard was down a miserable cobbled path that ran down the side of a mill. At the end of the path was a row of terraced houses that seemed to me to hang their heads in shame. Like us children, they looked a pitiful sight. Their whitewashed walls were covered in soot from the ever-present smoke belched out from the chimney mills that towered over the town. In these sad buildings lived other sad, scruffy kids who didn't have much to do with their lives. How I envied them because, whenever we were forced to do the 'rag run', they were outside playing and what joy for them to see three or four kids coming into their territory carrying bags filled with rags.

They hit us, threw stones at us and taunted us with name-calling. The worst of it came after we got the rags weighed by the unscrupulous Tommy, who usually gave you a shilling no matter how much more my mother found to put into the bags. We would then have to go back down the same path where the kids would be waiting to do it all over again and then threaten us that "if we came back again, we would get a real pasting next time". They knew we would be back.

On our way home, we would have to call into a shop where my mam didn't owe money in order to buy food to eat for that particular day. Looking back, it was heartbreaking seeing my sisters and brother crying to my mam when she would put their clothes into the bag for the ragman. There was a place where the poor could go which was run by the welfare state in order to get some more clothes. But it was a terrible large bleak building straight out of a Charles Dickens' novel; run by Dickens' characters the sly ones who made you feel that they were doing you a favor. My mam would rummage through the stalls with all nine of us kids, making us try on all kinds of horrible smelly clothes. These were second-hand, probably leftovers from a jumble sale that nobody wanted. She would sometimes make us put some shirts or skirts up our jumpers. We were only allowed so much. If we ever saw anything we liked, we would usually be told we couldn't have that by the man who ran this poor charity place and he never gave a reason. When my mam had managed to kit us out with some form of clothing with us pleading, "We can't wear these," we were told that we couldn't come back for another month and we must make them last, "no taking them down to the ragman" he would say. He knew, as did everyone, that what we wore today would be back in the rag yard soon after.

CHAPTER 11

Oh I do like to be beside the seaside
Oh I do like to be beside the sea
But there's not much joy when there's little in the jar
Beside the seaside beside the sea

Summertime Blues.

Blackpool, the Lancashire Riviera, with its famous tower, the golden mile, amusement arcade's, trams, pleasure beach, donkeys rides, bingo stalls, everything to entertain you if you've got 'the brass'.

Bolton holidays - last week in June, first week in July. We were all packed for our fortnightly stay at a caravan site in Squires Gate, just opposite the airport. Now bear in mind there were 11 of us and this was still the age of the steam train, so this convoy had to be planned with military precision. My mam would set off with the girls; all six of them, then my dad would take me and my brother (the trouble makers) on a later train. The reason for this was so my mam could get the caravan ready for when we arrived. My dad controlled everything and everyone.

Even though we knew what to expect on the holiday we all still felt excited to be able to play on the beach, even if it was just for a short while. It was like letting prisoners outside to walk around the jail yard a change from the cell, eh. Once we arrived there, the routine was the same every day as it was every year.

First thing every morning, two of us kids (we took it in turns) would have to 'slop out'. We had to carry the 'wee' bucket we had used during night which took two of us to carry it cos me dad went out with my mam to the pub every night so he would fill most of it up. It was one of the worst jobs to do, carrying that bucket out. You hoped that you didn't bump into anybody and 'cos it was full to the brim, you had to walk slowly so as not to spill any. My dad had warned us what we could expect if we spilt any on the floor. I know that some of the campers knew we where being beaten inside the caravan cos they would look at us sympathetically and ask us if we were ok.

Then us kids would get dressed. And bliss! We were allowed to go to the beach for an hour. Once again, this was so my mam could 'bump start' my dad with a cup of tea, his daily intake of pills and also give him time to get his head round.

We had one hour - any later and we were in for it. "You've got tongues in your head ask the time, nine o'clock and no bloody later" he would shout in our faces (with his own tongue screwed up inside his teeth). We would bloody run as fast as our little legs would take us to get there. Oh to be free: playing on the beach, paddling in the sea, shouting, singing and laughing. An hour was not enough but my dad had to have control and depending on how bad he was feeling we would sometimes get longer. This was rare. We had to make sure there was always someone around to ask for the time. I suppose it's hard to imagine. For most kids these days, just to be a little late is no big deal. For us, we would be kicked and punched black and blue. It was a big deal for my dad and was a personal challenge to his authority and he took it very, very personally. We were never late. After our time of freedom, we would make our way back to the site, mostly singing and definitely playing. We had to make the most of it. Once back at the site, my mam would give us our breakfast tea and toast. Then we would sit inside the caravan waiting to go out with my mam and dad for a walk along the prom.

Sitting in silence again, watching all the other kids on holiday playing around the camp site was torture. My mam challenged my dad as to why we couldn't go out and play. "They're on bloody holiday there's no neighbors around here. Let 'em out from under my feet," she'd say. But my mam was always given the same response, no matter how much we said we'd behave and looked pleadingly at him. The answer was always the same. "Them lot don't know how to behave, there's other people on this site". There it was again, "other people". I suppose that's why, to this day, I have problems relating to other people.

It would usually be about 11am when my dad would say, "Put your coats on now" and we were off for our daily walk along the prom. When we all went for a walk, this had to be done in an orderly fashion. Me and my brother would walk either side of my dad, then the six girls in front, on either side of my mam. We would be at the rear so my dad could keep an eye on things. Our Michael, the youngest, would be in his pram pushed along by me mam. My dad would shout out to my mam if we were to turn left or right or stop at the shops on the front to read the funny postcards. These were moments when I saw a side of my dad me and my brothers and sisters craved for. For a start, on these walks he would sometimes whistle, grab one of us and give us a tickle. But if we responded too much, he would say, "Alright, that's enough, you're getting out of hand now".

Now the reason we went out at 11am was that, after an hour or so walking down the prom it would be time for lunch. My mam would buy a loaf of bread then we would find a chip shop, there were loads to choose from, and we looked for one that sold the cheapest chips with the largest portions. The order would be for five bags of chips for us kids to share and fish and chips for my dad. He would break bits of his fish off and give a piece to each of us kids. My mam, bless her, would just have a chip butty. She was always going without. There was a time when we were all stood outside the chippy reading the price list, when a car pulled up. A man got out and gave my dad a fiver. "My treat," he told dad. Well, there were six bags and two fish that day. We would eat our lunch in the shelters on the prom and then we would slowly walk back to the campsite.

On some occasions we would go on to the pleasure beach but without money to spend it's no fun watching the other kids enjoying the rides. Once back at the campsite we would sit down again and wait for tea. This was usually sandwiches; beef paste butties, sometimes with lettuce and tomatoes. After tea we would then wait for the time when my mam and dad went to the pub. I'm more than sure my mam would have preferred to have done something else with us kids but she loved my dad and did what he wanted. He ruled the household.

At precisely 6pm we were once again told to "get your coats on" and off we'd go to the pub. When I say 'we', my mam and dad went inside the pub, we could play for a couple of hours in the park next door. Now you'd think we'd be happy. It was fun at first playing on the swings until the local kid's saw us, and then it wasn't so much fun. We became friends at first but, as kids do if there is a fall-out, we just couldn't leave and go home. So we would walk away from the swings and sit on a bench outside the park and wait. Halfway through the night my mam would bring out some crisps for us to share, tell us she wouldn't be long, and then disappear back into the pub.

Eventually they would both come out. At last my dad was okay to talk to and have a laugh with, thanks to the booze. On those walks back to the campsite, he would sing songs, pick us up and swing us round. We all loved this side of him but as we approached the campsite everything went back to being orderly. "No noise now, people may be in bed," my dad would say. Once inside the caravan, it was straight to bed. Us kids slept in one half, squashed on seats that turned into beds. Mam and dad would slide the dividing doors and they'd sleep in the other half. "Now get to sleep. I don't want to hear a murmur out of you 'till morning," said my dad, and he never did.

That was it until the next day and then it was all repeated again and for several years after. When I was a lot older and I had a car, I took my mam and dad to Blackpool for the day. We stopped off at the beach we used to play on when we were kids, and I said to my dad,

"Do you remember when we used to come here year after year for our holidays?"

"Yes," he said, with a smile on his face. "I do."

"Well, you know what," I said.

"What?" he asked. "I bloody hated it," I said. I'd 'waited years to tell him that.

CHAPTER 12

The little boy stood in the playground yard
Scared of the bullies who stared at him hard
He knew he was scruffy, smelly as well
Please hurry up and ring the bell

There was never a smile that lit up his face
Just the words in his head repeating
You're a waste of space
Saturday night piss up that's all you are
Get out off my sight you bastard boy

Marks on his legs made by his wellies
Some others put 'em there but tell if you dare
That hungry feeling he felt every day
Even after tea never went away

Birthday and Christmas were just the same
Like snakes and ladders his life was a game
Up one minute but never for long
Always ended up down that's where you belong

Hands covered his head as he wet himself
The beatings stopped he'd run away, given the chance
Stop that crying or you'll get some more
Thrown into backyard then the slamming of the door

In the outside toilet he could lick his wounds
He wished his dad would stop having these moods

The little boy stood in the playground yard
Just another day never easy, always hard

Chocolate Chains

Aye, life was bloody hard. There were some funny
moments too but looking back they certainly weren't
funny at the time. Like the time my dad got a job working for
the council on the bins. He came home one day carrying a big
box. He told my mam, "Look what I've fetched home for the
kids." We all gathered around the box. My dad had fetched
something home for us kids; I thought whatever next. This was
something we were never used to. We all gathered excitedly
around the box. "Dad, what's in the box, we all spoke at once.
"Wait a bloody minute while I get out of these work clothes,"
he shouted.

We waited, irritably pushing and shoving each other so we
could be first in line when he opened it. Eventually he came
downstairs and took his time opening the box. I think he was
getting some form of sadistic pleasure out of this. When at last
it was opened, he removed its contents and our little eyes all lit
up. He spread out onto the table bar after bar of chocolate.
Well, you could imagine the look on our faces, not to mention
the feeling in our bellies. The only time we ever came this
close to chocolate was looking through a shop window.
"Right," he said, "pick one bar each but no more." There were
so many different kinds of bars to choose from, we didn't know
which one to pick because we wanted them all. "Hurry bloody
up or I'll put 'em back and you'll get now't, and don't open
them 'till I tell you", he said. At this instruction we all eagerly
picked one. "Okay, now sit down and when you're all sat down
together you can open 'em."

We were down on those chairs quicker than you could blink an eyelid. "Go on, open 'em," he barked. We eagerly ripped off the wrappers. Now comes the sick, funny bit for my dad, for inside the wrappings what we thought was chocolate was in fact shapes of chocolate made from wood. Dad had gotten these from his rounds outside a shop. They were just display bars. I remember him laughing. Now you would have thought he would have at least brought a couple of real bars back home that we could share just to soften the blow.

"What the bloody hell's up with you all he said as we began to frown. "You can take 'em to school and play jokes on your mates." Yeah right. This was Lancashire in the 1950s. Nobody had nowt and that type of a joke would have got you a beating. We were still not allowed out to play, so we played 'shop' in whispers with the wooden chocolate bars. Any form of noise like talking a bit too loud was never tolerated. If we violated this rule, we where severely beaten with the buckle end of the belt. On numerous occasions I was taken to the casualty department at the local hospital, and it was only years later, whilst reading some of my early childhood medical records, I saw it stated 'injuries suspicious'.

Once upon a time in a world long ago
Lived nine little children that nobody would know
In dreams they traveled to places of make believe
But they where the forest the others the trees

There was the time we got our first television set. We had only ever had a wireless, which we would listen to on a Sunday if we'd been good. We listened to the Blackpool comedian, Jimmy Clitheroe. For those of you who don't know or remember him, he was a man that looked like a boy and also had the voice of a child, he was considered very funny.

Our first telly was a small black and white set. It was known as a 'slot' telly and, at the back of the set it had a meter into which you put a tanner. This lasted for half-an-hour. So if we were allowed to watch a film, dad would put two tanners in. Now in theory this should have lasted for an hour, which was about the length of a film in those days. So you can imagine nine kids sat silently together, watching the Lone Ranger. The film was just coming to its climax. At last, the Lone Ranger was going to have it out with the baddies. We would be sat on the edge of the worn-out sofa, excitedly leaning forwards to get more into the film. "Go on Lone Ranger. Get 'em," we would say excitedly, then, suddenly the meter ran out. The telly went off automatically. We would all cry in unison "Ahhh!" and look pleadingly at our dad, who would say, "I've only got enough for a couple of pints tonight and Jesus Christ wouldn't get that".

I don't think he meant to blaspheme. In fact, I suspect he did believe in God. He was just being truthful. He needed his beer money and later on in my life, so did I. The telly stayed off and once again we would sit silently, each child wrapped up in their own thoughts.

We were kids. We should've been outside playing. My dad's excuse as to the reason why not, was it upset the neighbors. I suppose that's why I have trouble with people today. I'm a friendly guy and get on well with people but I still have a low tolerance of them.

Pita pata pita pata pita pata pita pata
Tick tock tick tock tick tock tick tock
Pita pata pita pata pita pata pita pata
Tick tock tick tock tick tock tick tock

Rain against the window ticking of the clock
I'm sat here all alone forget me not
Thoughts racing, imaginary games
A knight in shining armour rescuing the dames

The fire in the living room is a dragon's lair
I see his eyes burning into my golden hair
My white trusted steed carries my sword and shield
And just like the creature my fate is sealed

Pita pata pita pata pita pata pita pata
Tick tock tick tock tick tock tick tock
Pita pata pita pata pita pata pita pata
Tick tock tick tock tick tock tick tock

Time moves on trapped in a world
Where children should be seen but never heard
Poverty and violence bread and jam
Clothes for the rag man packed in a pram

Nine green bottles huddled in a hall
One by one they're all gonna fall
They have no smiles just a pleading frown
A'tisho a'tisho we all fall down

Pita pata pita pata pita pata pita pata
Tick tock tick tock tick tock tick tock
Pita pata pita pata pita pata pita pata
Tick tock tick tock STOP THE RAIN, STOP THE CLOCK.

On a Sunday when we got back from church, my dad would go off to the pub for a lunchtime 'session'. This was good because my mam, who would be sat rocking in her chair, would let us out into the backyard to play so long as we were quiet. She didn't want the neighbors complaining about the noise her kids made. I don't believe we ever did make much noise but my dad installed this belief in us all. It was only a tiny backyard and with nine kids playing in it, there wasn't much you could do. We didn't have a ball or skipping ropes. There were no toys so we would play 'Cowboys and Indians' or 'Cops and Robbers' in hushed whispers. We once tried playing 'hide and seek' but the only place to hide was the outside loo. Still, we were outside so it didn't matter. My mam argued nearly every day with my dad. "Let the bloody kids out to play, will you?" she shouted. This always ended up with her getting her hair pulled out violently by my dad. Sometimes she would fight back. These were the worst moments of my life. I would have sooner took a pasting rather than watch my mam get one.

Me dad would get back from the pub five minutes after closing time which was at two o'clock on a Sunday afternoon, 'it wer' just up t'road' so he hadn't far to stagger. Opening the front door, he would walk in to be greeted by us all sat down quietly, have his dinner and trot off upstairs to sleep off his lunchtime 'session'. We would then sit still and talk in whispers watching our mam darn one of our clothes, as she rocked away in the chair. The frustration I felt listening to the other kids laughing and playing outside ate away inside me so much I wanted to scream. It was only when my dads snoring got louder that we could relax for a while and even get up and move around the house, even if it was just to peek outside the windows to watch the other kids having fun outside. I could tell me mam so much wanted us to be out there as much as we did cos she'd get out of her chair come over to the window stroke my hair and put her arms around me. She once said whilst doing this "don't worry you won't always be kids, he cant stop you growing up". Hope! A life line I will always thank her for.

Close your eyes to what you saw
Go back in time to when you were a boy
Sat in silence to the ticking clock
Close your eyes and watch your mother rock

Remember the days with the towering mills
The cobbled streets and the jack and Jills
The rag and bone man who cried for scrap
Remember the days of the pony and trap

Listen to the women as they gossip round back
Look at the kids dressed in rags and flat cap
The oil lamps that lit up the road at night
Listen to the men brawl in a drunken fight

Watch the coalman unload his cart
The Salvation Army band, play as they march
Go to the shop with credit book in hand
Watch the pitmen climb on the trams

Stop for a minute and remember tin bath
Or snakes and ladders played without a laugh
The old slot telly, have you a tanner to spare
Stop in time and have a good stare

Close your eyes for the last time
Those days have gone but they were mine
Clay pipes smoked clogs were worn
Close your eyes you weren't on your own.

I have to say, I know nothing of my dad's upbringing. I only remember my mam telling us his father was just the same, handy with his fists and dishing out the mental cruelty so I suppose it was handed down.

Whenever he took me and my brother Roy out for his walks which were often, we had too walk one on each side of him. We had too walk in step with him and all again done in silence. If he noticed anyone he knew walking towards him he would do a body swerve around the first corner to avoid having to engage in any form of conversation with them.

The walks for two little kids (we would only be around 8 and nine years old) were long and sometimes we'd be gone from home for at least two hours and all we did was walk during that time. Looking back I suppose I can thank him for giving me the endurance I was later to need in life. If he ever did stop to talk to anyone we were told to walk on a few yards and wait. If it was a women, he would threaten us not to tell our mam when we got home. "If we knew what was good for us". I don't know why he bothered we already had the fear of the devil installed in us.

In summer he would take us to the Queens Park in Bolton. This is a town a couple of miles from ours so we would catch the bus and if he was in the right mood we could sit on the top deck. Once off the bus it would be about half a mile walk to the park where we would sit under the same spot next to a large oak tree. Further down the park was the paddling pool were the kids where having fun splashing about inside it, me and our Roy would pick daffodils talking in whispers whilst making a chain.

I remember the time when we left our little two-up-two-down terraced prison where we had spent most of our childhood. The year was 1961 and the council had eventually listened to my mother's pleas that we needed a bigger place. Remember we had no bath, except the tin one that hung on a nail on the wall outside the backyard. It was now difficult to bath us all. Before, when we were smaller, she could fit at least three of us in the bath and would have to boil the water in various pans over the fire. So we were given a new house in George Street, New Bury, which was a couple of miles up the road from our old one at the other end of town.

The decorators were in doing it up, the council official told her, but he said we could go up there to use the bath until it was complete. This house had five bedrooms, two living rooms, a kitchen and yes, a bathroom. The reason for it being so roomy was that the council had extended it by knocking through to the other house it was attached to in order to accommodate larger families, and there were plenty of them around after the war had ended.

Can you imagine the excitement we kids felt when the day came for us to go up and have a bath. The house to us was a mansion. We had been told that we could have our own room, one just for me and our Roy and the girls also would no longer have to share one bed. Things were gonna be different, my dad had announced, and they were for a couple of days until the novelty wore off and he told us, "Don't think you're going outside to play, I have the neighbors to think about." There it was again, other people, he was always worrying about other people and what they would think.

Life returned back to normal for my dad. We were to live in this house for about three years but my dad hated the neighborhood and had asked the council for an exchange to another area, his reason was that the area was too rough to let the children out to play - bloody cheek.

25 Brookhouse Avenue was our next and last move with mi mam and dad. We were getting older and my dad was finding it hard to keep us from going out to play, so eventually we were allowed out but only until six o'clock as that's when mi dad and mam went to the pub. How embarrassing it was making up excuses to our mates as to why we had to go home, but eventually we would say that we had to do our homework which was a laugh in itself 'cos our dad didn't agree with us doing homework. "You tell them bloody teachers that they have you all day and when you come home you have work to do around the house." In fact he even phoned up our school to voice this opinion to the headmaster.

> Mary had a little lamb she also had eight more
> Bleatingly they went for milk
> But there wasn't much in store
> One by one they grew up to be sheep
> And set off to find pastures new
> The grass was greener on the other side
> But they hadn't learnt how to chew

Don't bloody chase me round this room my dad would scream holding the belt in his hand, I mean just curling up in a ball to protect yourself never worked the belt always found its mark so running to escape the onslaught and fury of my dad was the only choice it brought sometimes. I knew that this only made his temper worse and I would beg and scream, crying, I was sorry for whatever it was I was supposed to have done, but it fell on deaf ears and once he finally caught up to me, I curled up under the table and the lashing would start.

My dad used to say whilst waving the belt under our noses "your all gonna bloody get it then I know I've got the right one". Right one, we were to scared to do anything wrong. Our fault was that we had even been born. He used to say "your not bloody wanted, none of you should have been born". God how he hated us you could see it on his face. His tongue would curl and he would clamp it between his teeth and look at us with shear hatred in his eyes. He would shout "get out of my sight ".

We were even punished for being ill. Being sent home from school at a young age for being poorly was a nightmare. My class teacher at my junior school once walked me home I was about eight at the time. Our house wasn't far away from the school. I kept telling the teacher I would be fine even though I'd been sick in the classroom. She held my hand and stroked my hair reassuring me it would be fine and also questioning me why I didn't want to go home. "You need to be in bed with your mam looking after you", she said. Little did she know? I remember the house was silent as she knocked at the door; my mam opened it to be greeted by the teacher who explained that I'd been sick in class and also had a fever. I knew by the look on my mam's face she didn't know what to say or do. My dad was sat behind the door listening to every word she said. Eventually the teacher left. I walked inside and stood at the doorway looking up at my dad, "so you've a bloody fever eh, get over here he shouted". I walked nervously towards him and he lifted his hand to my forehead to feel my temperature then whack right across the back of my head. He accused me of getting out of bed at night when he was out with my mam at the pub. He grabbed me by the scruff of the neck and dragged me upstairs punching me then threw me onto the bed telling me that if I was ill "tha won't need owt to eat". I had to stay there all day, every now and then I could hear him standing at the bottom of the stairs to listen whether I'd got out of bed and was moving around. It was awful I couldn't even go down stairs for a pee in case he hit me so I would just wet the bed.

My mam would come up after I'd heard them rowing and check out how I was, telling me she would try and sneak something up later. If my dad had caught her we would both have been beaten. So my mam learnt how to box clever, it was her way of protecting us.

Years later after my dad had died, my mam told my partner Bridget, that she would have left him years ago but that there just wasn't the help back then. It was the old saying " tha's made thee bed, now tha mon lie on it.

We all suffered at the hands of my dad.

Our Barbara who was the eldest bore the brunt of my dad's violence in the earlier days but when I came along I was the eldest boy and expected to take the punishment. Barbara has never been right since and has lived most of her life in a world of her own as does our Brenda.

The spider spins its web of deceit
So fine and intricate so callous and neat
Hidden it lies patiently in wait for its prey
And I'm so confused I've lost my way

Time moved on and my mothers words started to bear fruit in me. I was getting older and just a little bit bolder. It was almost like I was becoming used to the belt and fists smashing into me, not just from my dad but also the school bullies. The fear inside me never went away. In order for me to get my dad to allow me out to play, I would ask my few friends to call round for me. When they called they knew that something was wrong, not that I told em owt but they where my friends and kept asking me why I couldn't play out. I made excuse after excuse till I finally said my dad was a bastard and wouldn't let me out in case I got into any trouble. Even though he would say no to them they persisted until the day he gave in. I was young and getting stronger whilst he was old and getting weaker. Young bucks eh?

By now our Barbara and Bernice had flown the nest, and also our Eileen and who could blame them. Our Roy was coming up fast on my heels and he to had his friends calling round. Then our Jean also had her mates so between us he finally caved in. Still we had to be home by 6pm "not a minute bloody later", he would shout. We were always on time.

The dye had been cast and freedom was born. Our appetite for it grew and grew and we pushed against the boundaries. We eventually managed to push the time further back from 6pm till 7pm. Bear in mind I was now approaching the age of 14 and only one more year to go and I would be leaving school. I couldn't fucking wait, cos when I did boy was I gonna have some fun. I could feel it growing inside of me, the hate and frustration, the fear and pain, the poverty and violence I was gonna hit back and get revenge on it all just fucking watch me I would say to myself,

Just fucking watch me.

CHAPTER 13

Starved of affection and so much more
The prisoner walked out from the locked door
Kissed by the sunshine and the daylight outside
He ran into the world, happy free and wild.

Mods, Skinheads and Crombie Boys.

The first job I got after I left school was as an apprentice Butcher at Mark Schofield in Deansgate, Bolton. My dad had gotten me this job. The take-home pay was £3.2s.6d and my dad got £3 of this and I got the 2s.6d. Before I left school I'd got myself a job on a paper round that my dad knew nothing about. As it was an early morning paper round, my mam would get me up at about 6am. My dad never found out about this job as he never got out of bed 'till we all had gone off to school. My dad used to get up around 8 o'clock and we would be expected to be out of the house before he got up. This was too early for us to go to school so we would have to stand around in an empty playground until school started, no matter what the weather was like.

Anyroad, back to the paper round. I would get at least 7s.6d for doing that round from which I gave my mam 4s and I kept the rest (3s.6d). So you can see that when I went to work at the butchers for five and half days a week - I was 1 shilling worse off and working harder for it.

Every Friday my dad would make his way down to Bolton to collect my wages. He knew that they were usually ready by lunchtime and I had to make sure that I had them for when he turned up. This went on every week until I was 16 years old, by which time I was beginning to fight back a little; by this I mean I would challenge him about waiting until I got home to give him my wages. I told him it was embarrassing for me and that some of the lads who worked there were beginning to take 'the piss'. I didn't use those words - I would have ended up in casualty - but I told him I was sick of being laughed at. He eventually gave in but I was still only getting 2s.6d until I reached 16. At age 16, my wages then went up to £3.7s.6d and my spending money rose to 5 shillings.

Rows between my mother and father went on all the time. I found any way I could to escape the past and present situation that life had dished out to me. It wasn't fair and without knowing it at the time I wanted revenge. I so much wanted to be a part of the 'in crowd' but I felt I just didn't fit in. Maybe it was because I just didn't know how too. Starting life in extreme poverty never leaves you, no matter what. The clothes that I wore were a second-hand version of what the other kids had. My blessing was, that once inside the clubs, it was dark but I had no confidence or self-respect to mix so, as usual, I was on the outside looking in. For most of my life - even up to the present day - I still feel like that.

> Tamla Motown sounds mingled with the Who
> *Ain't no sunshine in my life,* who are you
> Put on your boots and braces
> Its pay back time
> Tool up snort line poverty is crime.

'Ain't no mountain high enough?' Diana Ross and the Supremes belted out this great Tamla Motown sound, as me and my mates danced in a circle alongside the girls. I was smashed out of my head on Blue's otherwise known as 'speed'. It was 1969. What an era: The Who, The Kinks, Small Faces, Mods, Skinheads, Smoothies in their bottle green suits with loafers on their feet, sex, Drugs and Northern Soul. I had arrived but little did I know this would be the slow slide into hell. I say 'slow' because it took another 23 years to get there.

When you have spent most of your life in poverty, violence and being 'kept in your place', where children should be seen and not heard and then suddenly you find freedom with choices, you grab it with every fiber in your body. Not that anything had changed in our household. My dad still ruled with strict Victorian authority. It's just that we were older and bigger now, so he couldn't dish out the violence, though he would find other ways to subdue us. For instance, we weren't allowed a record player and if we weren't home at a certain time we were locked out. We still had to hand over our pay packet and wait until he gave us our pocket money. Friends were seldom allowed around, not that we wanted to bring any home. I was so ashamed at the way we lived; we still lived in a hovel.

I was sixteen by now and getting bigger, either that or my dad was shrinking. He also wasn't as handy towards me with his fists, only his mouth. He was still violent towards my mam. The very first time I stood up to him, is burnt into my memory. I had just walked through the door and they were shouting and screaming at each other. Suddenly he moved with fist clenched towards her I jumped up and stood in between them to protect her. He was yelling and cursing at what he was gonna do but he couldn't get at her with me in the way and the shock on his face when he tried to push me away is one I will never forget. I never even flinched like in the past when I would cower just in his presence. I just stood there. My mam, by this time had realized something that I hadn't and said to my dad "I bloody told you that one day he would grow up" this remark didn't help the situation.

So in order to calm the situation I turned, grabbed my mam and led her into the other room in order for him to save some face. I have to admit though I was shaking like an alcoholic with the DT's. His crown as king of the castle was slipping and he knew I knew that. I was waiting to knock it off. It would be another year and more of these confrontations before his crown fell and by that I mean he knew his control over me was over.

I was 17yr when the final confrontation with my dad came to a head. The incident happened as I had just walked thru the door. Our Michael the youngest of the brood would have been about seven. As I walked into the back kitchen I could hear screaming coming from the other room. I had just finished work so I threw my workbag down on the floor and ran in, it was like a flashback from the past cos our Michael was cowering on the sofa with his hands above his head to fend of the blows just like I had when I was his age trying to fend of the blows from the belt.

I fucking grabbed him demanding to know why he was lashing out at him like that. His only pathetic excuse was that Michael had been fighting with some other boy in the street, "So what". I said, leave him alone your bigger than he his. He looked at me and I knew this was gonna be the decider for the crown. His reply was to challenge me on what I was gonna do about it. I replied that I was bigger than our Michael and if he still wanted to lash out then lash out at me. His face was red with anger, his tongue bent between his teeth; he always did this when he was in a rage. He suddenly threw himself at me with his fists swinging wildly, by now I'd been in a few skin head fights so I dodged him and grabbed him by the neck slamming both of us to the floor holding on to his neck tightly.

His face was turned up towards mine he knew I had him and that it was all over. I knew he could feel the gripping power I had on him. I looked into his face the memories of the past came flooding back, all those beating he had given me with the evil look on his face where not there anymore. This time I could only see fear, fear for himself, for he knew it was over. He knew it. I knew it. For a moment our eyes met and I wanted to say sorry I wanted to hug him and tell him I loved him but I didn't get the chance cos suddenly my mam came in and hit me over the back of the head with the brush, shouting "leave him bloody alone and get out, get out of this house. This is true love eh? Call it what you want, judge what you will, she was the protector of the household, whenever she could, she was there for everyone and this was her husband. Even if she wasn't able or strong enough to carry this roll, she tried her best. I let go of the grip I had on him and ran from the house. I ran and ran until I was in the backstreets then I broke down and cried.

I went to our Bernice's and lived with her for a short time, there was no going back even if I had wanted to it was over and my life was to begin.

> I don't want to be me let me be you
> I have nothing and am nobody inside
> Just for a moment let me look thru your eyes
> Back at me a bastard boy who can't hide

I wanted to be a mod; I just loved the clothes that they wore. Bottle green suits, three buttons down the front, and a long (14 inches) single vent down the centre of the back. With a pair of brown loafer shoes on your feet, purple silk shirt, thin colored tie, you certainly looked 'the bee's knees'. But in order to be a mod you had to have money, a big problem for me. I suppose because I was always dressed as a tramp, to be a mod was the perfect choice: the desire to look smart and be accepted was my driving force. We had a Burton's tailors in our town and it was where the local mods would go to get measured for a suit. For a small deposit and a weekly payment, you could obtain one. For me, it was a mountain to climb, as I only got a couple of shillings a week 'spending money'. I had to save a bit each week in order to get the deposit. In the meantime, I wore a poor version of the dress code. I didn't have a suit, so I possessed a 'mix and match' outfit: a pair of black trousers, a brown coat, white shirt, thin black tie, and ordinary black shoes.

The trouble with the mods was they were always changing the fashion, so by the time I managed to get the deposit together and fitted up with a single breasted suit, double breasted suits were in. There I'd be turning up at the local club (Hollings School on Market Street) dressed in my bottle green new suit and the rest of the mods would be wearing double breasted brown ones. I may as well have gone dressed as 'Batman' for all the looks and sneers I got. Mind you, it did take at least a year for me to save up for it so I was gonna wear the bloody thing.

What a relief it was for me when the skinheads came into fashion; gone were the suits and loafer shoes. Now it was a pair of Levi or wrangler jeans, a pair of Doc Martin boots, a Ben Sherman shirt, braces, and hair cropped to the bone. Though this fashion was less expensive, it still cost a bob or two to buy Levis and Doc Martin boots but once you had em that was it you were in with the in-crowd.

I really enjoyed my skinhead days. I was in the local gang and also accepted as one of them. Now I had an identity. I ran with them, fought with them, got pissed with them; they were the family I always wanted.

I got in with a lad called Brian Howarth his dad owned a furniture business so because of this wealth he had a car, (A Mini Moat) which we would all pile in and cruise around the forbidden town of Little Hulton. If we saw some local skinheads we would pull up, pile out and have a fight before driving quickly back to the safety of our town before word got out that the farnworth skins were here. Brian eventually left Bolton and went to live in Blackpool where he lived in a static caravan. I was bumming around at the time with nowhere proper to live so he invited me down to live with him for a short while, which I did. I got a job in a crisp factory, but my drinking was increasing and my urge to travel was getting stronger so eventually I moved on. Me and Brian became great lifelong friends and I owe him a lot for his acceptance of me and the help he gave me in the past.

> Black leather jackets and Doc Martin boots
> Angels and skinheads bring on the troops
> Battles and booze lets have a party
> Life is good, when you're naughty.

We used to go to the seaside resort of Blackpool each bank holiday to fight with the bikers (Hell's Angels). We would meet up at the local bus station, and double up on scooters with those who could afford one (not me). On our way there we would join the other skinheads from Bolton and Bury plus the surrounding towns. What a sight it was; a couple of hundred scooters, with their dozen or so wing mirrors on the front, long aerials bearing little union jack flags on the back end, and parka-wearing skinheads and some mods cruising down the road passing through the different towns. We certainly looked a force to be recognized and made the local police sit up and stare.

We would pull up just on the outskirts of Blackpool at some roadside pub, and go in and sink some 'fighting fluid'. I would be completely on a high, full of excitement, fear, and the rush to get the show underway. After knocking back a few beers, we would be outside doubling up on the scooters for the parade through Blackpool. The atmosphere amongst us was, to say the least, invigorating and exciting.

Driving along the prom' was such a buzz. I knew that pretty soon I would be on the beach fighting with the bikers, and I didn't care whether or not I took a kicking as having 'battle scars' gave you a certain amount of credit, like collecting a scalp - even if it was yours.

We would make our way to the South Pier. This is where the action would be on the beach. It didn't take long for us to see the line of motorbikes parked up around the green shelters that one associates with the seaside. Usually there would be a few bikers dressed in their black leather jackets, decorated with chains on the back, posted as look outs. Now the ones to watch out for were the biker girls; these I believe had as much, if not more, bottle than the lads. They would come at you like wild cats, spitting and waving some bike chain in their hands. This would be a job for the skinhead girls to sort out and they could give as good as they got.

The moment we pulled up, all hell would break loose. The look-out bikers would shout down to the rest of their gang waiting on the beach - who were drinking bottles of booze and 'tooling up' for the fight - that the skinheads were here. The bikers or 'hell's angels', as they liked to be called, didn't have to wait long for us to join em; we were off our scooters quicker than they could start singing the Rolling Stones song 'Jumping Jack Flash'. It must have been a sight for the holiday-makers and I reckon more photos would have been taken of us than Blackpool's famous tower. The moment we set foot on the sands the fighting would start and soon it would become a free-for-all. I never got chance to see who I was fighting with; if they had a leather jacket on just 'kick its fuckin teeth in'. I can, however, remember seeing 'stars' as blows rained into my face from all angles. The whole scene would become 'completely manic' and you hadn't time to look around to see how your mates were faring. You could hear the moans from some of the wounded and the screaming from the girls which just accelerated the situation. These battles with the Hell's Angels never really lasted long before the cops arrived. By the time they did, however, it would be nearly over and many a time during the fight you got glimpses of them stood on the prom', just waiting, and weighing the situation up before they moved in - and who can blame them?

What a buzz it was driving along the prom; two hundred or so scooters certainly made everyone stop and stare. I know I wanted to let someone feel the pain I felt and, though I was scared of the fighting that was about to start, I would run straight into it, fists flying, just to vent out my anger. I wanted the gang to see me getting stuck in, even though nine times out of ten I came off worst. I needed to be accepted.

Once, mi dad caught a lad who lived in our street bullying me as we walked home from school. This lad was bigger than me, and stronger, and was giving me a 'right good hiding'. I ran off and into our house. My dad was stood at the window, and I noticed his face was pale and he was shaking. He came right up to my face with his tongue screwed up between his teeth. Standing nose-to-nose, he told me I had two choices; I either went outside and gave this kid a thumping or take a beating off him. I went outside, much to the surprise of this lad. I knew my dad was watching every move I made. I ran up to the lad and hit him straight in the face. He was completely taken by surprise and I could see on his face the same fear I saw on my brothers and sisters whenever my dad went to punish them. Something happened to me; for the first time in my life, this lad became my dad. I was crying and shaking as I laid into him and this time it was he who ran off. If I thought I was gonna get a pat on the back from my dad after that little episode, I couldn't have been more wrong. Once back inside the house my dad laid into me, stating I must have done something wrong for this lad to start on me in the first place.

Running with the skinheads certainly brought me out of my shell. I was no longer alone. I was with a gang that had a fighting reputation to keep up and the skinheads around my home town of Farnworth took this quite seriously. We would meet at the bus station and go down to our 'hunting ground' of Little Hulton. There we fought with the local 'skins' almost every week. Our local disco club was called the Big Apple in Peel Street. It was a small club and dimly lit inside. Here we would dance along to the Tamla Motown sounds, whilst dropping 'speed', always ready should some other outsider gangs come to try and take it over. For a small town, many came but none succeeded.

It was at this club where I started to become a D.J. At first, I would just go down there on a Saturday afternoon for the kiddy's disco to help out on the cloakroom. It paid me a 'couple of bob' and I was also 'knocking off' one of the female attendants. One afternoon the resident D.J didn't show up so Kev, the owner, asked me to play a few records. I got on so well with the kids, making them laugh, sing and dance along, that I discovered the showman in me and just loved the attention, so Kev invited me to do an hour spot each weekend. Slowly, I was moving away from the skinhead scene and getting quite a following playing records; so much so, that I got head-hunted by the owner of a club in Little Hulton (Uncle Tom's Cabin). What a buzz that was, but my reign was short-lived. Some of the locals knew I used to run with the Farnworth 'skins', and one night was waiting for me when I left the club. I'd gone outside with a local girl and I was gonna walk her home. She told me she lived on an estate which was heavily populated with the local skinheads and was certainly a place no Farnworth skinhead would walk along on their own. But I was young and full of that hot-headed blood you only have as a teenager. She had warned me about walking her home in case I got jumped. I told her, "I don't give a fuck" and that they didn't bother me, but inside I was shaking with a sense of battle fear. I never reached the estate cos they were all outside waiting to get me.

Now, to explain what happened next, I have to go back a few weeks. It was Friday teatime and I had just finished work at Fletcher's body repair shop, just off Albert Road. It was around 4.30pm and I was on my way home. Just like every Friday, I was excited the weekend was here; time to 'sink a few beers' and 'snort a line or two'. It was whilst I was in these thoughts walking home a lad run from outside a side street and bumped right into me. I knew straight away he was a Little Hultoner; he was wearing there colors. They wore red (Little Hulton was built as an overspill from Salford, Nr Manchester, and most supported Manchester United, hence the red). Farnworth wore ice blue (never did find out why).

I remember looking into his eyes and seeing the same fear I saw in my brothers and sisters when my dad was going to beat them. I didn't need to ask him what was up I knew he was being chased by some of my mates. I believe in one-to-one fighting and many a time during fights, I and some of my mates have pulled one of the lads off kicking someone else if it was two against one. I shoved this lad into a doorway as my mates came flying around the corner. Trying to look excited I pointed in the direction of the big local supermarket whilst saying, "The little bastard ran in there". When my mates disappeared, I grabbed this lad and took him through the shortcuts of the town to get him out. We didn't speak and it felt strange somehow, but also good, to be able to save someone from a kicking - something I had wished all my childhood and schooldays for. There was a border line the two gangs had on Cleggs Lane. I guided him to it; it was an unwritten law between the two rivals that once on your side, you were safe. Once at the border, we departed. Not a word had been spoken.

The gang of Little Hultoners gathered around me after I'd come out of the club and this girl, who was desperately pleading with them through all the taunts and shoving not to give me a kicking, this lad appeared out of the gang. He took one look at me, grabbed my arm, then told the rest what I had done for him whilst also saying, "If ya gonna beat him up, you will have to beat me up too". With one final shove from the leader I was left alone hence the saying 'what goes around, comes around'. After that little episode, I never went back being a D J at that club again.

CHAPTER 14

I'll never forget what's his name
I bumped into him t'other day
He was carrying one of those thingy mi jigs
He's trying to learn ta play
We agreed to meet in the what dost thi call it Arms
For a pint and a game of dart's
But I can't remember what night it was
Still he is a bit of a lost cause.

Then I traipsed up thingy mi street
Tha knows up that there road
I bumped into stammering john
Who mithered on about his cold
I thought I'd catch the summat 71 bus
That stops at that there place
But I couldn't get it together
Then again I'm outta my face.

I knew I had to buy a thingy mi bob
To fit my hosepipe together
But I'd left mi money on't mantelpiece
I'm always in a hurry
There's a light on but know one's in
I shud'nt be left out alone
There's only one thing left to do
I'll have to shank's pony it back home.

Be Young! Be Foolish! Be Happy!

Northern Soul and Wigan Casino, yes it certainly was good to be alive in the era of the 70s, even though I still lived at home and still shared a bed with my brother. I was enjoying this new-found freedom.

On a Saturday night the soul gang would meet in a pub in Market Street for the all-nighters at the casino. These soul sessions went on all night and we danced all night. This required a certain substance to enable us to dance and stay awake and this substance was 'speed'. We also took with us a little hold all which contained a towel and another t-shirt to change into during the night's sweating and dancing. Dressed in bell-bottom jeans, complete with braces, a Ben Sherman shirt and a pair of loafers on our feet, we were the 'bee's knees'. This same style of dress was also worn by the girls in our gang.

The night would start off at the local pub, which we had taken over as our meeting place. I remember getting dressed and 'buzzing' just walking down Market Street. How I enjoyed those Northern Soul nights. It gave you the chance to show off your dancing skills and I considered myself a pretty good mover on the floor. One of the moves was to semi-split onto the floor, then come up and spin around, put your hands together and move them from side to side with the Northern Soul beat banging in the background. It was sheer bliss and I felt so alive. We would sink a couple of lagers then find out who would be bringing the 'speed', how much it was going cost and how many we would be swallowing. This had to be done just right. If you took too many you could end up not sleeping for a couple of days, which had happened to all of us. It was no good when it was time to get up for work on Monday. 'Speed' can give you a very bad come-down, so sleep was needed if you were going to work on Monday morning. On the other hand, if you didn't pop enough then you would crash-out at the venue which was a 'bummer'. I have to say, we almost always took just enough.

The downside to this kind of lifestyle of 'dropping speed' was if you had a girlfriend or pulled one that night, sex was out of the question. Now maybe some people out there reading this may have been fortunate enough to get an erection on 'speed' but I certainly never did. It was common talk among the lads who took 'speed' that this was the only downside to the drug.

I remember one night a friend of mine had got his hands on some 'sleepers' (barbiturates). It was known at the time that the great Jimi Hendrix - not that I listened to his music - was the 'king' of these pills. Sadly it was to kill him or that was what the official report in the papers said. My mate asked me if I was up for popping a couple. You have to remember around this time that drugs were still in their infancy. I was up for anything. With years of being kept a prisoner, I had plenty of catching up to do, so we agreed to meet one Sunday night at the Post Office pub in Farnworth.

I was still only 17 at the time and always felt excited whenever something new came my way. But if I thought I was in for a good night, I was greatly disappointed. We met, drank a couple of beers to pluck up the courage to take the pills, then off we went to the toilet to 'pop' them.

For the next hour or so I felt pretty relaxed. It was not something I was used to. Then I noticed my speech was becoming slurred and when I had to go to the toilet, I had a 'stagger on'. Being in a packed pub, I upset a couple of regulars by bumping into them accidentally but in my drugged state of mind I just said "sorry" and tried to smile at them. I couldn't seem to focus on who I was speaking to and I don't remember much after that except being woken up by the pub's landlord. How I got home remains a mystery. I was the kind of kid that liked getting 'stoned' but I liked to be awake and enjoy it, so this was the end of the 'barbs' for me. Sadly, a couple of my mates died from taking this drug.

There was a record around at the time by the Elgin's called "Be Young Be Foolish but Be Happy." This to me summed up everything I had been deprived of. I literally loved this tune. I followed its words in my thinking and everything I did. To be honest I still do. I think we would all probably live a bit longer and get on a bit better if we put those words into practice. I don't think there would be as much depression around.

I'm up at seven and out of bed
Not really knowing where I've left my head
It's time for work and I must go
The foundry awaits me ho ho ho
Hot dirty work, mates miserable and snappy
And I'm singing be young, be foolish, but be happy

"D'ya fancy taking a trip?" my friend Frank asked me as we sat in his upstairs bedroom at his parents' house in my home town of Farnworth. The year was 1970 and I was 19 years old. I knew he wasn't meaning a holiday trip. No, the kind of trip Frank was on about was the kind that went on in the mind. "I've got some great acid (LSD)," he announced. "It's called

'Strawberry Fields (after the classic Beatles song)." One of the verses of the lyric goes:

> '*Let me take you down*
> *Cos I'm going to Strawberry Fields;*
> *Nothing is real and nothing to get hung about;*
> *Strawberry Fields forever.'*

He opened up his bedroom drawer and pulled out these microdot tablets.

"D'ya fancy a full one or half?" They were known as microdot tabs 'cos you could hardly see them.

"Hang on a minute," I said, "I've not agreed yet."

I had recently read an article about Keith Moon and Pete Townsend, two members from the rock group, *The Who.* They had both decided whilst flying to the USA, to 'drop a tab each' and experience what it was like tripping out of your head on a plane. Acid, for those who may not know, is a hallucogenic drug that takes one's mind out of reality and into a world of strange illusions.

From all accounts, Pete and Keith had a bad time hallucinating on that plane, seeing weird images, like watching the plane melt in front of their eyes. At one point they both felt they were gonna die. Being on a plane, they couldn't just get off. On reflection, they both agreed this was not an experiment they were likely to repeat; it had left them somewhat mentally scarred.

As my mind drifted back to this story, I turned to Frank and asked him what the effects of acid were. I was no stranger to drugs, having already experimented. I still took marijuana, amphetamines, and barbiturates. Frank turned to me and smiled. "It's just like smoking dope," he said, "but gets you a bit higher."

I knew Frank had tripped before. We had known each other from secondary school and kept up this friendship into our teenage years. I trusted him and so I agreed on giving it a try. Remember I was just nineteen and full of the young dare-devil blood that knows no fear. Plus, having been kept a prisoner as a child growing up, I wanted life and all it had to offer.

"Shall we drop a full one or half?" Frank asked. Now, I never do anything by halves and you could hardly see these pills, so I just said, "a full one."

Frank's dad had offered to drive us to the Odeon Cinema in Bolton that afternoon. It was showing the film *Live and Let Die* starring Roger Moore. We sat on the edge of Frank's bed as he handed me a tab then put one into his own hand. It felt like a kind of religious ceremony. We looked at each other placing the tabs inside our mouths, like one would take Holy Communion at church. "Here we go!" said Frank, as we both swallowed the tabs together, "heaven or hell!" We both fell about laughing. To be young, eh?

The journey in Frank's dad's car to the cinema in Bolton took just twenty minutes. We both sat in the back seat talking quietly. I was feeling nervous and wondering when the drug was going to take effect and what those effects might be. Frank had said that he hoped there wouldn't be a queue but, as it turned out, there was one, a bloody long one that twisted from the foyer to the outside and round the back of the cinema. It was at this point, whilst queuing, that Frank gave me his entrance money saying. "Here, you get the tickets."

I didn't give it a second thought as I took his money. It had been about half-an-hour since we had taken the acid but whether or not it was my paranoid imagination, but things began to feel strange to me. I turned my head towards the main road just as a car was passing. I looked at the car as it passed but it was like a strobe light effect, a slow motion, seven cars-blending-into-one illusion. I was feeling stranger by the minute, my heart was pounding, the palms of my hands were sweating, and my brain was racing with all kinda weird pictures. I turned to Frank who was happily smiling away. "This is fuckin' scary," I said. "Relax!" he replied. "It gets better once you are used to it."

We reached the pay desk and I asked for two tickets. The lady behind the counter pressed the buttons and what seemed like a reel of tickets came flying towards me. The woman's eyes behind the cashier's desk seemed to have snakes crawling out of them. I stood frozen to the spot as I handed over the money. I just didn't know what I was supposed to do next. Frank picked up the tickets and then, taking me by the arm, guided me towards the entrance.

Those were the days when cinema's had usherettes waiting to take your ticket and, walking backwards, guide you by torch to your seat. Frank followed the usherette and followed her torch light in a hypnotic state. She kept moving her torch up and down the aisles in her quest to find us both a seat and I kept trying to follow its light like a moth. I just wanted to be in that light! This was the second time Frank took me by the arm and guided me to our seats.

The lights dimmed and the film got under way. It was at this stage that I was beginning to feel how Keith Moon and Pete Townsend must have felt on that plane. The cinema screen started to melt, as did Roger Moore's face. I was sensitive to every bit of sound coming from the screen and also inside the cinema. My brain became highly aware of someone eating popcorn. Every chew and swallow they made, I could hear it. Loose change rattling in people's pockets as they walked past our row sounded like strange music to my ears. I became highly aware of every cough, every whisper, and every sound. I started to panic. I didn't like the suffocating darkness that enveloped me. This blackness, I felt, was hiding demons waiting to get me. "I've gotta get out of here," I said to Frank, panicking as I rose to leave. "Relax, man! Take it easy," he said as he gently pulled me back into my seat. "Do what I do," he whispered, "look at the colors."

I turned my head towards the big screen and, just like the episode earlier with the usherette's light, I found myself transfixed by the colors. Frank was right. Roger Moore's blue coat - if in fact it was blue! - was the bluest I'd ever seen. All the colors seemed to beg me to look at them. Eventually, I began to relax and watch this color light show. I was not just watching this film, I was in it! The car chases, gun fights, beautiful women, I caressed them all!

The next thing we both became aware of was that the cinema had emptied and was being cleared up by the cleaners.

"What the bloody hell are you two still doing here?" said a woman with a Hoover in her hand. Me and Frank looked at each other and started to laugh uncontrollably. We got ejected from the cinema.

Once outside, things were completely different. Daytime had been replaced by nightfall and it was drizzling with rain. Added to this, the street lights, having been turned on, offered us another mind altering show.

Being a Sunday the buses were every hour, so me and Frank decided to walk the two miles back home to Farnworth. I was enjoying the trip as we walked home. Me and Frank were laughing at everything we saw. Passing by a cemetery we shouted for everyone to wake up. It was completely insane. Unfortunately this relaxed state did not last and as we entered the Post Office pub things took a turn for the worse. Friends that I worked with started to enter the pub and coming over to me, started up a conversation, like, "Where have you been today? Are you working overtime tomorrow? Do you fancy a game of darts?" I tried to respond to their conversation but I was tripping and drugs being in their infancy in the early 70s, were taboo.

My brother Roy came into the pub and by this time I was seeing all kinda monsters in my mind. Things had become unreal and in this paranoid state, I thought people were after doing me some harm. My brother took control of the situation when I told him I had taken some acid that afternoon. He took me outside the pub and to the local park to try and bring me round. We had smoked pot many times together and he lit a joint up. He offered me some and I declined. I just wanted to get back to normality.

"You need a beer," he said. "Let's go somewhere where it's quiet." We went into a pub called The Saddle in Market Street. This was more up-market than the ones we visited (or so we thought). Sitting down in a corner, Roy handed me a pint, telling me the trip would be over shortly. In fact it wasn't until 2pm the next morning that sleep came my way, I had been tripping for twelve hours and for eight of these it was a bad trip.

Now, you would think after that experience I would have learnt a lesson about the effects of taking acid, but no. The next week I was back at Frank's wanting another tab. Talk about demons in my head! I don't know whether I was born an addict but I certainly lived my life like one!

The 60s is regarded as the explosion of music and fashion, and it certainly made people sit up and think; after all, it was only 15 years since we had had a world war. All the big names were making their entrances; legendary names such as The Beatles, The Rolling Stones and The Who to add just a few. Mini skirts had come into fashion and it was great seeing all those lovely legs walking around on a summer's day (or any day for that matter). Well, if the 60s was the 'explosion', in the late 70s we were to see the 'eruption' when Punk Rock hit the scene and we had new names to look for in the record shops; names like The Sex Pistols, The Jam, and The Clash, again to add just a few.

Just outside Bolton is another industrial town called Bury and it was here I went to my first punk rock festival. Armed to the teeth with magic mushrooms, speed, dope and booze, me and a couple of my mates set off for the three-day event where the great punk poet, John Cooper Clark (from Manchester), along with The Dammed and some other punk bands were appearing. We didn't take a tent; we just went along. I don't know how all those hippies got on back in the 60s at Woodstock but as for me and my mates we had a party. We danced to the bands in the fields, crashed out in the fields, pissed in the fields, threw up in the fields, and made new friends around the campfires in the fields.

One particular day, when The Dammed was on, the group organized a joint-rolling contest. Just before the festival began, it was reported in the local paper that there would not be a police presence. Instead, the whole event would be watched by three local council officials and a rumour went round that they spent most of the time in the marquees eating the home-made, dope-laced cakes and drinking coffee. By all accounts they had a bloody good time. In fact they where quoted in the local paper as saying after the event, that is was drug-free and that the punks were well-behaved and mannered people. They also said they would be happy to marshal another event. And I agree with them. Everyone shared their 'spliffs' with each other and 'banged' their heads together.

To get back to the joint-rolling contest, I was sat on the grass trying to get one together but I was that smashed I just ate mine and smoked what was passed along. When the time came for the contest, various punks managed to stagger on stage holding what can only be described as 'abortion-looking' joints, and the group had to try each one to make sure that they had dope in them. After all it was a dope-rolling contest. When it came to one youth's turn, he just about managed to stand up but had no 'spliff' with him and, when asked where his joint was, he replied, "I'm so full of drugs, you can fuckin' roll me," and guess what ...he won.

The punk era certainly put me in touch with a new bunch of friends. One lad I remember, called Robin, was born a punk and was a punk before punk came along. He was an albino-looking lad: thin, gangly, with white hair and eyebrows. He was quite knowledgeable on various subjects but he took punk to the extreme. He hardly bothered to wash or take care of himself but he would help you out whenever he could and, like me, he loved his drugs; it didn't matter what it was, he would take anything - to quote him "as long as there's drugs, I'll have some".

CHAPTER 15

Day 3

Tuesday 24th July
Stage 3 - A Los Pies Del Lascar
(In The Footsteps of the Lascar)
Distance: 40 kilometres/25 miles
Elevation: +260m, -150m

No sleep again, only catnaps. Another night bloody freezing whilst lay inside my sleeping bag. No bloody appetite for breakfast, and no bloody room to get near the camp fire.

I'd climbed into my sleeping bag each night wearing the same gear I'd been running in. I was so exhausted. I didn't care, I was becoming animalistic.

It was 5.30in the morning and another 25 mile run in front of us. Today we were to be introduced to a short stretch on the salt flats. These are lakes that over the centuries, due to no rain whatsoever, have dried up. Thus the salt in them has formed into sharp crystals like icicles which mash your feet up as soon as you step on them. I had read about this particular stretch of land, The Salt Flats, as had the other competitors, and I don't think anyone relished walking over them, let alone running. It's like when you are walking barefoot on the beach and you hit a patch of rocks and stones: you run across them, ooh-ing and ah-ing, lifting your feet in the air. Well, imagine doing that for six miles or more!

It's also worth mentioning that the Atacama Desert is 15 million years old, and fifty times more arid than California's Death Valley.

Pierre did his usual 8am course briefing, and also handed out maps of the course to those who wanted them. He may as well have handed me a book on the sociology of modern Britain, for all the sense it made to me. Now don't get me wrong. I was still feeling good, both physically and mentally. It was just that I was so tired through lack of sleep.

The run got underway; I turned on my music and set off at a slow, steady pace. I was still sticking to my plan of starting like a tortoise and hopefully finishing the 150-mile marathon like a hare. No matter what, I had to finish. This was not only about finishing an extreme marathon in the desert; it was about putting the demons in my head, inflicted on me from the past, to rest once and for all. And to prove to certain people that a leopard can change its spots! My pace was good and I was in the middle of the field of runners. The temperature for me once again felt very hot; it fluctuated between 32 and 38 degrees Celsius (100° Fahrenheit).

I was ten kilometers into the run and was silently thanking God that I hadn't got any blisters when, suddenly, I felt a hot spot sting on my big toe. We had been advised, when we got a blister whilst out on course, to stop and treat it immediately with our blister kits, and then get it treated at the next CP. I stopped, got out my kit and popped the blister with a needle, then stuck a plaster on it; put my trainer back on and carried on to the first CP. I hate stopping once I have got myself into a pace, as I always find it difficult to settle back down again. When I got to the CP, the American doctor asked me to remove both of my running shoes so as to check both of my feet. Well, surprise, surprise! Here was me, thinking I only had one blister, when the doctor informed me that the soles on both of my feet were mashed and blistered! He was going to make me two new soles out of plaster tape he said, and they should protect my feet from further blisters throughout the race. That was the second time I thanked God because how long I'd had these blisters is anybody's guess. They must have been there for some time but I had not felt them.

Having got plastered at the CP (sorry about the pun!), I was on my way, running and walking fast. I didn't want to spend another night on my own out here in the desert.

I eventually hit the salt flats even though this part of the flats was short it was bloody painful. The moment I stepped onto them the ground attacked my feet. I felt the sharp pain with every step and there was no-where else to put your feet to avoid the icicle looking rocks that surrounded you. I covered the flats slowly taking each step carefully I'd heard that this was the place where it was quite possible to receive an injury either by twisting an ankle or knee. It was uneven, rough, hard terrain and took me an age to cross it. I thought, if this is just an introduction to the salt flats then God help me on the big one. Thoughts like these have to be battled with on these extreme marathons cos they will deflate your spirits, it helped me to just try and laugh them off with the words "bring it on, no fuckin surrender". Having finally crossed this nightmare stretch of salt flats I thought if I could get through that then anything else would be a peace of cake. I was wrong, cos the day was to get worse.

During the day the winds would get high and the sand would blow against your legs stinging like biting ants. The course also ran through what can only be described as a small bamboo forest. Here it was difficult to follow the little red flag markers; some had been ripped up as other runners ran past them. The bamboo sticks were very tall and, once you entered this forest maze, the sky disappeared and you got the feeling of being small and insignificant.

Once through this forest of bamboo, we moved on to the next CP. Every time I reached a CP, it felt like a little victory. That was part of my plan: one CP at a time. I like to read poetry by the greats. It was one of these poems that I kept bringing to mind when needed some inspiration. A poem by Rudyard Kipling, called 'If', part of a verse goes like this:

> If you can force your heart and nerve and sinew
> To serve your term long after they are gone,
> And so hold on, when there is nothing left in you
> Except the will which says to them hold on...

I recited that verse every day, plus others.

I wasn't eating very well, as I didn't like the food I had fetched with me. My own fault really, I hadn't done enough research about it, and when Bridget asked me what flavors I would like, I just said,

"Get us seven of those beef stew and seven porridge. It'll be reet." Clever arse me cos it wasn't!

Steadily running and walking along through the heat and wind, with Kipling and music in my head, I soldiered on and munched the miles up. Time was not on my side and night-time fell with the same uncaring vengeance, blacker than black, freezing cold, and deathly silent. The only bonus (if you could call it that) was the stars. I'd never seen as many stars before in my life! It was like God had tipped a skip full into the sky! There were thousands of them! What a show the sky put on at night, with all the shooting stars that sped past you. Pity I hadn't time to lie back and watch the display.

The only advantage or disadvantage, depending how you look at it, of being in the dark is that you can't see what's in front of you. It was only when you saw the green glow sticks rising up towards the sky; you knew you would be climbing up something. Or, if they suddenly disappeared you knew you were about to descend down something - usually something big, rocky and rough. I saw the camp lit up to the right of me, but a gorge separated us. I could have reached out and touched it! I could see the other competitors milling around the fire, eating, drinking and most off all keeping warm. Though it was to the right, the glow sticks veered off and rose to the left, so I found myself running away from the camp and climbing up rugged mountainous rocks. Scary, when all you had to navigate your footing was a small night-light worn on your head! Imagine, you had to point the light to see where you were going to put your hands to climb and then turn and point it to your feet, taking it steadily in the darkness. Careful not to loose your footing and fall back down the height you had just climbed. Whilst going through this nightmare alone, at the back of your mind all you wanted to do was to be back at camp in your sleeping bag.

This was the night when I really lost my way in the dark and thought that I had blown it. If they had to come out and find me, then take me back to camp, I could end up getting a D.N F.

I was following the glow sticks as they steadily rose up and disappeared somewhere high above me. I felt knackered and also pissed off 'cos I could see the camp. My feet kept tripping over rocks and whatever bloody else that lay on this hostile ground. I remember at the time I was listening to the Hollies, He ain't heavy he's my brother, on my I Pod and thinking, 'Don't worry, Roy, I ain't gonna fuckin' surrender". I must have been lost in my thoughts cos, looking up, I couldn't see any of the glow sticks and nothing at all in front of me. Everything was in complete darkness. I stopped, turned off my music, took off my headphones and listened to the silent night. Looking around I was filled with a feeling of emptiness. Not only that but all around me was void of anything. I couldn't even see the campsite anymore.

As I said before, I can get lost in Tesco car park but at that moment I didn't know which way to turn. I tried to assess the situation. I knew the campsite was to the right of me, but also the glow sticks had been rising up to the left. Remembering the warning about not straying off the course, I was momentarily frozen to the spot. I decided that I must have missed a glow stick and that it now stands to reason that the course had altered and I should be heading to the right of me where the camp lay. Up until that moment I had been making my way in an upward direction but, as I started to head back, I suddenly found myself climbing down a very rocky ravine and as my light had limited distance I couldn't see the depth of it.

I was cursing and swearing as I steadily climbed down. Sometimes I would lose my footing and ended up sliding down on my arse. If it had not been for my backpack, I would have probably injured my back. I must have been at it for a good half-an-hour and could just about see the rocky ravine I was on in front of me.

We were told that the terrain changes very dramatically and as I was slowly and very carefully making my way down this rocky ravine, my light shone into an empty darkness. There was nothing there - no rocks to put my feet on for my next move. I must have come to a sudden drop and I could hear a powerful river rushing a long, long way below me; at least I thought it was a river, it could have been anything in my tired imagination. I was so tired and being on your own in a desert for long periods can send you a bit strange. Whatever was down there, I wasn't about to take a look.

Panic struck me. I hate heights and had a mental picture of me stuck on a cliff face with a bloody long drop below me. I desperately started to climb back the way I had come, but there were no familiar signs it was pitch black save for my little light it all looked the same to me, I seemed to be climbing for ages before I finally got back onto level ground and back into the empty desert. I just wanted to sit down and have a fag, but I couldn't because, according to the rules, we weren't allowed to have cigarettes or matches. It was too cold to stay still; in fact I was bloody freezing. So I had to keep moving, but where? I hadn't a clue which direction to take. I silently said a prayer asking God to direct me and off I set, by now just walking. Each step was taken slowly as I followed my night light, not knowing if I was going in the right direction. I plodded on. In the far distance I felt certain I could see the glow sticks but I wasn't sure if these were stars. I had no choice. I knew I was completely lost and had to keep moving to keep warm. I was tempted to get out my emergency whistle and blow it for all I was worth. I could feel my teeth chattering and I didn't know which way to turn and I was once again panicking. I'm no wimp, but this was a desert and I was all alone I could end up being here all night, till someone came to find me and I didn't fancy chancing my arm in case they gave me a D.N.F.

I tried to keep my spirits up with the thought that I had made it to the last CP at the required time and also that I had seen the campsite, so it had to be close by somewhere. Slowly but surely I plodded on. I convinced myself that the bright dots in the distance were glow sticks and not stars. As I got closer to them, this indeed proved to be true and before I knew it, I was running up to one and throwing myself on my knees kissing it. I was so relieved. I was back on track but it had given me a bloody good fright.

The camp lay perched at the top of a high plateau and on the final quarter of a mile, I literally climbed a steep sand dune on my hands and knees, stopping several times to catch my breath. With each step, my feet sank up to my knees in the soft sand. The next day I overheard one of the top runners describe this last climb into camp as "the mother-fucker of all dunes". I saw the headlights of a truck, parked at the top of this high mountainous sand dune, and then I heard a voice call out to me, asking if I needed any assistance. I answered back, lying, saying I was fine. The voice came down to me and offered to carry my backpack. I asked if they had carried anybody else's, the voice said no, and I replied, "Then, you won't carry mine!" Now the reason I am using the terminology, 'the voice', is 'cos that's all it was to me at the time, just a voice. I was all in, both physically and mentally; there was nothing left in me. The voice turned out to be Mary Gaddam's husband and was a great help and encouragement to me during the marathon.

I finally made it into my tent, having had my number taken and my passport stamped. I went straight to bed, not bothering to eat anything, I had eaten peanuts and chocolate energy bars during the day and just didn't feel hungry. Instead, I needed feeding on James Herriot to get out of this nightmare, cos it sure was turning into one. Three more days to go and one of them a distance of 50 miles! It didn't bear thinking about.

I found out the next day, that my timing on stage 3 to cover the 40 kilometers (25 miles) was 11 hours, 51 minutes, 55 seconds. Still, I covered it! Unfortunately, several runners had already withdrawn. I silently quoted our Roy's words once again, 'No Fuckin' Surrender!'

CHAPTER 16

Bob Marley's stoned jammin' all the way
Lou Reed's laid back havin' a perfect day
Not so good for Dylan though
Knocking on heaven's door
Shooting the sheriff was a definite no no
Bryan Ferry finding it hard, his rain is gonna fall
While Dave Bowie dances John's sat in the hall
Jagger's got a stagger on, Jerry looks on
Lennon walks in, here comes the sun
Keith Moon's ballooning he's got that look on his face
They're all here in body but their heads are in space.

Drinking Dens

The room was dimly lit with two red bulbs. Jimi Hendrix was blasting away on the record player and I was completely smashed outta my head. My mate Frank's parents had gone away to Australia to visit a relative for three months and about eight of us had unofficially moved in. The night before we had gone down to Moss Side in Manchester to one of the illegal drinking dens run by the Rastafarians. If you don't know Moss Side, it's one of those 'No Go Areas' you didn't go into. Well, not back in the 70s if you were white. Like most things, there was an exception to this rule: if you wanted to buy drugs, this was the shopping mall. So the rule was; buy drugs then get "ya white arse outta the place".

The den was down a side street. It was one of those places where you knocked on the door and someone on the other side would slide back a peep hatch. You would state your business, then the door would open suddenly and you would be quickly ushered in. Once inside the place, it was like entering another world. Smoke from the 'grass' that was constantly smoked hung heavily in the air, mixed with the loud reggae music and Jamaican jargon; one got a feeling of being on a Caribbean island. The good thing about this place (which we constantly visited) was once you were accepted, they really went out of there way to give you a good time. The grass, along with the booze, was passed around and we were forever being dragged onto the make-believe dance floor by the women to dance along to the songs by the great Bob Marley. We could be in there for hours before we got down to the business of 'scoring some weed'.

There was many a time we would fall outta this place and couldn't find our way home for ages. We would just wander around the town trying to remember where the car was parked. We never parked it near the club as we didn't want any of the Rasta's to know the make and licence number; not that we thought they would do anything but, you know, you can never be too careful.

Once back at Frank's we would divide the dope into two sections, one for selling on the street to pull some money back, the other for personal use. It goes without saying that we never sold much.

I remember one night me and my mate Millsy had devised a plan for the next night. It was coming up to the weekend and someone had got some acid. The plan was that Millsy (who rarely stayed at Frank's) would drop his tab at 6pm and me likewise, then he would catch the bus and meet me at Frank's. At exactly 6pm, I dropped my tab. Millsy turned up at Frank's around 7pm and I could tell by the look on his face he was on his way to tripping. We sat down with the rest of the lads smoking, drinking and generally having a laugh. After about an hour or so, Millsy asked me if I fancied going to the pub. Most of the lads were tripping by now and I mean 'full on', so they just stared at him in astonishment at such a suggestion. To go outside and mix with the straight heads is a no-no, not unless you want the trip to turn bad. But at that moment the trip was good. It seemed a good idea to take a trip round the local pubs, sink a few beers and have a laugh. Laughing off the taunts from the lads, we decided to go to The Saddle on Market Street. This was a pub we used quite regularly, so it was no big deal or so we thought.

The moment we entered the pub which was packed to the hilt, we both knew we had made a big mistake. Within a matter of seconds we became separated as the crowd enveloped us. Eventually we met up at the bar (homing instincts, eh!). We ordered a couple of pints and Millsy asked me how I was feeling. My reply was "Fuckin' wrecked, how about you?" He laughed and said the same. This false joy only lasted a matter of minutes, then things (or rather the acid) started getting outta hand. Suddenly heads were floating around the place without any bodies, the walls were melting in front of us, and there was an electric noise (one assumes coming from a pylon) vibrating all around us. I didn't take a sup of my beer and just said, "Fuck this, I'm off" and panicking fought my way to the exit with Millsy quickly on my heels. We'd only left Frank's for about 10 minutes before we were back, much to the amusement of our mates.

We had an unwritten code that, apart from the gang, no-one else was invited around. Frank respected his parents and it was a nicely kept house. Each morning we would clean up the nights mess and then settle down to messing it all up again. This code was kept to the letter and no-one broke it; no-one except for one night when we were all tripping and one of the lads broke the rule. I will not mention his name to save him from embarrassment, but he had a habit of turning a good trip into a bad one. I don't think he ever did this intentionally it was just his nature.

Anyway, this particular night we were all sat down listening to the rock band Hawkwind blasting away from the stereo, when there was a loud persistent banging on the front door. As I was the one sat nearest, all eyes turned to me to go and see who it was. These were the early days of drugs, so we had no worry about the police coming calling (though we did stash the stuff whenever a knock came). I opened the front door to see this lad sheepishly grinning and moving around nervously (something he always did). When I beckoned him to come in, he reached to the side and pulled a girl he had 'copped off with' into the hallway light. I smiled at them both, shook my head in a 'no' gesture and went to shut the door. Now bear in mind I was tripping on acid. He asked me to get Frank. I said, "OK", shut the door and walked back into Hawkwind.

Sitting myself back down on the carpet, it took me a minute or two to realize that Frank was asking me who was at the door. I laughed and mentioned this lad's name and also that he had brought back 'a bit of skirt' with him. At first Frank and the rest of the lads were angry but seeing as we were all having a good night, it was decided that perhaps a bit of female company wouldn't go amiss, and for this one-off we would break the code and let him bring her in. Fatal. The moment this lad came into the room with his nervous twitching and constant questions about how the trip was (he was not tripping at the time). Within a short time the atmosphere had changed from a relaxed nice trip into a paranoid fuckin' nightmare. No-one could settle down and enjoy the trip; the dye was cast and everyone became nervous and edgy. Eventually we put on a bit of *Moody Blues* and let the calming sounds embrace us.

The morning found us sat on the floor staring into space. It had been a long drawn-out night and if it had not been for some whisky one of the lads had fetched around, I think I would have gone insane. I dragged myself up from the floor and went into the kitchen to grab a beer from the fridge. One of the lads was making beans on toast. I nearly threw up.

"What the fuck ya playing at, breakfast! Are you ill?" I asked jokingly, 'cos most of us were supping beer and smoking a spliff as soon as we woke up. "Shh," he said, putting a finger to his lips. "This is for that little fucker and his tart." I asked him why he was cooking breakfast for him when he nearly cracked us all up last night. He poured the beans over the toast, and then went inside his jeans pocket and pulled out a tab of acid, mixing it with the beans.

"This," he said, "is for him. Now it's our turn to fuck his head up." Now I don't go in for 'lacing' people, so I objected, which I have to say fell on deaf ears.

"Ya not gonna give the girl one," I asked pleadingly. He reassured me that this was just for the lad. I watched to make sure as he poured beans over the girl's plate. He didn't spike it. Then I grabbed it and took it to her.

My mate came in from the kitchen and handed the beans on toast to the lad. Whilst he was eating his breakfast, the lad who had cooked it started telling a story about a pal of his who regularly took acid and how one day, for no apparent reason, started tripping. As his job involved welding, he had to clock out and take himself home. All of the lads by this time had found out about the 'delicate' dish our mate was eating and started telling made-up stories about how some of their friends also found themselves tripping for no apparent reason. It was eventually explained that this experience was known as 'having a flashback'.

Our mate, who was ravenously eating his brekkie, listened with great interest as the stories unfolded. We had all decided the night before we were going to go out to the pub today and as it was around lunchtime, we made our minds up to go to The Saddle for a few beers. After last night's bad trip, the house had become a bit of a nightmare and we needed to get out. We told our mate to go ahead whilst we cleaned up the house and stashed our drugs (that was our excuse anyhow). The idea was that we wanted him in the pub alone with his girlfriend and we would time it just when we knew the acid was beginning to take effect. Then we would make our entrance and set about cracking him up. Pay-back time.

Timed to perfection, we entered the pub. Because this was mid-week, we knew it would be empty. We also knew where our mate would be sat cos we had our own little area just next to the door (easier to leave should you need to). Our mate was sat just behind the door when we all walked in. Sitting down next to him, we began to flick the beer mats up into the air like you do with your fingers. We knew he would be tripping and the effect of beer mats flying around when you're on acid can certainly crack you up (give it a try and see....only joking). Then we all started to talk at once, whilst intentionally leaving words out; you know, like when someone is breaking up on their mobile, talk about 'cat on a hot tin roof'. He was jumping around like Mick Jagger on 'speed' shouting "I'm having a flashback, I'm having a flashback". I thought he was having a stroke the way he was panicking. My mates were just loving it and I was at first, but to me it's just another form of bullying and - forgive the pun - I eventually spilt the beans and told him he'd been laced with a tab. He asked over and over again for me to tell him this was true 'cos he felt he was going insane. My mates have all been there before with bad trips so collectively we all set about reassuring him that this was indeed the case, and after a while he began to settle down and somewhat enjoy it.

We were still to get more sweet revenge 'cos this 'piece' he had picked up was a student at Liverpool University and she was off to catch a train back that afternoon. This lad, being outta his tree, decided he would escort her all the way back to the college gates 'cos, as he said, it was the honorable thing to do. Lying bastard. We knew, as well as the girl, that he just wanted to get his leg over. This girl tried to talk him out of it but he wouldn't listen, which resulted in him catching the train to Liverpool and this girl saying "Ta and goodbye" at the gates. From all accounts, whilst now tripping on his own, he had a bastard time making his way back to Farnworth. After this bad incident, Frank banned him from the house for a while, but we all loved him in our own way and he could also make us laugh. He was one of us and where I come from, that goes a long way.

CHAPTER 17

Give me another one
Just like the other one
All I want is more
It doesn't have to be the same
So long as it hits my brain
All I want is more

Taking A Trip

The moment I decide I am off out for a drink, which is often, it is usually always accompanied by some drug or other. I feel such a rush of excitement that flows throughout my body. I only have to walk into a pub and the smell of the place exhilarates me. It's the same feeling I get whenever I roll a joint or take a line of 'speed' or whatever mind-altering substance I'm on. I'm completely buzzed out, waiting for the hit. I remember the first time I tried amyl-nitrate (poppers). This stuff is apparently used, so I'm told, to bring around 'stiffs'. I was sat in The Queen's pub in Farnworth with some of my mates, when suddenly one of 'em brings out this bottle and invites me to take a big sniff.

I asked the usual questions like "What does it do and what is it". That's just like me, first ask what affects I can expect to have, then ask what it is. I didn't really care what it was so long as it gave me a buzz and got me outta my head. Not that I cared; I was always willing to try owt for the first time. It was a Saturday afternoon and we were all getting ready for a weekend bender. I had some 'charge' (pot) in my pocket, beer down my neck and it was time to 'start my engines'. I took the bottle off my mate and ignored all the taunts and laughter from my mates, who where busy telling me that this stuff separates the men from the boys. Giving them all a big smile with the words "heaven or hell", I shoved the end of the bottle up my nose and inhaled deeply, then nearly fell of the fuckin' chair as the drug hit my brain.

It felt like I was being pulled away from the crowd and pub in a fast backward motion; either that or they were moving away from me at warp 10. I could hear their voices getting more distant as I tried to keep a grip of reality. The whole experience lasted only a few seconds but I'd just been blasted far into space. When I finally touched down and my heart returned to some sort of normal beat, I was aware I was gripping the end of the table so tight my fingers had turned white. I just wanted to go to the toilet to throw up but stood my ground in order to save face from the laughter going on around me. After getting a few pats on the back from my mates and a very large whisky down my neck, it was my turn to sit back and watch the other lads who walked into the pub get 'initiated' into this new found drug we had got our hands on. We spent that day drinking, smoking and every now and then, taking a sniff of the amyl. It was good once you had got used to the sudden rush of brain space travel and accompanied by the booze and smoke, we had a bloody good day.

The next morning, however, I had one great big thumping head and I knew the reason why; it was definitely the poppers. So I made my mind up that I would give this bugger a wide berth - that's not to say that, over the years, I haven't still tried 'a hit in the pit'.

Every time I decided to go out I would always say the same thing to my mates, "Tonight I'm gonna get so smashed they won't be able to put me back together", and when they reminded me that I had said that the last time, I would reply, "I know but tonight I really am gonna get completely wrecked," and I would too, until the next time then I would repeat it all again. As I got older, the drug/drink-fuelled benders were taking longer for me to recover from. It's great when you're full of young blood. You have a resilience that can handle almost any session but each one takes its toll and, just like me, it can be years (if you're unlucky) before you realize that in fact you ain't drinking from the bottle now or taking the drugs, it's the other way round - the bottle is drinking from you and the drugs are taking whatever sanity you may have left.

It's a long road back to some sort of recovery but there is a road and it took me years and a lot of pain and heartache before I found it, unfortunately some of my mates didn't. I thank God he showed me the way.

CHAPTER 18

Day 4

Wednesday 26th July
Stage 4 - Atravez Del Salar
Crossing the salar de la Atacama
Distance 42.8km/26.75m
Elevation +155m/-294m

Another bloody sleepless freezing night tossing and turning in my sleeping bag. This bag was supposed to be the bee's knees of sleeping bags; it cost me £130 and was guaranteed to keep you warm in temperatures minus -2c. The thing is it did keep you warm, but only if you fully covered yourself with it, head and all, but after a minute or so I would have to unzip the top to pop my head out for some air, then the temperature would drop inside the bag.

Whilst lying inside my sleeping bag, I needed to take a leak. Reaching for my wee bottle, which was within easy reach, most male competitors had them and I don't know what the women did, I relieved myself, still lying inside my bag. As I went to put the bottle back, I spilt some of its contents inside the bag. By this time I couldn't give a shit, not until the warm wetness turned cold then I started to feel pissed off laying on this wet pool of urine; I eventually was forced to climb out of my bag to turn it inside out. I'm sure you know that feeling; lying in a warm bed in the middle of winter and then having to leave it to visit the toilet. You lie there hoping the need to go to the toilet will go away and you will fall back to sleep again but 9 times out of 10 it doesn't and you're forced to leave the comfort of a warm bed.

Having climbed out of my bag, I quickly turned it inside out not caring by now if I woke up my fellow tent dwellers. I then decided to get out one of the emergency blankets, you know the kind? They are the ones you see wrapped around marathon runners as they pass the finish line; they are like a long roll of tin foil. It was a compulsory part of the kit to have two. I climbed into my backpack holding the emergency blanket and then fiddled around for an age trying to wrap it completely around my body. Eventually I was wrapped up like a turkey and the bloody thing worked. At last, for the first time since sleeping in the desert, I felt warm. Unfortunately, I still couldn't get to sleep, but unknown to me sleep was to come my way tomorrow.

The scene in the mornings around the camp reminded me of the TV series *Mash;* you know, the hospital campsite where the wounded and injured received treatment. There were competitors bandaging each others feet up and others outside the medical tent getting treatment for their more serious injuries, and also queuing for medication. The worse pain for me was when the doctors had to remove the plasters from my feet to put new dressing on. These American doctors were real cool; they would be listening to music, singing and moving along with the sounds, as they smilingly (but with concern) ripped the old plaster off. This mood for me was infectious. I too found myself jamming along with Bob Marley, whilst gripping the sides of the chair, humming along through gritted teeth.

Same old thing that day with a briefing by Pierre in the morning, then off on the course by around 8am. Today, we were informed, was the day we would face the hardships of the salt flats. Pierre had told us up until today that the salt flats we had already covered were only an introduction, and that today the salt flats were to be longer and the ground surface much tougher than we had previously experienced. Ting Bresnahan of the U.S.A. describes this terrain (and I quote her from the official *Racing The Planet* blog) 'This was the type of place that one would consider taking a gun to one's head if one was inclined to such things'.

8am came, and as usual, I was right at the back of the line. I was pleased each morning with my starts 'cos I still had the ability to begin with a slow jog and keep this up for an hour or so. There is nothing new to tell you about the scenery except to say "it's a bloody desert out there".

I'd already passed through the first CP having run mile after mile across loose rocks that lay scattered on the hard sand. Then on through a canyon and down into a river valley. At about 2.30pm, I finally reached and set off from the second CP which lay at the edge of a forest. Now I was to face the hardships of the salt flats and, unbeknown to me, another high head-on wind later in the day. How does one describe the salt flats? I can only liken them to a farmer's ploughed field in winter, the ground looks hard, jagged and uninviting, with the white frost laid over it. Well, that about describes the salt flats.

It was going to be a hard slog to the third CP over the flats. With each step it sounded like breaking glass underneath my feet, and in fact my already mashed up feet were getting more and more cut up with each step. My Achilles was inflamed and causing me grief. It took me over four hours to reach the third CP, with still 10k/6m to run to base camp. If I thought I had had it bad running/walking the other nights, well going across the flats was bloody manic. On and on I plodded, trying to find a not-so-jagged piece on which to place my feet; it was like trying to piss in the wind and not get wet. Each time I looked up from the ground it seemed as if I had gone no-where at all, the flats just went on and on. I'd managed to overtake a couple of competitors who like me where struggling to cross them and I thank my training on the rocky beaches of Whitby for giving me some kinda preparation even if it was no comparison at all.

I felt that if I was gonna get beaten in the desert on this race, well this was the place. I knew even though the salt flats were difficult to cross, I had to put in some form of run to reach the required time at CP3. When the going gets tough, eh? Eventually, and I mean eventually, I had crossed them. I had made up my mind that at the end of the flats, I was gonna piss on 'em and I did - pity it wasn't a bloody long one.

Then just when I thought the hardship of the flats were over and things couldn't get any worse, a gale force wind kicked off. The wind was taking my breath away; I had a bandana wrapped around my mouth, my face pointed to the ground trying to catch my breath. I remember at this point thinking about the flats I had just crossed. The terrain is supposed to be the closest thing on earth that resembles Mars. I remember thinking and laughing to myself, I now know why the Pope kisses the tarmac when he steps off a plane; he's probably just come back from walking across the salt flats. Once again that feeling of being the only living thing left on earth enveloped me, and my mind became paranoid with all kinda black thoughts rushing through it. This was not the first time I was pleased that I had my I-pod player with me. The mood of the songs determined my pace. Say, for instance, I was listening to Pink Floyd, I would take it easy for a while on the course, but if the music turned to the Rolling Stones, then I would break into a faster run as *Jumping Jack Flash* blasted my eardrums.

Things got worse for me at the third CP. I had taken off my running shoes to tend to my blisters and massage my aching feet, but when I tried to put them back on again I just couldn't. My feet had swollen up to two times their normal size. One of the American doctors informed me the only way to get them back on was to cut the shoes at the back of the heel if they where to fit me again. He asked me if I had fetched another pair. I hadn't so I was left with no other choice but to have them cut. He then said that if they did cut them and they fell apart, I would not be able to complete the race and that the decision was entirely up to me. What choice did I have? Like a surgeon he expertly cut each shoe down the centre just above my heels asking me to try them on after each delicate short cut so he did not cut too far. Eventually they fitted my swollen feet with a little force and I was off again to complete the last 10k.

Now my head was racing paranoid overtime. Here I was with bad swollen feet and tomorrow was the big one, fifty bloody miles of desert and already I was one of the walking wounded. I have to say though, I did manage to run; well, just about faster than a walk. I tried to keep my spirits up with the fact that I was nearly back at camp and tomorrow was another day, plus I was becoming a bit of a veteran and this added hardship just spurred me on more. I've always liked a challenge so to charge myself more, I shouted out to my past 'call me a loser, bastards, watch me fuck this desert up see if I don't...' brave words. Had I have known what the next couple of days had in store for me on the biggie, I'd have kept my bloody gob shut.

I was in a bad state as I neared completion of this stage but I did it; again on my own through the desert in pitch darkness. The whole 26+ miles had taken me 12 hours: 14 minutes: 15 seconds and I was all in, both physically and mentally, and tomorrow was the big one, 50 miles.

After the marshals had taken my number and stamped my passport, one of the volunteers (a young women whose name I cannot remember but I shall call her Florence Nightingale for she certainly helped me) asked me where my food was after helping me off with my backpack. "I know you have not eaten anything these last two nights," she said, "so tonight I'm gonna make sure that you do". She got my food out of my backpack and took it over to the camp fire to put some hot water into the sachet. Coming back, she then found my spoon, grabbed my backpack and taking me by the arm led me to my tent. If you are Florence Nightingale and you are reading this, thank you xxxxxxx.

Inside the tent as usual everyone was asleep. I didn't try to keep quiet; in fact I said quite loudly that I didn't care if I fuckin' woke anyone up as I was all in. It was at this point a fellow tent mate greeted me with, "Tough one today eh, Billy?" I remember saying, "I don't know how you all manage to sleep in the bloody freezing cold." He laughed and said "Sleeping pills". "You're joking," was my reply as I'm no stranger to sleeping pills having been given enough in the hospitals. "Don't they make you feel groggy in the mornings?" I asked. "Not these," he said, "they are special ones". Well I never got to find out what they were. He asked if I would like one as he had one left to spare. I nearly ripped his arm off as I said yes and he handed me one. Throwing it down my neck, I started on my food. It's funny really; up until that point I hadn't felt hungry, but as the beef stew went down my throat, I suddenly felt ravenous.

Having taken the pill and finished my supper, I climbed inside my bag still wearing the clothes I'd worn since day one - as I've already mentioned, I'd gone past caring. With my night light still switched on, I got out James Herriot and started to read and that's all I remember until I woke up the next morning. Bliss, I had slept well; it was 6.30am when I woke up and I didn't feel groggy. If you are planning on taking part in a desert marathon and you, like me, are a bit of an insomniac, I'd do some research on these sleeping pills. I wish I had known about them beforehand. Still *Que Sera Sera,* eh?

CHAPTER 19

I've been a skinhead, a hippy too
I've even touched on Krishna for something to do
I've trekked the highways byways and the bars
Met all kinda people even some from Mars
I've chased the dragon powered my brain
L.S.D left me a bit insane
Pink Floyd's *wish you were here*
Took me to places when I was high on gear
I landed in the park I had no opinion
Mick Jagger sang *you can't get no satisfaction*
I was off again but where to go
My yellow brick road held no rainbow
Then along came Sid Vicious with his words
Well fuck you peace this is something I ain't heard
So I punked along banged my head a few times
But the music moved on and I was still outside
Mozart maybe he held the key
So I listened to a few of his symphonies
But it just weren't me my spirit was trapped when it wanted to
fly
The drugs where taking longer to get me high
Fear gripped me I wandered around lost
I walked into the future but lived in the past
Until at last it came to me
Thank you Shakespeare
To be or not to be
I'm free.

Everywhere and Nowhere

I'm gonna go and work down in Newquay my brother Roy said to me one day. I hadn't a clue where Newquay was but I couldn't have cared less we were gonna work away I was both scared and excited at the same time. We agreed to meet in town on the Friday when we both got paid and then head for the motorway that was just at the end of our town where we planned to hitch it down.

Back in the early 70s, Newquay was a small Cornish fishing town that was inhabited by the hippie culture, with their drug-taking and free love; it was a dream come true. Not being strangers to drugs, we both loved this new found lifestyle. What we couldn't get used to was all this love they constantly pedaled. We just couldn't understand it, now don't get me wrong we enjoyed the free love, it's just that we couldn't understand how someone could say that they loved you, I'm sure, neither did some of them. Here we were, me at the age of 20 and our Roy approaching 19 but because of how we were brought up, we were both still little kids inside.

Life took on a new meaning but the best was being free. I couldn't get used to the fact that I could come and go as I pleased without having to answer to me dad. Talk about kids being let loose in a toffee shop, both me and Roy embraced this new found freedom. We were still in our teens and still bearing scars from the past. Having a front door key was a buzz in itself. When we lived at home we had to be in at a certain time. When we were eventually let out and as we grew older and started to bring a wage home this rule was still enforced. If we didn't make 'the deadline' we were locked out. Rebellion like any teenager kept us away from obeying this and when we did eventually end up home after the deadline had passed, we would have to quietly tap on the door and my mam, who would be listening out for us, would silently creep downstairs to let us in. Then in whispers we would make our way upstairs.

In the morning, my dad would enquire what time we came in. He would have been fast asleep from the booze and sleeping pills he took nightly. We would lie, of course, but inside we still felt the fear of disobeying him even though he could no longer dish out the violence. Psychologically our upbringing had damaged me to the extent that I carried fear with me all the time.

That first year we found a job at one of the local hotels that had live-in accommodation. We shared a house with the other staff and also a lad that we had met in the town on the first few days of arriving down here. His name was Millsy and guess what? He came from Little Hulton. He was to become a lifelong friend to me and my brother, Roy, and one year we all went to work on the island of Jersey.

Unbeknown to us, Newquay was to become our home. (My brother Roy and Millsy, both still live down there and are married with families. What a place to run away to; it was full of young people who, like ourselves, wanted something different from life. Newquay - for those of you who don't know it - is a surfers' paradise and we met plenty of Aussies down there who were traveling around Europe for a couple of years before returning home. I would listen to their stories in the Sailor's Arms over a beer and be enthralled as to the countries they had visited. A yearning to go the same places and visit them for myself began to grow passionately in my heart.

Apart from the occasions of eventually traveling and working abroad, I stayed down there for a wonderful, exciting 10 years. I have so many tales I could tell you about the times spent down there, it would warrant another book. However, I will touch on some of them.

I met so many wonderful people that summer, and also chanced my arm at surfing. Surfing! My mates back home wouldn't believe me I thought, when I first entered the Atlantic surf on Fistral beach. I had got myself a surfboard and it was orange with a road runner sticker on it. Me, Roy and Millsy would go to the beach after we finished work at lunchtime in the hotel. On the walk there, we would smoke a couple of joints and buy ourselves a couple of bottles of Festival vat cider (known locally as *fessi vat*).

What a feeling it was, sat on the beach smoking and drinking, surrounded by the bikini- clad, tanned, bronze-bodied girls around. Stuck in the sand were our surfboards; this always attracted the talent and there was plenty to choose from. I would not recommend it today, but being young it was great trying to ride a wave stoned 'outta your crust'. We spent some happy hilarious days like that in the surf, then after, still wet, we would lie on the sand listening to music on the little cassette player we took with us, getting nicely tanned, then it would be time to go back to work.

After work in the evening, we would all meet back at the staff quarters, roll a few joints, drink some more fessi vat, listen to some sounds, and then off we would go to the Sailor's Arms.

The Sailors was the place to be as it buzzed with the sounds that were hitting the charts back in the early 70s and almost everyone I knew smoked dope or took speed.

It was a large pub with a dance floor in it. In the early years some more of my mates had come down from Farnworth to work the summer. These were the lads that used to go to the Wigan Casino, and soon they were getting the D. J. to play some Northern Soul.

It certainly made some of the hippies sit up and watch as me and my mates spun around on the floor to Northern Soul. Boy! These lads could dance. There was Wilkie, Baz, Paul Worthy, Steve Fay, Tilley, Tony Cunliff, Mickey Bullis, Ian Rothwell to name but a few, and they certainly made an impression when they took the floor over.

Because of the hippie influence my taste in music began to take on a new meaning. I still loved Tamla Motown (always will do) but we were being introduced to rock. Suddenly instead of The Four Tops, we began to listen to the likes of Pink Floyd, Genesis, Yes, Mike Oldfield. Everything for me was changing from the only world I had known as Ian Drury sang 'Sex and Drugs and Rock and Roll' and I loved it.

One summer I got myself a job working at The Bay Hotel that overlooks Fistral beach. I was a silver service waiter and enjoyed every minute of it along with the lads I worked with: Pete, Fitchit and John Wray. We all lived in the hotel together and had some great parties. I remember one day phoning our Roy up, who had gone back to Farnworth for some reason or other, to send me some dope through the post. This was still the early 70s so I thought it would be safe….. Wrong.

He phoned me back a couple of days later to say it was in the post. On the day it arrived, I was working in the dining room when the head waiter Mr. Lawrence (an elderly gentleman with silver hair who had once worked on the royal train) asked me to go to the manager's office. This was unusual as the staff were usually 'bollocked' in front of everyone else in order to get the message across to the rest for whatever misdemeanors they had got up to.

I knocked on the door trying to figure out which 'piss up prank' I was gonna get told off for. I opened the door on the command of Mr. Hicks, the owner/manager, to be faced by the secretary and a tall, suited man who introduced himself as a detective sergeant. I then noticed, stood behind the door, two uniformed constables. The detective asked me to confirm my name and then produced an envelope with my name and lots of other graphic comments written on it, and, on close inspection, a drawing of a long rolled joint with the words 'beware blow your head off' written above it.

He then went on to ask if I had any reason why he shouldn't open this letter in front of me. I knew straight away it was from our Roy but asked him what he thought was in it and why were the police here. He didn't answer but asked me to confirm that the name on the envelope was mine and also that no other person who worked and lived in the hotel had the same name as me. I confirmed it was my name and that I didn't know anyone else here with that name. He then opened the envelope; my heart was pounding like a good 'un.

He stuck his hand into the envelope and pulled out one of those plastic money bags which you get from a bank, and inside this was a large oxo looking cube I knew to be pot. He asked me, whilst waving the bag in front of my face, what I thought it was. I replied, "A money bag."

He smiled and said, "I meant the brown stuff inside." I shrugged my shoulders and told him I hadn't a clue. He went on to inform me that he had reason to believe it was a controlled substance namely *Marijuana.* Well it was time to put on the well-rehearsed innocent act I had perfected over the years.

"Drugs?" I said in a shocked voice, "someone is trying to stitch me up".

He asked me, "Who would want to stitch you up and why? Because this," he said, "has come from the town you were born in". I replied that sometimes when I go back home, I knock about with the women a lot and maybe it's been sent by a jealous boyfriend or husband. I knew that this statement had him cornered for it was a plausible comment.

I had to go down to the local nick and make a statement whilst they held enquiries. When I returned to the hotel I asked the manager if I could take a few days off to go back home and see if I could sort summat out. He agreed, considering I was a good waiter, and also because no charges had been brought so he had no choice. I went back up north to be told by our Roy that the day he sent it he was a bit stoned himself and was also with some of the lads but didn't remember writing anything on the envelope. I told him that if the local cops come by to deny sending me anything (which he'd already figured out).

Whilst at home I decided to party for a few days and ended up dropping some speed, quite a bit really and I was still speeding when I got back to the hotel. I was speeding so much the day I got back that I had a party in the staff quarters. The party went on most of the night 'till eventually people went home and I managed at last - after being awake for nearly three days – to fall to sleep. I was woken in the early morning with a loud thumping on my door and when I opened it the detective who had first opened the envelope was stood there along with the other constables. He produced a search warrant for my room. I figured that the manager must have told him that I had gone home and when I would be back. But it wasn't quite like that as the police had asked him to keep them informed should I make some sudden movement.

Anyone who has worked and lived in hotels knows that the staff quarters are just about big enough to hold a bed and a set of drawers and mine was no different except I had a wardrobe, which made moving around inside very difficult, still, I didn't need to chase the girls around the room too much...know what I mean! It was from this wardrobe that he pulled out one of my coats and he inserted his fingers in the top pocket and pulled a plastic bank bag out with some brown stuff inside it. I knew this was a stitch up and told him so, explaining that after the little envelope session I would be daft to have anything in my room, also that I didn't do drugs.

The result of all this was I was charged on two counts of possession of marijuana - one of these being an 'attempt to possess', meaning the envelope one. Now being that drugs were in the early stages in this country, I had to appear at Bodmin Crown Court. It was a hot sunny day on the morning I appeared in court and I was shitting myself. In those days possession of drugs always meant a prison sentence and especially down in Cornwall where time had stood still.

My solicitor had told me it would be a two-day trial. They would have to swear a jury in so I wouldn't be expected to go into the witness box until the last day and also that the prosecution had to prove the charges. I sat there whilst the jury were sworn in. Looking up at the rays of sunshine that filtered through the skylight above me, wishing I were somewhere else. In the dock beside me was a prison officer who, on my arrival to court, arrested me in case I was going to be sent down. I was totally freaked out.

At lunchtime the court adjourned 'till two o'clock. In the court sat my brother and some other of my mates who had come over from Newquay to give me some support, or so they said. What a load of bollocks! They had come over for a piss up and to check out the local talent and bars in Bodmin. Here is an amazing twist. The prison officer who was there to guard me came from Farnworth and had noticed my mates. When he asked if they were from our home town and I said yes, he let me go and have lunch with them, with the words, "I'm only doing this 'cos you're from Farnworth. Be back, don't let me down". We have a bond amongst each other, those from Farnworth.

I believe he knew I'd be back; there ain't nowhere to run in Cornwall. Still, it was good of him to let me go.

"I've got some *blow* hidden down my bollocks," announced Roy, as we went into a pub". Bless him, he meant well. Still, I couldn't believe it. Here was me up on a charge for drug possession at crown court and our kid brings some pot into court with him. Still, we were young lads and when you're young, you know no fear. I'm gonna cut to the chase here. As I wasn't expected to be put on the stand 'till tomorrow, I went outside the pub with the rest of my mates and smoked a joint.

After lunch I went around the back of the court to meet up with the prison officer as arranged and he took me once again up those fateful steps in the courtroom that lead to the dock. Crown Court is a scary sight, what with the judge in red robe and wig, the lawyers all in black and also wigged up, plus the jurors. But this time after lunch I was pretty relaxed after the smoke and sat back to enjoy the suns rays once again that danced around the court 'till the next minute. Surprise, surprise my name got called out.

I looked up at my lawyer who had called my name and beckoned him over asking him what he was playing at. "I thought I wasn't being called till tomorrow," I asked nervously. "Tactics," he replied. I was led completely stoned to the witness box and sworn in.

My lawyer asked me all the right leading questions portraying my innocence and I thought all was going well and it was until it was time for the prosecution's turn. The lawyer for the prosecution stood up, altered his cloak behind his back in that intimidating manner then holding his shirt collars, he cleared his throat suddenly and like a predator lion he pounced on me. His questions came fast and furious. I thought I was handling it well considering I was 'out of my tree' then he tripped me up, it went something like this.

Lawyer, "So tell me, Mr. Isherwood, have you ever smoked marijuana?"

Me, forgetting to just answer yes and no, as I was instructed to do said, "No, I have never had a joint in my life".

Lawyer, "A JOINT? Mr. Isherwood, A JOINT? Kindly explain to the court and members of the jury what A JOINT is".

Me (whilst unwittingly demonstrating with my hands how to roll and put dope in a joint), "Well, from what I know, you get these skins" (cigarette papers).

Lawyer, "SKINS? Mr. Isherwood, SKINS?"

Me, "What I mean is..."

Lawyer, "That will be all, Mr. Isherwood".

Me, "but you don't understand, it's just that when you're working in Newquay, you hear this jargon".

Lawyer, "NO FUTHER QUESTIONS, Mr. Isherwood".

The jury retired and I was taken down stairs to a holding cell. I couldn't believe I had been so stupid as to smoke a joint whist at court but I had and I did. I could only expect nothing less than prison after my stoned testimony. The jury stayed out for a couple of hours then my mate the prison officer came for me, "Don't worry," he said, "you'll probably go to Launceston prison. It's ok in there". "Thanks," I said. And here's me fretting, eh?

"Members of the jury," I heard the court usher say, "have you reached your verdict?" I was aware of the guard gently pulling me from the seat and turning me to face the jury. On count one, attempting possession of a controlled substance, namely marijuana, how do you find the accused Guilty or not Guilty? GUILTY. On count two, possession of a controlled substance, namely marijuana, how do you find the accused, Guilty or not Guilty? NOT GUILTY.

I wanted to kiss them all. I could hardly believe my ears and neither could the judge, who gave me a fine of £100 which was a lot of money back then but what the heck, I was free. I had accused a police officer of planting dope on me and I had got away with it. Only because it was true, so I'd discovered there was such a thing as 'good old British justice'.

Before I left the court to go out and celebrate, I was interviewed by another police officer regarding my accusation of me having dope planted on me and put up on a possession charge. He said that because of the not guilty delivered by the jury, I could press charges against the officer involved but life would be hell back in Newquay 'cos this officer was well respected and also had a family. On the other hand, if I didn't bring any charges against him then off the record I could walk around carrying any amount of drugs 'cos no-one would want to arrest me, as I could claim police harassment. Guess what I chose? Well let's just say I had a good time in Newquay and never once got arrested again, well not for drugs 'anyroad'.

I became friends with a lad who had lived in Newquay since he was about 8 years old but came from Manchester. His name was Billy Turner and he was a big lad over 6ft tall with an infectious laugh. We had some great times together. One that sticks in my mind because it was so funny is the day we went to watch Newquay football team play at home. It was a Saturday and we'd been out during the afternoon drinking and smoking some pot when Billy asked me if I fancied going along to watch them. Well I mean we're talking Cornwall here not a nation of footballers, sorry I love Cornwall but you have to draw the line somewhere. I screwed my face up when he reminded me that the pubs would be shut at three nowt else to do so why not go along for a laugh. I said ok; let's have another quick pint and joint before we go. We arrived at the ground completely smashed but being young still able to get it together. We paid and went in to the crowd. I think Newquay where playing St Austell that day and there was a crowd of about 200. I know don't laugh.

It was strange being stood in a small crowd with gaps in them, when you're used to being crammed among 20,000 to 30,000 fans. The game got underway when Billy said he was off to the bar, I looked at him in surprise telling him that he'd kept that quiet. He told me it was only for the directors, players, and trainers of both teams plus their spouses. I asked him how we were gonna get in. He said just follow me and keep your gob shut. I thought if he can get us both some booze I'd keep owt shut.

We went upstairs towards the bar and walked in to be met by someone from the committee. Billy didn't give this guy the chance to speak he told him straight away that we were the trainers of the St Austell team and had just popped in for a quick drink. He accepted this and then lay into us verbally about how our team were gonna get their arse kicked today, we both smiled (like we could give a fuck). Billy said, "we shall see".

This man was true to his word cos every time St Austell scored a goal he was over to us taking the piss. Me and Billy kept pretending, discussing team tactics and who we were gonna drop after the first half; I've failed to mention there was a large window inside the bar where you could watch the game but we never went near it instead we were shooting some pool at the far end of the room. By the time it had got to something like 9 goals to 2 for St Austell or some ridiculous score like that. We were onto our fifth pint plus a couple of chasers and the committee man had cottoned on, took him long enough. He came over and told us that he'd sussed us out and had just been down stairs talking to the real trainers, we didn't give a shit by then we were so out of it laughing and falling about we just told him that we just fantasized about really wanting to be the trainers for Newquay and would he put a good word in for us to the director. I thought he was gonna have a heart attack cos he went from being red to turning blue, spluttering and splattering, he escorted us from the bar and out of the ground. What a day! I remember reading in the Sunday papers the next day that St

Austell had won by about 14 goals to 6. No mention of me and Billy.

Another mate of mine who followed me down to Newquay from Farnworth was Benny Davies a very likeable fellow. We too spent many a happy boozing time together. Benny worked at the same hotel as me for a short while and was liked by the hotel owner. Benny had a problem with getting up early in the morning for work and was always late which was a sack-able offence. All the owner did was to make him head chambermaid over the girls. They just loved him and would take him his breakfast down into his room you just couldn't help but like him he was always laughing and up for owt.

Another mate was John Lambert (Reggae) he to was up for owt but was a bit of a gambler, he liked the horses and was nearly always having a bet or two. One particular Saturday we had just been paid our wages, when Reggae says to me that he couldn't do owt with such a small amount. We were making our way down to the pub when he suddenly stops and walks into a betting office. Without really studying the form of the runners he just put all his wages onto the first favorite horse to win. I told him he was off his trolley and asked him what he was gonna do if he should lose cos he wasn't getting any of my beer money on such a daft act. He just smiled and shrugged it off. The race got underway with Reggae nervously playing with his betting slip. After 10 minutes he gave me the ticket and said he couldn't listen to anymore his horse was about the 8th in a race of about 20 horses so he walked out. I stayed and listened to the end of the race and the horse he backed came in like a train winning by about 8 length's. I went to collect his winnings and as an afterthought picked up a used ticket from the floor, by the time I went outside Reggae was halfway down the road looking up towards the betting shop. I looked at him from the distance and shook my head ripping up the ticket I had whilst I held onto his winnings. I was gonna have some fun for a short while and maybe teach him a lesson. "C,mon" I said, "I'll buy you a drink you silly fucker". I wasn't gonna lay up till I'd thought he'd regretted his actions which he did for a short while, then laughed it off with the words "easy come easy go". I finally gave in and gave him his winnings, he didn't get the face on with me it wasn't his nature instead we both had a good piss up that day.

During the summers I worked in Newquay, I held many jobs in different hotels, starting off working in the kitchens and eventually ending up as a waiter. Of all the hotels I worked at, The Beresford Hotel was the place I enjoyed working at the most. Most of my mates from Farnworth who went down to Newquay either worked or had connections with the Beresford. If they didn't work there, they at some point slept in the staff rooms. It was an outpost somewhere to stay and eat 'till they found a job elsewhere so the lads would put them up in their staff room and sneak food out for them.

The staff numbers there were large and consisted of Chefs, KPs (Kitchen Porters), chambermaids, waiters, waitresses, porters, and bar staff, and most lived in. They came from all over: there were the Scouses, (from Liverpool) the Brummies, (from Birmingham) the Scots, the Welsh, we even had some Aussies, and of course the Farnworh gang. The order of the day was to have fun and party.

This was also the place where I met two girls from Manchester, Helen and Jane. They became great friends. In fact I went out with Helen for a couple of years off and on we even went to Crete together to work at the end of one season. Helen and Jane worked as waitresses; they were about 17 years old and had a love for life. They became 'one of the boys'; going on to the beach with us all, drinking, smoking, listening to our cares and woes, sometimes sewing a button on a shirt or maybe ironing some trousers. But they also were definitely liberated females and even though they sometimes reluctantly did an odd job like this for you, they would certainly let you know the only reason they would do this was 'cos they liked you. It was a two-way thing and I know the lads certainly looked out for them and also loved having them around, especially when stoned, as there is nothing better than having a couple of dizzy broads along (sorry, only joking).

This was the hotel where I tried my hand has a waiter. I remember one Saturday as the guests were going back home after their week's stay, the waiting staff were coming into the kitchen counting money out on the tables. I was stuck behind a large dish washer and in front of me, on a long table, were all the plates, cups, teapots and toast racks piled all in a disarray waiting for me to load in the dish washer. This hotel catered for about two hundred guests so the job was hard. Plus the heat of the kitchen and the gorgeous Cornwall hot summer outside, soon had you sweating 'your nuts off'. When I asked the waiting-on staff what was all this money that they were counting I was simply told "Tips" they had got from the guests.

Wages in the hotel trade are not all that brilliant, so I made my mind up to become a waiter. I asked the manager if I could be a waiter and he told me to get myself a white shirt, black trousers, shoes and a tie and I could start that evening. Off I went after service and collected my wages and, instead of making my way to the pub with the rest of the staff, I was off hunting around the various charity shops 'till I got kitted out. I took to waiting-on like a duck to water. I have always been a bit of a cheeky chap - a proper Lancashire lad - and this went down well with the guests. Come the following Saturday, I was in the kitchen counting out my tips. Not that I managed to save up ow't, it just meant I had more money to spend on drink and drugs…happy days.

Winter found me sharing a room with our Roy and Millsy and at least five other mates: Jimmy Rothwell (a Little Hultoner, as was Millsy), Steve Fay (Bolton), Paul Worthy (Farnworth) and Baz Hindley (Farnworth). This room had five single beds in it. In winter, unlike the summer, Newquay became 'dead'. Once the visitors had left, Newquay resembled a ghost town and also the weather was very wet and windy. We all made a claim for income support and when they came round to visit, they mentioned to the landlord (Arthur, a Cockney) it was overcrowded. He said fine I'll kick 'em out then, but the authorities didn't want this so we all ended up staying.

We shared everything together; food, cigs, booze, and dope but there were times when we had to improvise in order to get stoned. On one occasion when there was little to go around, we decided to inject some brandy. One of my mates came up with the idea, so we sent a young girl who used to knock around with us to the chemist to tell the pharmacy that her mother was diabetic and she needed a needle. That night being a weekend we were all off to *The Sailors*. We clubbed together to buy some *fessi* vat cider and a small bottle of brandy. I have never liked needles so as everyone prepared to let this lad inject them; I was at the back drinking the cider in order to get some form of Dutch courage. Eventually it was my turn; my mate tied a home-made tourniquet around the top of my arm and plunged in the needle as I looked away. As soon as the tourniquet was released, I stood up to let the next one get a fix and bang, I was staggering all over the place just like my mates had done before me. The brandy went straight to my head. I don't remember much after that, except trying to dance and getting thrown out of *The Sailors*.

The winter became a bit of an ordeal. We still had some fun times with the friends we had met who like us hadn't saved up any money during the summer months to go abroad and also like us didn't want to go home. The only thing we could do was to try to survive and have as much fun as we could find. I remember one day I had left Roy and Milssy in the flat whilst I nipped out to the corner shop to buy a bottle of milk. As the shop was just a couple of doors away I didn't put any shoes on. I had got into this habit of not wearing shoes during the summer months; it was a bit of a hippy thing.

'Any road', I walked into the shop around 10am, bought the milk and as I came outside I met a mate of ours called Frank. He was stood leaning against the wall and by his appearance he was well stoned. He said "hi" and asked me what I was up to. I could tell by his eyes and constant smile on his face he was lit up alright. I told him I was off back to the flat with the milk for a cup of tea. He said if I had nothing to do he was just going into the shop for a bottle of wine, then back to his place for a smoke and did I want to come - ducks and swimming, eh? He told me he had just received a back-dated giro so was off to the pub later. We trundled off back to his flat, smoked a couple of joints, drank the wine, listened to some sounds, then Frank asked me to go to the pub with him and it would be his treat. So with no shoes on and carrying a bottle of milk, we hit the bars. When the pubs shut at 3pm, we went back to his flat with a carry-out and continued to smoke and drink 'till the evening came and off to the pub we went again.

That evening, in the *Sailors Arms,* I was given two pairs of shoes by some of the lads who knew me. When they asked me why I wasn't wearing any I said I couldn't afford to drink and buy shoes as well. What a day! It started off going to the shop at 10am for a bottle of milk and ended with rolling in at gone 11pm, stoned 'outta my tree'. I remember going into the room where Roy and Millsy were laid in bed asking me where the fuck I'd been. I fell onto my bed laughing saying, "Out for the milk".

Once the summer came around again, everything became rosy once more. I would find another hotel to work at just for a change but my lifestyle with the booze and the drugs just increased to the point where enjoyment for me meant getting drunk and also stoned on whatever drugs were knocking about.

"We're off to a cider farm," said Millsy. The season of '72 was underway and it was coming up to my 21st birthday. I was working at the Beresford Hotel along with our kid and Millsy. The hotel employed at least 30 workers and most of them lived in. A party was arranged for me that night after work hence the reason for our trip into Devon and the cider farm. A whip round by all the staff was taken up and I think we collected about £5. Now the hotel wages were only about £12 live-in and considering most of the workers went out every night £5 was a good collection. One of the workers had a battered old mini. So after serving breakfast we set off to find a farm. I can't remember who came along but I can remember pulling up into the cider farm. We were greeted by an old looking man carrying one of those long sticks you see shepherds holding with the obligatory collie dog running around him. I just love the south west accent, slow long drawl, kinda spoken with a tune in it. We told the farmer we were after buying some cider and when he asked us what kind we wanted we just said the bleeding obvious "strong" what else?

I noticed after this remark the glint in his eye and the mischievous smile spread across his face. He led us into a barn that was full of those metal milk churns one associates with country people. Still smiling, he took a metal cup that was hung on a nail at the side of the wall, removed the lid from one of the churns and plunged it inside, pulling it out when it was overflowing with a strong foul smelling gold liquid which he invited us to taste. It really was a putrid smell but it was alcohol and that's what we were here for. It took some swallowing and after we all managed to stop coughing with him smirking in the background he took the lid off another churn. He repeated the same gesture, holding up the tin cup with the words "try this bugger" delivered with another cheeky grin.

This time as we tasted the honey of the South West it went down better than the first and also we didn't cough. I have to say we tested about five different kinds of scrumpy but we all agreed they tasted the same and, after you got over the initial desire to throw up, the pleasant glow we got from the effect was very intoxicating (forgive the pun). Eventually, and just because we were getting pissed, we chose one. We asked how much it was for a bottle. The farmer just laughed and said he didn't sell it in bottles but in churns, so we asked then how much a churn was. "10 bob (50p) to you lot," he said, whilst adding that he wished he was coming to the party with us. "I could do with a bloody good laugh," he said. We managed to squeeze three of these churns in the mini with us and set off back to Newquay, stopping every now and then to get *scrumpered up.* I can't really remember much about the party except someone throwing up over me, but I can remember that that cider lasted for a couple of days. The reason for this was it soon got you pissed and the female staff didn't like it.

I enjoyed every minute of those working summers. I'd been down there every summer since I was 19 years old, staying for the season then traveling abroad for part of the winter. This was what most of the seasonal workers did in the winter; we all traveled abroad, working if possible. I'd worked picking the champagne grapes in France. I'd picked oranges on the island of Crete and even worked for a short time in Zermatt, Switzerland, where a close friend (Hank) from my home town worked. He had kindly invited me over at the end of one summer season to join him. I was working at that time at Kay's catalogue mill in Bolton and on receiving his invitation; I immediately gave my notice in.

What a time I had over there. I worked in a little restaurant situated high on one of the ski slopes. I used to catch a cable car to work then Hank eventually lent me some skies and taught me how to ski. I would catch the cable car to work, where my job was to wash up and stack the bar, helping myself to a beer or two, then ski back down the mountain into the town of Zermatt.

I remember the day Hank had decided to meet me at work and bring me a set of skies to teach me how to ski. The sun was shining and bouncing off the slopes. It was lunchtime and I was outside on the veranda collecting plates and empty glasses from the tables. The view was spectacular. I was surrounded by the white-tipped, snow-filled Alps full of skiers. Right there in the middle in all its majestic glory, was the Mattehorn. I just drank it all in, along with the booze. One day, whist clearing up the empty tables, I came across two young good looking girls who were having a right laugh between themselves. Well, I was young free and single so I made my way to their table. As I approached I instantly recognized the smell of marijuana coming from their direction. I approached their table and said, "That sure smells good". "Do you toke?" enquired one of the girls. Now I'd heard this expression before whilst working in Newquay (there is an American army base there) plus her accent was American and toke meant smoke dope.

"Slightly," I said, laughing. She then produced this rather bent looking spliff the way the yanks roll them and gave it to me, she then told me, "This is home grown Carolina bush. Be careful, it's strong stuff". I thanked her, laughed, and said, "Heaven or hell," and stuck it inside my pocket. Hank came along as planned that evening with a spare set of skis. We sat inside the restaurant where I'd just finished work and we ate a fondue and drank a few beers together then it was time for my lesson and to ski home.

My heart was racing as Hank showed me how to put the skis on. From outside the restaurant there was a slight downward slope that led to the ski run and it was on this that he showed me how to brake with my skis on. We were nearing the run and I was excitedly shitting myself, it was then that I remembered the joint that the yanks had gave me. Pulling it out, I showed it to Hank. He was like me (we had worked together in Newquay) and he liked a good laugh and was full of life. "Spark it up," he said, laughing". We stood at the end of the run smoking this joint whilst I kept looking down the run where I was going to ski. The town looked like a little dot from high up on this mountain and I heavily inhaled the joint when it was passed to me. The smoke had the desired effect and pretty soon

I was completely relaxed and laughing off the adventure I was about to take.

With the joint finished, Hank asked me, "Are you ready?" I said "no, but let's go for it". Hank jumped onto the run shouting, "Farnworth!" and I laughingly followed. All was going well for a short time and I was managing to stay upright on the skis, then suddenly I lost control and was speeding along uncontrollably along the piste. Now try to imagine this next part; here is this out of control maniac on skis and in front of him is a family having a ski day out. They are all in a line together, mother, father, son, and daughter and suddenly this mad man on skis flies passed unable to stop. He grabs the mother, who then grabs one of the children, who then grabs...well, they all grab each other. The end result is we all came tumbling down head over heels sliding down and down until eventually stopping at what seemed a mile down the side of this mountain. Fantastic, I was loving it in my stoned head, not so the family. The father was shouting at me in German (I'd worked there so recognized the language). I apologized but to no avail and just left them on the side of the mountain. Putting my skis back on I wanted more of this skiing lark. It reminded me of when I first went surfing in Newquay; the more I fell off the board, the more determined I was to stand and ride the surf. That's what I'm like, beaten as a kid, but fuck if I'll be beaten when I've left home.

I was having a ball with this kinda lifestyle, the traveling, booze, drugs, women, and not a care in the world but little did I know a price had to be paid, and the bill was on the way.

Crossroads

Show me a way to a home
I'm lost on a road with many paths
I've been up a few and back down them again
But times moving on too fast
I walk along with a heavy soul
Worn out by my weary heart
But the words in my head
I've already said
Show me a way to a home.

The season of '74 in Newquay had drawn to an end and I decided to stay for the winter. I was skint so no going abroad this year. I found myself a little flat on the outskirts of town. I had started to get flashbacks from the acid I had been taking. I got really scared when these attacks came on me. Try to imagine, just sat talking to someone or walking through the town centre and suddenly you start to hallucinate and become totally spaced out. This experience leaves you totally paranoid. The flashbacks got worse for me once the season had ended as I had more time on my hands. As I mentioned before, in those days during the winter months Newquay became a ghost town.

This was a period in my life that should have served as a warning about the kind of lifestyle I was leading, but I was too stoned to notice that my behavior was becoming erratic. I couldn't sleep, eat, stay in my room, go out, watch telly, not watch telly, be sick, not be sick; it was madness inside my head. I wanted to escape this mental torture, and the only way for this to happen was to get stoned, which was in fact the cause behind it.

I'd visited the doctor as I was totally paranoid and depressed. He prescribed valium, but this only gave me a short tranquil rest from my anxious paranoid thoughts. Strong drink was the only medication that really brought any relief but once I'd sobered up, the demons in my head seemed stronger. I stayed in this depressed, paranoid state for about six months before I walked out of this dark tunnel of my life.

The will to live, to get back to some degree of normality, was my driving force through this dark period. One morning I was pacing the room, bottle in hand, looking at the mirrors I had covered up with a towel so as not to look at my face (which, when I had a flashback, appeared distorted). I reached for a valium, popped three down my neck, took a long pull from the bottle of cider, and then angrily threw it against the wall. I fell in a heap crying at the side of my bed. Holding my head in both hands, I screamed for the demons to leave me alone, for the black paranoid thoughts to give me rest. Then I got angry, shouting at them, "Fuck you!" Do your worst, heaven or hell! If yah gonna live inside my head, then I'm gonna give yah a good time". Crazy as it may seem, it worked. I had made the first move to be in control. From that moment on, I became stronger, but the demons remained and continued to haunt/taunt me for many years.

Just because I'm paranoid
Doesn't mean they aren't out to get me.

CHAPTER 20

Sun, Sand and Sangria

Under the hot Mediterranean sun of the island of Crete, I relaxed on the beach with my friends, Pete, Bodge, and Harry. The year was 1977 and we had decided to come over here to work and have some fun after the season in Newquay had come to an end.

We travelled on the Magic Bus from London; I think it got its name from the hippies back in the sixties. There was nothing magic about it except the price as it was very cheap. The downside was it took three days from the moment we set off to arrive travelling through France, Germany, Yugoslavia, then onto Greece, and from there we then had to make our own way over to the island, which meant a ferry crossing from the sea port of Piraeus, which was an overnight crossing. We met up with two other Brits and spent the entire journey getting pissed (what else). We also had a bit of dope with us so we all smoked that together. I've forgotten to mention that we met up with them at the ferry port of Piraeus. They were supposed to be catching a ferry to another island but after a few beers/smoke with us, they joined us on our ferry.

I can't remember what happened to them when we arrived on Crete, except to say they had sobered up and took off. Pete and I had been here before a couple of years ago; unfortunately he became ill on the journey and spent three weeks in a Greek hospital on the island when we arrived. He was diagnosed as having infectious hepatitis. I later found out he had been using dirty needles to inject some kinda drug or other. He was a great guy and a true friend as were also Bodge and Harry, and we had all spent a lot of time together partying in our home town of Farnworth and also working in Newquay. Sadly Pete died about 10 years ago and took with him a part of me. I miss him a lot. Pete would not want me to get morbid about him as he enjoyed life to the full, so enough said.

What a beautiful island Crete is, with its white-painted churches, villas and buildings. Added to this the lovely hot climate, the white sandy beaches, blue coral sea, friendly accommodating local's and, back in the seventies, cheap beer/food; what more could three lads from Lancashire want.

We were sleeping on the beach, and each morning at the break of day we would make our way to the town square of Chania, this was a local meeting place for anyone who was looking for work for the day. What would happen was we would get up early, cross the road to a local taverna, which was owned by a large sixty-something Greek woman who had taken on a motherly role towards us (we actually addressed her as *Mama.* Then have a bit of brekkie, usually a coffee Nescafe and a Greek salad with chips, and if we were hung over from the night before (which we usually were) a couple of beers. Then we would stash our gear with Mama and walk along the beach to the square. It was a wonderful way to begin a day, strolling along a white sandy beach in the Med at 5am. Anyone who as been to the Med will know the day starts early as the hot sun begins to rise.

We would arrive in the square half-an-hour later and then - along with the throng of other young Brits and Europeans - await the arrival of the local farmers. Most of the jobs were on a daily basis, that's because people were just passing through; traveling, sightseeing, and working their way across the island.

You never really knew what work to expect when a farmer picked you up in his truck or if you were unlucky, on the back of his moped. Mostly it was working in the fields tending to his olive trees. Back-breaking work under the hot sun was the order of the day, whether it was picking the olives/oranges or spreading manure around the trees, the sun drained you leaving you very tired. The work would last from sunrise till sunset, and come noon it was siesta time but not for us donkeys, just the locals. We were expected to carry on working (except for a short break to eat) unless the owner was a friendly Greek guy (and there were some).

The money was poor, usually 100 drachma (about £1.10) but back in the seventies on the island this could get you a good meal and piss up, which is all we wanted. I remember one day when there was no work, we were sat at a bar next to the harbor. Earlier that day we had pawned our passport to the bar owner, which was the usual custom. They knew you could not leave the island without it and also when you did get work (which was most of the time), you would go back to the bar to redeem it and spend your money there. It was a good arrangement and suited us as we were there just to party.

This day, after pawning and spending the money on drink, we were wondering what to do. We could always go back to Mama's but this meant going out of town as the beach we slept on was a bit remote, the reason being was to keep away from the local police who sometimes moved you on, plus it was full of beach bums like ourselves and they'd probably be as skint as we were. Little did we know it but today good fortune was to come along and bless us. This was in the shape of a young, long-haired American guy who politely asked if he could join us at our table. He was the usual kind of hippy looking guy you saw traveling around the island, dressed in jeans, with a picture of Bob Marley smoking a spliff printed on his T-shirt, Jesus sandals on his feet and the obligatory guitar thrown over his shoulders. The difference with him was he reeked of money, you could just smell it.

He pulled up a seat after we agreed to him joining us, and then asked us if we would join him in drinking some local wine, c'mon 'can a duck swim?'. He bought two large jugs of Retsina (the local wine) then we all settled back, drinking and chatting. He said he was on a year's vacation from the States and that he was island-hopping around the Med before flying on to England. It soon became apparent why he chose to join us he wanted to know all about the English girls.. Apart from our accents, whenever I went abroad, I always had a union jack hung on my pack and he had spotted this.

We told him we were working over here and also hoping to tour the island but work was short and we were skint, and also we had pawned our passports. He was shocked that anyone would pawn their passport and immediately set about redeeming them for us. I have to say me and the others were tick tacking each other with our feet under the tables as well as rubbing our hands together knowing we were in for a good night's piss up with our new found rich yank.

As the drink flowed so did our spirits and tongues. Our friend was very generous (most Americans are but, had the shoe been on the other foot, so were we). We drank, ate and drank some more all through the day. The conversation was kinda mixed; but being young it usually centered on women with him wanting to know what the English girls were like and vice versa. Things were going great, the sunset across the harbor was relaxing, and the smell of Greek food mixed with the musical strings from a local bazooka player added to the harmony of the evening. Then this guy crossed the line into a taboo subject, politics. He started by attacking Britain's involvement in Northern Ireland. I myself have no interest whatsoever in politics of any kind. I do have opinions but, being a veteran of bar talk, two topics that are certain to cause arguments are politics and religion. Pete, on the other hand, was very patriotic. He was also a skinhead. Standing over 6ft, dressed in jeans, doc martin boots and a t-shirt, you'd think twice before tackling him plus he could handle himself. I had to take Pete away from the table a couple of times to try and calm him as he had a quick fuse. Though Pete was a 'live and let live' person, if you rubbed him up the wrong way, watch out.

The inevitable was about to happen though as this guy (pissed by now) continually bad-mouthed the British government. Suddenly Pete sprang up from the table, all 6ft of him; he verbally laid into this guy reminding him of America's withdrawal from the Vietnam War leaving the people at the mercy of their oppressors. He continued about the way they stole the land off the American Indian, and his icing on the cake was the resignation of their 'bent president' (as he put it), Richard Nixon. If he was trying to gall this guy into a fight it failed, 'cos the guy stood up, picked up his guitar, said he was back off to his hotel, threw 500 drachma on the table, and bid us goodnight. If his final gesture was meant to shame Pete, it didn't, as Pete's only response was, "I should think so too", and he shot off to the bar. When he came back with the wine, he proposed a toast to Richard Nixon.

This guy really didn't need to go. Pete didn't hold any grudges; he was the kinda man that would step outside a bar with someone if they wanted to fight, then walk back in with them and have a drink together - 'live and let live', that about sums him up, plus we did like the yank.

I remember an incident we had the first time we visited this island together. One day me and Pete were in the square drinking. It was late afternoon when we decided we would explore and go up into the mountains to find a real local bar and mix it with the locals. It was a hot day as we walked to the bus station and caught the first bus that was leaving. We decided to buy the cheapest ticket and get off where the driver told us to. The bus set off and was soon into the countryside and mountains.

We passed a few local tavernas, but they seemed quiet and uninviting. We didn't want to go too far as we both knew we'd be drunk before the evening was over and we may have to walk/stagger back to town. The driver made our minds up for us by indicating it was our stop. Don't yah just love fate? (as you will read) the bus pulled up outside a large taverna that was cut into the side of a mountain. The sound of local Greek music invitingly invaded our ears, along with the laughter and singing of the locals, and as we walked up the steps we could smell the mouth-watering succulent lamb kebabs that would soon be finding their way down our necks. Both me and Pete rubbed our hands together at the same time and said "let's start our engines". We opened the door and went inside; what happened next was like a scene from an old cowboy film where two drifters walk inside a saloon and the music stops and all eyes are on them, Well, it was like that except the music didn't stop, just died a little. We were shown to a table by an inquisitive Greek waiter, given a menu, then he left us and we stayed left for quite some time that is 'till Pete stood up and in the kinda sheepish way that he possessed, signaled the waiter over with a clicking of his thumb and finger in a friendly but thirsty gesture.

We ordered the lamb, Greek salad and chips (what else?) and a large jug of Retsina. On the dance floor was a Greek guy dressed in traditional costume. He was holding a handkerchief in one hand and a woman in the other, and she was also holding on to several other women, he was leading them around the dance floor in motion to the lovely Greek music. Every now and then he would let go of the woman's hand, slap the back heel of his black boots, go down on his knees, shout out, jump up, twirl around, grab the woman's hand again and continue leading them. It was infectious. After me and Pete had finished eating and 'wetting our whistle' a few times, whilst clapping along with the rest of the crowd, it was time for us to have a bit of fun. I went into my pocket and fetched out an English coin, "Heads or tails" I said to Pete, "What for" he asked. "Well," I said, "whoever loses gets up and has to dance". 'Never say your mother raised a gibber', that's what we say in Farnworth. No best out of three and all that crap, Pete lost and immediately stood up and went onto the dance floor. Picture the scene if you can, there's Pete all 6ft of him dressed in skinhead gear dancing around a group of Greek dancers in a kinda skinhead stomp. I was laughing so much I nearly forgot to have a drink.

The next thing, and as is the Greek custom when they are enjoying the show, plates came crashing all around Pete as the locals threw them from where they were sitting, and (if you don't know this) you can purchase cheap plates to throw as the night goes on. Pete, however, was not aware of this custom and thought they were having a 'pop' at him and, before you could say last orders, he had a huge Greek guy by the throat and was ready to 'hang one' on him. I immediately knew as the plates began to crash around Pete that trouble along with the plates was in the air. I jumped up and before Pete could do any damage I stepped in between them explaining to Pete that this was their way of saying 'nice one' and that they loved his dancing. Fortunately Pete's actions were taken in good humor by this guy and we were invited to sit and join his friends at their table. The rest of the night was a party as they piled me and Pete with wine and Raki (a local strong spirit). Considering that none of us spoke the other one's language, we had a whale of a time.

By the time we all left the taverna daybreak was dawning. Earlier in the evening with the help from a waiter who interpreted for each side, the guy who Pete had nearly made do the chicken (this means grabbing someone's neck, putting it to the floor and pulling his head up and down like a chicken would peck at seed) had invited us back to his house saying that he had a son who could speak English. We all piled into his jeep (no worries about drink and driving laws in the mountains) and were on our way to his house, stopping several times to take a pee as we all carried on drinking wine from an ever-flowing supply in the truck. When we got to his farm, he went upstairs to wake his son; He then came back down the stairs with his arms around a tired protesting 12 year old. The conversation went like this exactly, Boy," Hallo what is your name?" Me, "Hallo I'm Billy and this is Pete." Boy "Hallo what is your name?" that's all the English he knew end of conversation. We didn't stay long. I'm sure that sooner or later they would have dragged us off in a friendly way to tend their olive crop and we were too pissed to do any work so after a bit of brekkie and more wine we made our excuses and bid them goodnight, then remembered it was morning but what a piss up.

On the night we bid farewell to our long-haired American friend, we decided to have a couple of more beers with the 500 drachma tip he had left us then make our way back to hotel beach. Our sleeping bags were arranged around a cluster of trees on the beach; these came in handy to hang your clothes on the branches to dry and also as a shade from the sun when it started to 'crack the flags'. (Another Lancashire saying: 'flags' are the paving stones and 'cracking' means they begin to crack as the sun bakes them.) We made it back to the beach on a stagger and song and fell into our sleeping bags. Due to the large consumption of wine, we went out like a light. Now being a light sleeper, I was woken up with something dripping onto my head. I soon realized that it was spitting (rain).

We had been warned by Mama that rain was on the way, and that when it started to rain on this island, with it being in the middle of the Med, it really started to rain. I shouted over to the other three to wake up as the spitting started to open up; I would have got more response in Farnworth Cemetery. I climbed out of my warm (but getting wetter by the minute) bag and went over to each of them giving them a gentle shake; it doesn't do to wake up someone drunk too quick, eventually I stopped trying to 'wake the dead'; the rain was beginning to turn into 'cats and dogs'. Lovely language flowed from each sleeping bag as they became wetter, eventually three drunks emerged cursing and swearing into the night. Rumbles of thunder could be heard far out at sea. We gathered all our belongings, bumping into each other like silly clowns performing in the ring, and quickly found a shop doorway in which to shelter, and that's where we stayed until the morning. It pissed it down all night.

Drowned tired rats that's what we must have looked like in the early hours of the morning, walking along the streets towards the town square. I had decided during the long rainy night that in the morning I was going to cash an *only to be used in emergencies* traveler's cheque and rent one of the cheap rooms with four beds for us all so we could get some kip. It was nine o'clock before we found one suitable for us all. The moment we all hit the pillows we were off into the land of nod. I awoke about noon and found Harry already up and getting dressed, and the sun was out in full force. He said he was off for a beer, and by this time my throat felt as dry as an Aborigine's armpit.

Getting dressed and grabbing my gear, we left a note for the other two telling them we were off for a beer around the square and we would see them when they were up and about. Walking down the road we heard some 60s music coming from a bar somewhere. We followed the sound and found this little taverna up a side street. It was dark inside, lit up by blue lights and flicking colored ones that danced in time with the music. We ordered chips and Greek salad, plus of course beer. The music was a change from all the Greek stuff we were getting used to listening to.

We stayed there for quite some time getting relaxingly pissed and singing along to the music. In the middle of the floor was a fire stove with a pipe coming from it and leading out through the ceiling, even though it was cracking flags outside (know what I mean?), it was lit. Well, I don't know what made me do it but I lifted my feet and laid them on the top of the stove. Being somewhat slightly intoxicated, my foot caught the pipe and knocked it away from the stove it sprouted from, and the next minute the room began to fill up with this choking thick black smoke. Now, coming from Farnworth, and not wanting a bill for the damage I may have caused, I was out of there faster than I was at getting to the bar for last orders, followed as quickly by Harry. It soon became apparent that we were being chased by some angry coughing locals who finally caught up with us as we ran into a dead end. They set about us for a minute or two but being an ex Bolton Wanderers football hooligan, their kicking was kids stuff and we soon got away and told them to Fuck Off even though their kicking didn't inflict any real harm, our pride had been wounded and, being pissed, we wanted revenge. We formed a drunken plan to petrol bomb the taverna; all we needed was a milk bottle, a rag and to siphon some petrol from one of their fuckin' mopeds and 'ding dang do' result. But this was Greece so no milk bottles, which meant no petrol, bomb, thank God. In my drunken /drugged stupors I've had some crazy plans for revenge. I once crashed out only to wake up with a meat clever in my hand ready to cut some-one up, and once again I thank God I didn't. I was by now getting drunk nearly everyday and just loved it, my past as a lot to answer for.

Eventually we bumped into Pete and Bodge and decided to go on to a night club. Harry was older than us all but you would not have known it, as he kept his age well. He was about 5ft 8in, medium build with black curly hair, and around his neck he wore surf beads. Harry, like the rest of us, was up for anything so long as it meant having some fun and a beer or two. Bodge was a bit smaller in height but broad, and like Pete wore a skinhead hair cut. Bodge just seemed to laugh off anything; no matter what it was he found a funny side to it. When he was not wearing his t-shirt he turned some heads, for tattooed on his chest was a clenched fist representing the logo for Northern Soul.

We stayed and worked around this part of the island for about a month and decided to move on. We had heard about some caves where the British, Australian, Canadian and other troops had hidden during the occupation of the island by the German Army in the Second World War. Also, back in the early sixties, that great American singer Janis Joplin had also stayed in them. The caves were on the western side of the island in a place called Matala (and for anyone visiting this wonderful island I recommend that you visit them). The caves were overlooking the beach and the scenery was splendid. We found a sizable cave and stayed there for at least two weeks. Unfortunately there was no work around this place, it was typical tourist visitors only, but we had a great time, swimming and snorkeling in the blue/green Med sea, then of an evening entertaining the locals with our singing and larking about and the best bit of it all was we never once went without a drink money or no money the locals just loved us.

I still visit Crete a lot these days and though I'm a lot older, I could still live it all over again even now at my age. I'm still trying to make up for my lost childhood and do you know what? I don't think I ever will.

I know I'm a little bit paranoid
Whether you talk about me or not
I also have a touch of Alzheimer's I think
Can't remember I've just forgot
My agoraphobic Illness isn't just a waste of space
Hypochondriac I don't think so
I'm having a panic attack in any case.

My insomnia keeps me awake at night
Bastard there goes my torrette
The walls are closing in again
And I'm feeling claustrophobic
My manic depressive mood swings
I now have their ups and downs
And if I wasn't sick doctor
I'd make a bloody good circus clown

Now all these phobias are not just me
That's my other schizophrenic side
He thinks that he's a dentist
I don't, open wide
If this poem has left you feeling confused
And you're trying to figure it all out
Don't bother its just dribble
Or is it… you work it out.

CHAPTER 21

Day 5

Thursday July 27th
Stage 5 - Part 1 - Marcha de la Muerte
(March of Death)
Distance 81.5km/50.9m
Elevation +450/-390m

Huddled around the camp fire at 5am with the other few early risers who sat silently eating their breakfast. I wondered if they, like me, were planning and a bit worried about today's big 50 miler. I suspect they were.

The night had been bloody cold again, freezing all the water in the bottles. Today with the big one ahead of me, I knew the desert had chipped away at my physical/mental state, and left me wondering if I had anything left inside of me to complete what was regarded as the toughest and final stage. Really, the 50 miler seemed like the end of the race, even though there was yet another stage of 10k/6m before the end of the grueling 150m marathon. I silently thanked my friend, who had given me the sleeping pill last night; for being asleep meant I didn't have to endure the mental torture of freezing all night.

Looking down at my new cut shoes I wondered if they would hold together and not fall apart forcing me to withdraw from the race. I don't know how I would handle that. All that I had trained for, all those demons inside my head, my self-esteem, were all now riding on my shoes staying on my feet. I overheard some of the competitors saying that to get this far was a great achievement and that you could go home with head held high. Well not me. I wanted that bloody medal, nothing less would do. On one part of the race yesterday I did 2m with a couple who had successfully completed the Gobi marathon the year before. They had spoken to me about their plan for the big one today and seemed confident that they would finish it. I was hooked and asked them if I could join them. I knew I was in for a long night-time haul in the desert, and didn't fancy going through it on my own. They cheerfully agreed, saying it would be refreshing to have another person with them. They were a husband and wife team and said jokingly that after spending four days together in this desert, they were close to divorce.

With that in mind, I felt pretty positive for the long haul ahead of me. I forced some porridge down my throat and I mean forced. Hunger had left me a long time ago. Looking around the camp at the other runners, the majority bearing some form of pain or injury in their feet and legs, it seemed crazy that today they were going to take part in a 50m marathon through a desert, with inhospitable terrain and weather. But looking at their faces you would not have known it; most were smiling and chatting amongst themselves quite excitedly and there was a kinda festival atmosphere around the camp. I myself had the feeling of 'it's nearly over' however, this was to be short-lived.

At the 8pm meeting with Pierre he spoke about sticking to your plan that had got you to this stage so far. He also informed us that this one was going to be tough especially for the mere human runners. Today's course had 8 CP's. The last

CP being base camp, plus 4 stages to pass through. Pierre informed us that we had to be at stage 2 by 5pm; anyone coming in after that would receive a D.N.F (Did Not Finish). Just to refresh your memory, that would mean no medal.

Today the runners were to be split into two sections, which meant us mere humans starting at 8pm and the elite top runners two hours after. I still don't know the reason for this, it was probably explained to us all but I was past listening. I was busy looking for my companions for the day. Pierre then informed us of another cut off time at base camp. I was completely taken by surprise and not just me. I thought having got this far we would have plenty of time to cover this 50m section, but in fact we had until 3pm the next day to finish it. I was not sure whether failing this time would result in a D.N.F. and for any of you runners out there who may be thinking, that's plenty of time, I agree in normal conditions, but we are talking about a bloody hostile desert here. Having already covered about 90m in four days, this 50m stage was designed to test you both physically and mentally.

Let me go back to the point I had made earlier about my feeling that it was nearly over, but that this was short-lived. Well to explain this, I was approached by one of the organizers who had gotten wind about my intention to complete this stage with my new-found friends. She strongly advised me against doing this and to stick to my plan. She said she had every faith in my ability to complete this stage and that she felt the couple, who I was planning on running with, wouldn't. Her final words delivered to me with a hug were, "Go it alone, Billy, you can do this". If these words were meant to encourage me they didn't, as I saw my plans go crashing around me. I knew that today I would spend the last part of the run, during the whole bloody night through freezing weather conditions, on my own.

I walked away from the meeting and a little way from the camp, I needed to be on my own. Finding solitude behind one of the dunes. I took stock of my situation. Physically I was tired, my feet were swollen, I was wearing running shoes that could pack in at any time, my lower back was in constant pain, I had an inflamed Achilles, and I was dying for a cigarette. Mentally I was strong even though doubt as to whether I would finish this entire event crept into my mind. I had Capt. Picard and the rest of the team on my side, plus I came from Farnworth. We have a saying around our way, 'Never Say Your Mother Raised A Gibber' (a wimp). As I sat behind the dune chewing all these thoughts through my mind, I got fired up. "Fuck it," I said to myself, "bring it on, heaven or hell. If my shoes pack in then I'll fuckin' crawl, they will have to shoot me to get me to stop". Through all this bravado was the fear of getting a D.N.F. I'd come all the way to South America for that medal and I'll be fucked if I was going back without it.

The start of the race was pretty much the same as the other days, the only difference being I was not in the same shape physically. The first section of the run was over (yes, you've guessed it) more salt flats, but not as long as yesterday's. Then we had to cross this stuff that was like soft sticky fudge with a white coating over it; one minute you could be sliding along it, the next you sank up to your ankles. Three hours into the race with a two-hour start, the elite runners came charging passed me. It reminded me of the last orders at the Queen's pub in Farnworth where I used to drink.

On reaching the first cp I sat and took off my backpack. I was reminded by one of the volunteers that I could take a rest for as long as I wanted, bearing in mind though I had to reach the second CP by 3pm. I resisted the urge to rip off my running shoes for fear I may not get them on again. That morning it had took me an age carefully and painfully getting them onto my feet. I remembered saying once they were on that they don't come of again 'till the end of this 50m stage. It was whilst I was resting one of the runners informed me that because we had run more miles during the previous stages than what we were supposed to, the organizers had cut today's down from 50m to 43m. I just shrugged my shoulders. I was passed believing and caring about anything except getting that bloody medal.

I had reached the first CP at around 12.30am and set of again before 1pm. On the second stage we had to pass through 'The valley of the Moon'. It was indeed a spectacular sight, lunar-like terrain for as far as the eye could see. One did get the feeling of being on Mars. I stopped, got out my camera and took a picture of it. I could have stayed there all day drinking it all in - superb. Having passed through this section, I was once more into the hot hard-packed sandy desert. I would alternate my running/walking every 10 minutes constantly keeping my eye on my watch. Let me remind you that covering 2m in this hot hostile terrain really takes it out of you. I was constantly thanking whoever it was that invented the I Pod. I don't know how I would have fared without my music; it certainly gave me the mental boost I needed.

I figured it was around 3pm and I was getting near the end of the second stage as it was supposed to be 10k/6m from the last CP. I had crossed the dreaded salt flats, the dry river beds (soft fudge earth) but what hit me next took my breath away. In the far distance I saw huge sand dune, like mountain. On it I could make out tiny dots in a line climbing up it. I took out a small telescope that my brother, Roy, had lent me hoping that what I was seeing was a mirage and that I did not have to climb that bloody thing. Lowering the telescope, I sank onto the sand and sprawled out onto my back still wearing the pack. It was not a mirage. Those tiny dots I saw were my fellow competitors struggling to get to the top of this mountainous sand dune. Taking a deep breath, I stood up. I had little over an hour to get to the top of this and down to the other side where the CP was. I do remember Pierre saying that we had a sand dune (no mention of a 'mountain') to climb near the end of stage two and before our 5pm cut off time.

That cut off time was my driving force. Whatever it took, I was determined I would make it. With this attitude, I set off putting all my energy on reaching and climbing this mountain/sand dune. I reached the bottom of it at about 4pm. I felt so small and vulnerable just looking up at the bloody thing; I could see various runners staggering up it, some lay flat out, others at the top taking photos. It was at this point I cursed the police who had confiscated my walking pole at Madrid airport.

My back was aching, my calves, and Achilles were giving me pain, I was gasping for breath, and I was not yet a quarter of the way up this mountain. My only selfish relief was looking back at the distance I had covered where I could see other runners struggling up towards me. With several stops and 'a wing and a prayer' I eventually made it to the peak and as far as I was concerned this was my Everest. What goes up has to come down and if I thought I was on for an easy descent, I couldn't have been more wrong. Granted I went down quicker, which only added pressure onto my sore stiff knees, but also I was sinking up to my knees in the soft sand. When I finally made it to the bottom, I had no choice but to take off my shoes to empty the ton of sand I had picked up on my way down. Relief, relief, sheer bliss; you know that feeling you get when your feet are aching and you just can't wait to take your shoes off. I sat there for a couple of minutes as my swollen feet cooled down. I then spent at least another 5 minutes struggling with the pain to put them back on again.

I could see the international flags surrounding the CP. I checked my watch. It had taken me 25 minutes to scale that mountain and I had 35 minutes to reach the CP before the 5pm cut off time. Because I had already covered about 30m and was getting tired, the camp seemed farther than it actually was. I figured it was about a third of a mile away across hard sand. This was my goal. Once I reached this, I had until 3pm the next day to finish this long 50m stage. I made it with 15 minutes to spare and felt ecstatic, but I was aware that night would fall shortly and so would the temperature. There where only two other runners at this cp when I arrived, and they were ready to leave. One of the volunteers said it was another 10k/6m to the next but last CP and the same again to base camp. I wanted to set off and catch up with the runners who had already set off but I needed to rest and try to eat something before I took off again to complete the remaining 20k/12m through the night. One energy food that I had with me was salted peanuts. I just love them but they also make you thirsty, but no swilling them down with a nice ice-cool coke. No, for me, it was very warm water. I have never been a water drinker and struggled getting it down. It obviously had to be taken regularly, but it just doesn't push my boat out. How I dreamed of what I would do when I got back to England; drink loads and loads of iced coke, and eat portion upon portion of fish and chips, one of my favorite foods. I can tell you at this point that is exactly what I did on my return but, for now, it was warm co-operation pop (water) and peanuts.

Time to move on. I started to put on my thermal jacket, gloves, hat and night light, it would be dark soon. I noticed that the other runners I had seen leaving the camp were now far in the distance. I then suddenly became aware of the volunteers breaking camp. I looked again at my watch, just a couple of minutes to the cut off time and I saw two more runners just coming up towards the camp with worried looks on their face. I suppose seeing the camp being taken down, they feared they would receive a D.N.F. but that was not the case. However, I could see in the far distance other runners that I knew would not make it. I did ask if that was it for them, and would they get a D.N.F. and the reply was a definite yes. The other two runners were females and looked Japanese to me. I would get to know one of these runners very well on the course later on that night but that was a long way off.

Having changed into my night gear, I set off at a slow pace. There was no point in worrying now, I had made the cut off time and no matter what, I resigned myself to the fact that I would be spending most of the night in the desert.

Munching the miles in the dark and alone with my thoughts I remembered when I had my first taste of alcohol; I would have been about 14 years old at the time. I had a friend called Dominic who was an Italian. It was during the long school summer holidays and my dad was getting sick of pressure from my friends to let us out to play. He couldn't stand the sight of us anymore, which he constantly told us, so I would go 'round to Dominic's house. Dominic was very good at getting money; I don't know where from but I did have my suspicions. On this particular day it was really hot and we had been playing behind the local mill with our little gang, when he said he had to go home and go to the shops for his mam. He invited me along with him. Off we went, did the business for his mam, then he asked me if I would like a drink of wine. Because he was Italian he was used to drinking wine at meal times. My first taste of alcohol; what a glow! It felt like sunshine had entered my life.

During the course of the rest of the day I persuaded him to go back to his house for some more wine. The end result of this experience was I became violently sick and was walked around by Dominic and a friend until I became something like. When I got home I told my mam I was off to bed 'cos I didn't feel well. She always lived in the back room whilst my dad sat in the front room parlour as we used to call them, posh, eh! So I knew I wouldn't bump into him. The next morning I called round at Dominic's to play out and the first thing I asked for was some 'pop'. I did this for a week wanting to have that sunshine feeling in my life everyday. He told me his dad had shifted it and we were to have no more. That was when I was 14; my next taste of alcohol was at 16 and lasted 38 years up to the present stage of writing this book.

As night-time began to fall, I noticed I was closing in on a runner and from what I could see, be it male or female; they were having a lot of trouble with their feet. I seized upon the chance to have some company and put on an extra spurt in order to catch up. "You look like you're struggling," I said to the man, as I caught up with him. I introduced myself and he said his name was Paul. His feet were in a bad way and that he was unsure whether he could go on any further. I tried encouraging him and suggested that we could finish this together if he was up for it. I knew he felt relieved to have someone to talk to through the night. He said that this would be his first time on the course at night, and was surprised when I informed him I'd spent the last three nights on my own.

We stayed together for an hour or so. He was really struggling every step was painful on his feet. Added to this we could not sit for a while to get some rest as the temperature had dropped and once again it started to get freezing cold. We were struggling to follow the red markers on the course when it dawned on me that the glow sticks had not been set out. In the darkness, the course should have been lit up like a runway. When the last bit of light disappeared behind the curtain of darkness, it was apparent that we could no longer continue along a course we could not see. Paul, who by now was in a lot of pain, brought out his emergency whistle and started blowing it for all he was worth, after several minutes with me joining in with mine, we gave up and listened to the deafening silence. It was at this point that we were joined by the two female Japanese runners I had seen earlier entering the CP. We all looked at each other wondering what we were going to do. This was a 'first' for me; being a somewhat night-time veteran I had never known the course not to be lit up. We could only assume that somewhere communication had broken down between the organizers and the local Chileans, whose job it was to mark the course with the glow sticks.

We all knew it was dangerous to wander off the course, but paranoia set in. If the organizers were unaware that the course was not lit, we could remain here for hours. The night temperature began dropping fast, and standing around was not helping us to keep warm. The girls took out their whistles and took over where Paul had left off. This was a situation one is not able to comprehend, or even describe. I suppose the only way I could attempt to describe it is try to imagine being out on the moors in freezing temperatures, with nowhere to shelter, no form of communication, and no path to follow. It was bloody scary and I'm no wimp, but with Paul indicating that we could die of hyperthermia out here (and also being warned by the organizers that hyperthermia was a great danger at night), it did leave me feeling somewhat unsettled. We rifled our packs and put on any extra clothing we had brought with us but, for me, I only had the bare essentials. I'd never expected in my ignorance to get cold in a bloody desert. I was wearing long cycling tights and only had shorts for my bottom half in my pack so my legs were getting colder by the minute.

The girls had stopped whistling, and the cold and black silence entered our spirits. I began to wonder if I had come all this way to die in a desert. That's how serious it was getting. We could see only as far as what our night lights lit up, which was not far; certainly no landmarks, but we couldn't have followed them anyway. Paul was not helping the situation. Being in great pain, I suppose, was an excuse to let off his anger, but his outbursts were not helping our female friends. I had no plans on what to do, but I had a desire to get that medal, and not a D.N.F. I silently prayed, 'this can't end here…'.

CHAPTER 22

Turn the key crank up the car
The wheels are moving but you ain't going far
Open the windows let in some air
Light up a joint without a care.

Pop a pill and open a can
Bang up the music, freedom man
Don't be a fool, you're acting a prat
I don't give a toss, silly twat

Mile after mile up hill and down
Changing scenery smile with a frown
The road goes on where will it end
Not here, you gotta go round the bend.

Losing My Mind

The 70s in Newquay were coming to an end and so was the party. I had been there for a decade, but I didn't know it at the time. I was 28 years old and had been getting stoned since I was 17 from L.S.D. to magic mushrooms, speed, dope, booze, poppers, uppers, downers - all around the mulberry bloody bush - and I hadn't got anywhere in life except older. I was in that place again where I couldn't go outside, yet couldn't stay in, couldn't watch the telly, yet couldn't not watch it, couldn't eat yet couldn't not eat; to cut it short, I was a bloody mess mentally. I was suffering from flashbacks brought on by the L.S.D.

I went to the doctor who made an appointment for me to go and see a shrink; he diagnosed me as being extremely depressed due to my lifestyle of booze and drugs and prescribed valium. For the next three months I locked myself away in my flat in Newquay too scared to go out. I felt that I was going insane. The valium took the edge off the panic attacks but that was as far as they went. I wasn't working - it was winter time - so there was no need to get up, which was just as well 'cos I wasn't sleeping much. The only time I ventured out was to sign on at the dole, cash my giro and buy some booze. Then I would return back to my flat, taking all the back roads so as to avoid bumping into anyone I knew. Back at the flat, I would drink myself silly then climb into bed, hiding under the bed clothes hoping the monsters inside my head would go away but it never worked. Friends would call around shouting through the closed door that they had some dope and "Get your arse out," but I kept quiet till they went away. Dope was the last thing I needed; if this is what they meant by 'cracking up' then I certainly was. I had covered up all the mirrors in my flat, well all two of them, as again I couldn't look at myself. I had returned to this demon infested place again and would return here many more times in my future.

Christmas had come and gone and we had just started the New Year. I had ventured out for Xmas Eve, and also New Year's Eve. My mates had wondered what had become of me and bombarded me with all kinda questions. I avoided any honest answers, saying I was just having a break to sort my head out.

My mate, Martin, from London sparked up a joint and said, "This will sort your head out", "Yeah" I replied, taking it off him as he passed it to me. For the rest of the night it did sort my head out! We had just entered February and I was still messed up but I'd had enough of the mental pain. One morning, dragging myself out of bed after another night fighting the demons inside my head, I made that decision again not to let the demons take me, I got angry, "Fuck this".

Millsy and our Roy decided to go and work on the island of Jersey in the Channel Islands. I was still working at the Bay hotel with a lad called John Wray another good mate of mine and very funny. We both decided to leave and go and join them but John was courting the receptionist at the Bay whose name was Gill so he didn't stay on the island long and went back to be with her. Up to the point of writing this book they are married and still living together.

Roy secured me a job at the hotel he was working at along with millsy. They worked in the kitchen and me in the dining room as a waiter. Now I'd been a silver service waiter at the Bay but I was out of my depth at this place. The menu was written in French being as France was just further up the channel; also, this was the kinda restaurant where they cooked 'crepe suzettes' at the table a definite no, no, for me. Anyroad this owner decided to train me up and said I had a great future there. The Hotel was right slap bang in the middle of the country I shared a room with our kid and Millsy and by the time we finished work there was nowhere to go for a drink.

We decided to ask the owner if we could come into the bar when work was finished at the end of the night. It was left up to me to ask him. He agreed and said I was ok dressed as I was, but Millsy and Roy had to dress up smartly. He must have thought they only had the jeans and t shirts that they worked in.

After work that night Roy and Millsy went back to the room to get changed and then join me in the bar. The atmosphere was not good with all the so called upper class. The men were smoking their Winston Churchill cigars accompanied by their large brandies. Whilst the women with very large glasses of wine in their hands bitched about each other, they weren't shy at doing this at the tables' whilst I served them.

After we had drunk our second pint and were about to order our third the owner commented to us about our large consumption I suppose he wasn't used to people drinking pints and we were definitely setting him on edge. We asked him if we could have a carry out. He looked relieved and said yes, so we ordered 2 bottles of wine and a large bottle of whisky. Bear in mind Jersey is a tax exile, so no tax on the booze and cheap to buy. We took it back to our room put some music on and laid into these bottles. It didn't take long for three thirsty Lancashire lads to sink this lot and pretty soon the bottles were dry and we were still thirsty. Millsy got up and left the room. We thought he'd gone outside for a piss but a short while later we could hear someone kicking on the door, and when we opened it there stood Millsy carrying a large barrel of ale in his hand and two knifes he'd picked up from the kitchen in his mouth. What he'd done was to creep into the cellar and disconnect it from pipes which fed the ale up into the bar. His explanation for this was that "no other fucker was drinking it" so with two knifes pushed up the connecting end we siphoned it into a bucket and supped most of it before we all staggered back to the cellar to reconnect it.

I had been working for about two weeks without a day off and told the boss I needed one so after one particular busy weekend he told me I could have the next Monday off. On the Monday I was up and dressed by 9 o'clock. In Jersey the pubs open at 9am and stay open all day till late at night. The beer is cheap but they do have one rule and that is if you are pissed or even look pissed you won't get served. I caught a taxi into town and was in the pub around 9.30am and settled down to some cheap ale. I didn't know anyone and when I tried to set up a conversation the talk was short and sweet. The locals were suspicious of outsiders. It was around 4pm in the afternoon that I found myself outside this one pub trying to get my head together. I had formed a plan which was to have my money ready, walk in as straight as I could, and order a pint whilst looking around pretending to be looking for someone. All went well I managed to make it to the bar and order a pint. The barmaid placed the glass in front of me. I picked it up and took a large swallow, put the glass down, turned around from the bar to look who was in the joint and went to lean on the bar with my elbow and missed the fucker. Down I went and stayed down I was so pissed I couldn't get up and just laid there laughing. I remember arms grabbing me bodily to take me outside then I heard someone saying that they couldn't just leave me on the kerb in this state so they took me to a taxi rank asked me where I lived I managed to tell them and away we went. The taxi pulled up at the hotel but I was crashed out and don't remember owt else. My brother told me the hotel owner had come to their room to get him and Millsy to help me out of the taxi. I went into work the next day and the owner lays into me verbally telling me I wasn't to get drunk like that anymore. I told him it was my day off and I'll get as pissed as I like. We didn't stay long after that and soon made our way back to Newquay.

I didn't fancy another season in Newquay so I went back home to Bolton. I'd also got back with an old girlfriend who lived in Manchester. One day a friend of hers told me that they were looking for people to clean the buses at the Manchester bus depot, so I took myself along. It's funny how things turn out 'cos I went for a cleaning job and ended up as a bus conductor. After only four weeks into the conductor job, I was asked if I had a driving license. "Only a provisional one," I said. "That will do. "Report to the driving school on Monday," said the inspector. So after applying for a job cleaning buses, within six weeks I was bloody driving them. I passed my test the first time.

Give peace a chance
Cos here comes the sun
Imagine all the happiness if we live as one
Working class heroes you see them everyday
They've fuckin shot Lennon and I've lost my way

"Are you in there Billy"? I was sat on the loo at the bus station waiting to start work on the buses when my mate who had been looking for me walked in. Yea I replied wats up? Have you read today's paper he asked, nah I replied why what's up? John Lennon been shot he's dead, "don't fuck about" I said. He knew I was a great fan of the Beatles and especially Lennon. I'm not fucking about. He got shot today in New York. The year was 1980 and I was 29yr old. He pushed the newspaper under the door and there in big headlines was the announcement that Lennon had been shot outside his apartment in Manhattans upper west side opposite central park by an unknown crazed gunman. I read it and read it and read it but it wouldn't sink in I just refused to believe it. I left the toilet in a daze and went over to the bus I was working on that day. The driver greeted me with the words "have you read today's paper" I looked at him to see if he was taking the piss cos I wanted to smash some fucker in the face to get rid of the feeling of shock inside me but he to looked shook up. The bus left the depot and drove around the route stopping to pick up the morning workers. I issued tickets in a daze looking at everyone reading the shocking story and talking to each other about it.

A young couple got on the bus sat down and started reading their papers when I heard the young girl laugh out loud, I was on her quicker than going up to the bar for the last orders. "What the fuck you laughing about" I challenged her, the young guy must have seen the anger in me cos he kept his mouth shut. "I'll throw you off the fucking bus in a minute and you'll walk to fucking work, I was in a rage. Some of the passengers and the driver came over to me to try to calm me down, "fuck this" I said, took off my ticket machine threw it on a seat and stormed of the bus and into an off license to buy some booze and get smashed

I went on a bender for a week, then I heard they were holding a John Lennon memorial down in his home town of Liverpool. It was Sunday when along with a few of my mates we decided to hitch it down there, not a good idea I was still smashed out on booze and speed and so were my mates. We only made it has far as the nearest bar before we decided to hold our own vigil.

At the end of the bender I went back to work, to be disciplined by the chief inspector. I was only young so recovery from the booze/drugs was no problem but getting over Lennon death is too this day a thorn in my flesh. The music that genius could have still given us doesn't bear thinking about.

The next thing I knew I was being made redundant and got a £1000 pay out. With this I decided to go on an adventure and took my mate, Pete, to Crete for a couple of months. My life took off again!

CHAPTER 23

Driving on Liquid

On returning back to Manchester from Crete I secured a job driving coaches and became a coach driver operating tours around the country. Now why I said "my life took off" is because I'd never had so much spare money in my life. I would be driving around the country staying at hotels, food and board thrown in, plus the coach party each week would buy me booze of an evening after each outing. I never touched my wages.

It was during this period at the age of 32 that I met a girl who I was to marry. This marriage was destined to fail. I had too many issues to deal with though I didn't know it at the time, plus I was still drinking. I had lived on my own for so long and coming from a dysfunctional made up a recipe for disaster. The good thing to come out of this relationship were my three children; Hayley, Billy, and Bethany. I tried to be a good father, but looking back I was to busy fighting a battle within myself. I supposed because of this I failed them but not through lack of love cos I love them more than anything in my life. They are my treasure and even though we don't see one another at the moment of writing this book I live in hope that one day we will be united and happy together.

My coach driving career lasted for 5 years. I ended up leaving the tour driving when the kids came along. I had a break for two years then went driving the buses. Then late one night, as I was driving my bus back to the depot, I stopped off and bought myself three cans of special brew. I parked up, drank them then turning off my interior lights so as not to pick any passengers up for fear of them smelling the booze on me. I drove back to the depot. Now because I was the last bus in there should have been no-one else there. I only had to park up and lock the gates but, as I swung my bus into the garage, I noticed three other drivers in the yard. It took me three attempts to reverse into a parking space, one that I usually could have done with my eyes closed. They were duty bound to report me to the manager. The next morning he pulled me into his office. He was an old boy and very understanding, but he had no choice but to suspend me and for me to get a doctor's certificate to see whether I had a drink problem. The trouble was I'd been to the doctors a few times, saying I was drinking quite a bit 'cos of the problems I was having finding it hard to cope. The doctor had no choice but to write on my certificate 'chronic alcoholism'. I'd been lying to him in the past stating that I never drove under the influence of drink. My driving career came to an end and I've never driven a coach since.

Turn off the light shut off the TV
Pour away the booze I don't want to be me
Cover up the mirrors and draw the curtains shut
I'm hiding away in myself no answers just buts

CHAPTER 24

Booze Run

I awoke to find myself laid on the toilet floor covered in vomit. In its drunken, confused state, my mind raced to remember how I ended up here. I knew I'd had an alcoholic fit. I crawled back to the living room on my hands and knees for fear of 'fitting' again.

My drinking was now completely out of control, I was 44yr old and going on benders that were getting frequent and also lasting longer. The doctor by this time just didn't know what to do with me. The pills he was prescribing to help me withdraw were now being taken with the booze.

The living room was full of empty and full bottles of cider, plus empty cans of special brew. I crawled onto the mattress, opened the cider bottle and took a long swig, then threw up in the bucket at the side of my mattress. I had to hold the cider down, so I took another swig. This time it stayed down. I took account of how many bottles I had left. It didn't matter really, 'cos it would not be enough to last me through the next day which was just dawning. I knew a paper shop that opened at 6am. I had to venture out before anyone took to the streets. I looked at my watch. It was 5.30am.

I had been awake most of the night, drinking. I knew I was in a mess both physically and mentally. Fear gripped me with the thought of venturing outside but it was vital for me to get my supply of booze. The panic of running out was my driving force, for I knew what waited for me – delirium, tremors, bad shakes; dry heaving, and - the biggest one of all – paranoia.

I trembled as I put on my coat over the top of the clothes I had worn and slept in for the last few days. Stepping outside, I silently thanked God that it was still dark. It was winter, so, like a rat, I kept in the safety of the shadows. The streets were still deserted save for the road sweeper, postman, and the early morning buses taking people to work. I knew I too should have been on my way to work. I couldn't remember how long I'd been off and on the booze, but I didn't care. All that mattered now was to make it to the shop.

I stopped at the kerb to cross the road and, even though it was deserted, I crossed it with fear. I reached in my pocket for the bottle I'd brought with me for the journey and, with trembling hands, took the top off and took a long swig. Once again I threw up. My body had had enough but my brain wanted more. I took another pull from the bottle and managed to keep this down. Every little noise in the street caused me to jump. A car going by or a seagull flying past sent me into a panic. My heart was beating so hard and fast I feared I was going to die. I stopped a couple of times to have a drink. Eventually I made it to the shop and my brain raced. What to say to the shopkeeper? How many bottles to buy? My hand reached inside my pocket feeling for my wallet.

"Oh! No, God, no! Please tell me I haven't forgotten it".

I searched all my pockets over and over again but it was not there. What to do? I thought of going inside the shop and picking up the drink and saying I'd forgotten my wallet. I'd been in this shop many times. The lady who served behind the counter was elderly and I knew by her body language she felt scared of me. I only ever went in when drunk.

It was no good. I had to go home! Every step on the way down had been carefully taken. I'd held on to walls in case I had another fit. The day was beginning to get brighter. Time was not on my side. I reached for my bottle. This time, thankfully, I did not throw up. I had made it. Stepping inside my flat I dropped onto the mattress, held my head in my hands and cried, "Oh, please God, help me!"

The telly was still on. I heard the presenter say it was 6.30am. It had taken me an hour to get there and back. Normally I could have done it in twenty minutes, but I'd crossed the bridge from normality to insanity. "Get a grip!" I told myself again. "Think what to do. Yes, first - find wallet." It was on the table. I opened it fearing it may be empty. I had no recollection of how long I'd been on this bender. Nor did I care. If I had no money, I still had enough full bottles to see me through. Hopefully I could sort out my head to go stealing or borrowing later. I opened my wallet and found about £40 inside. I had a flashback. Of course! I'd been paid my wages! That's when I must have started the bender. I kissed the wallet.

The booze was beginning to have the desired effect. That, plus the morning air, had begun to bring me round a bit. Because of my normal binge pattern, I guessed I'd been on this bender for at least four days. Four days locked up in this flat, watching videos, playing music, cursing everything and everyone and drinking – yes, drinking! The devil's comforter.

"Right," I thought, "let's start again on the booze-run. First, put wallet into pocket. Then, check to make sure it's there.

Then, check again. Next, have a drink." As I swallowed, a crazy thought invaded my brain from the old telly commercial about petrol. *Put a tiger in your tank!* "Well," I thought, "I must have at least a pack in mine!" I smiled at the image. The booze was definitely kicking in. I put on a tape, Pink Floyd's, Dark Side of the Moon, 'Us and Them'. That's how it had been all my life. Bloody people! Authority! Hospitals! Rehabs! Counseling! Screw them all!

I walked into the bathroom to check myself in the mirror, and took a look at the face that looked back. I wanted to hit it – bloated, unshaven, hair all over the place, and eyes like pissholes in the snow. I could hear the music drifting into the bathroom. My favorite bit was coming up where they sing: *So lock the door and throw away the key; there's someone in my head but it's not me.* How true! I wet my hair and sang a John Lennon verse, "woke up one morning, got out of bed, dragged a comb across my head", whilst I brushed my hair. I was definitely feeling better. Pity the pubs weren't open! I could do with talking to another drunk.

Time to go I went back into the living room, turned the music off, checked my wallet again just to make sure it had money in it, got my keys and thought of myself as Bilbo Baggins in The Hobbit. THE JOURNEY BEGINS!

This time I made it to the shop at almost a run. I stopped outside, composed myself, took a deep breath then went inside. The lady was busy doing the morning papers. I said good morning to her, picked up a paper, went to pay for it, then as if as an afterthought, I went to the booze section.

I could feel her eyes watching my every move. We had played this game before. I had to be quick in case anyone came in. She wasn't supposed to sell it to me before 8am. But I remembered the first time I bought it. I had told her I worked on the boats and was going out to check the nets and wouldn't be back ashore 'till late. She may have swallowed it the first time but I suspect she soon realized I was lying. I believe she felt sorry for me.

I bought four two litre bottles of cider and four cans of Special Brew. As soon as I paid for it, panic once again took over. This had to last me all day and night. Had I bought enough? She gave me my change and I said, "Sorry, but I forgot I need a bottle of whisky". She looked at the door. I took this to mean hurry up before anyone comes in. Again I apologized. She took one from the shelf directly behind me. I was sweating and getting paranoid. She hesitated before putting it on the counter. I wondered if she had seen me stealing the extra two cans of Special Brew I had put inside my large jacket (which I always wore when I went out on a booze-run). If she had, she did not say. I paid her and quickly left the shop. My hands were shaking violently.

I hurried up the road to put as much distance as possible between me and the shop. Paranoia was kicking in again. Was she phoning the police right now? I couldn't be locked up whilst I was in this state. Doing cold turkey in a police cell is hell. Doing cold turkey is bad enough but in a police cell it is sheer mental torture. When I felt I was safe, after going down back streets, I slowed down. People were beginning to stir from their hobbit-holes. I thought, time to make myself invisible and put on the ring, or in my case, crack open the whisky.

I took a swig and threw up straight away. I leaned against a wall, my stomach heaving from the invasion of the whisky. I expected this. It would soon settle. My next swig would be okay. When my breathing returned to normal, I took another pull from the bottle. My stomach accepted it. Then came the glow! That feeling of comfort, security, that feeling of Zip-i-dee Doo-dah! I put my hands in my pockets and sang that Beatles song '*I'm on my way home*'. I felt good. I had done it. Mission accomplished. For a while, the booze would keep the demons away.

But they were waiting. I could almost hear them laughing and taunting me, saying, "Have another drink, Billy. You're easier to handle drunk than sober." Such was my booze-fuelled mind; I laughed with them, took another drink, and said, "Cheers! I'll see you in hell." Prophetic words, because that's where I ended up.

> My eyes can't hear
> And my ears don't see
> I'm not firing on all cylinders
> What's happening inside of me
> My nose won't lick
> And my tongue don't smell
> I'm walking backward thru life
> Its heaven or hell
> I need putting back together
> But where do you start
> I'm like Pinocchio
> I want another heart

"What are you doing sat up here watching television, Billy?" said the female counselor, "the party's about to start".

The reason I was sat upstairs in the TV lounge of the rehab clinic watching a Saturday night film was I didn't want to go to the bloody party that they held every Saturday night. The idea behind it was to simulate an occasion that we the alcoholics/drug addicts may have to attend when we go out into the big bad world. It was a bloody charade. They put on a karaoke night, complete with food and non-alcoholic drink, and then the counselors would mix with us in a pretend kinda party spirit, to show that you could have a good time without booze or drugs. The former addicts would never admit this pretence; they believed that this American claptrap psychology really worked and I suspect, for those poor unfortunates who had accepted this form of brain-washing, it did. I don't believe for one minute that any one of them was happy. I mean according to what we read about the American rich, they change their therapist at least once a month.

I had been here for three weeks, with another three to go. I didn't need de-toxing. When I arrived, I'd already been sober for a couple of months so the only tablets they put down my neck were vitamin ones. Apparently you would not be admitted if you were suspected of having a drink. The reason behind this was to protect the patients that were already staying there. I soon found out that this was a farce as I saw them sometimes carrying 'basket cases' into the joint.

My doctor had come to the end of his tether with me; he had given me all the medication at his disposal to ease my cravings for alcohol but none worked. I had been attending A.A. meetings for over a year but was still going on benders. In my defense, these meetings left me feeling so depressed. The first time I went along to an A.A. meeting, it was in the basement of a local church. It was dimly lit with paint peeling off the walls.

It reminded me of the prison cells of my local nick in Farnworth. We would spend two hours listening to someone go on about their problems (usually drink). Some would even appear happy but they didn't fool me; any one of them would have given their all to be able to drink normally. I had no intention of spending my life as a dry drunk (dry drunk means someone who isn't drinking but still has the mind of an alcoholic) and sometimes after leaving these meetings I would rush into the nearest bar.

The criterion for acceptance into this clinic was a referral from your G.P, then a least two references from respected professional members of the community (whatever that meant). The first one was easy as my doctor was only too quick to shift me on, the second not so easy. I used to take my children to the local church so they could attend Sunday school. Then after dropping them off, I'd wait inside the church sat at the back daydreaming whilst the vicar delivered that morning's service. Before going into church, I would visit a local off license and buy a four-pack of special brew and down them before I went inside. It wasn't easy to switch off. One day, Richard the vicar, who was one of them young modern day vicars with new ideas approached me and asked me if sometimes would I mind reading a short bible scripture before he delivered his sermon. I must have been drunk 'cos I agreed.

The thing is it back fired on me. What would usually happen was that Richard would warn me in advance, a couple of weeks before the reading, and give me the scripture to practice on. This meant that on the day I was to read I couldn't drink. One Sunday I forgot that it was my turn and as the choir came walking down the aisle dressed in full regalia carrying the cross, the vicar stopped at my seat, leant over and informed me that today was my turn to read. So when it came time for me to read. I somewhat staggered up the steps to the pulpit having consumed my usual four-pack and began to read or, should I say, slur the scripture. Here endeth the lesson, I slurred at the end, and ended my days as a reader. I confessed shortly after to the vicar that I had a bit of a drink problem and he set about counseling me. Bless him, I really liked him. I suppose I became a challenge for him, a sort of crusade to convert me and sober me up but it didn't work. I liked to drink. He did, however, give me a glowing reference for the clinic; in fact it was so good that if there was such a thing as a heaven, it would have got me in there.

To this day, I can't remember who gave me the other reference but no matter what, I was accepted. The counselor walked over to the TV and turned it off, "C'mon Billy," she said, "let's go and join the party". "Let's not," I replied, returning her patronizing smile. She sat next to me and attempted to put an arm around my shoulder, but I shrugged it off. "Let's get one thing straight," I told her, "when I leave this clinic, I would never, I repeat never, attend a party where there was no drink. My dad used to say, "Don't trust anyone who doesn't drink".

"This," she said, "will have to be taken up at the next group meeting with your peers and the counselors". So in my best Jack Nicholson impersonation (from the film 'One flew over the cuckoo's nest), with my eyes opened wide, giving her a huge smile and a wink whilst rubbing my hands together, I replied,

"Yum yum, I can't wait." She left shaking her head and tutting at me.

I did, however, manage to manipulate the group meeting when it was brought up; after all, I was an ideal patient, having entered the clinic sober and with 12 months A.A. attendance meetings under my belt, they had an easy time with me. I knew the right things to say that they wanted to hear, like not blaming anyone or anything for my alcoholism, and that I wanted to get sober for me, no-one else, also I had no desire to go to any party with or without booze. It worked, it always did but I didn't fool them all the time 'thank God'. As for the episode with the TV, I just told them how it was and that was the end of that.

Some of the patients were in a right old state, having being carted in by their family or spouse. It took them a week to come off the booze or drugs, then another couple of weeks to familiarize themselves in another world full of counselling advice and reading self-help books. Bloody scary, when all you want to do is 'get off your tree'. I remember one poor soul who the counselors couldn't reach; he refused to get involved with group talks though he had to attend, and would sit on his own during the times we went into the recreation room. One day I went over to him where he was sat at a table on his own, smoking a cigarette, I pulled up a chair, lit a fag and, taking a drag, I lent over to him and just said, "It hurts, doesn't it"? I broke down his defenses and also him. As a result of that statement I found out that he worked at an airport as a airline traffic controller, you know, the person who talks down the planes, I didn't know if he was in drink when he did his job but I'd put money on it that he was.

I stayed for my full six weeks' course, which was good really, 'cos not many did. They would last about half the term once they had sobered up. After you had been in there for three weeks, you were allowed to go to the shops without an escort. However, on return, you were randomly picked for a breath test or for those who were in for drug addiction, a drug test.

One poor bloke who was desperately trying to get back with his wife and family was kicked out with just two days to go. His family would come along each weekend and, along with the counselors, would undergo family therapy, and address his alcoholism. He seemed to be doing well and in the group talks, sounded positive about how he was going to cope and change his life around once he left. However, with just two days to go, he got kicked out.

What happened was that one day he went out with a few others including me to the shop. He said he was popping in to the bookies to put a bet on (this was not allowed 'cos the counselors had informed us that gambling was another form of addiction). None of us bothered too much about him going inside - I mean, where do you get off? If you took life as a whole, someone who plays golf every day and claims it's a hobby; this too could be likened to an addiction.

However, when we met up with him, his breath stank, and when we asked him what he was sucking, he said that he was coming down with a cold and had bought some 'fisherman's friends' to suck. Well, you can't 'con a con man', as the saying goes, and you can't con an alki. When it comes to the deception of trying to hide the smell of booze on your breath drinkers are experts. It must be said that we all tried to help each other to keep sober, so we challenged him but he remained adamant, claiming he would not risk getting kicked out with just two days to go. He also didn't want to risk losing his wife and kids. Poor sod. He managed to get through the reception without being stopped but that's only because several of us gathered around the counselor chatting and offering her sweets to distract her. She, being an ex-alki, must have known something was going on but she didn't let on; either that or she was being totally naïve.

Lunchtime finished at 2pm and we all made our way upstairs to the quiet room for our daily group meeting with the counselors. The head counselor used to live on the streets when he was drinking and from what he told us he was a real wino. He was a very quiet man and one could never tell what he was thinking, except today. The moment we all sat down he started looking suspiciously around at the group and raising his nose into the air like someone trying to smell his way to a fish and chip shop. The game was up for our 'fisherman friend'; the leader nosed his way to him and he was immediately taken away from the group and kicked out of the clinic. I felt very sorry for him, and saw him a few days later staggering past the clinic. The clinic was in Nottingham and this man was fortunate enough to live there, I say 'fortunate' because he got to see his family unofficially on a daily basis as they met him sometimes on his way to the shop. Being local, he managed to come along to the clinic on a daily basis to talk to the counselors should he need to, but they would never admit him again, or anyone that broke the rules which were 'no drinking or taking drugs' non negotiable.

At the end of my six week stay, I was given a medal for completing the course. I couldn't understand the reason for the medal at first but on reflection - after all the crap they fed us - I guess I deserved it. When I say 'crap', I knew I had a problem with drink. When I felt like taking a drink, I didn't want to have to go into a quiet room and put on some bloody dolphin music in order to "relax my spirit" or go and talk it through with someone; I mean they may try to talk me out of it and leave me feeling in a worse state. Please don't get me wrong, these things do work for some people. I just wasn't ready for it; I wanted to live and, for me, drink was a part of my life.

I left the clinic no different than when I had entered it except maybe a bit more Americanized and confused. And that's how I came to be back inside it a few weeks later. I told a good friend of mine who also attended the local A.A. group with me that because I had attended sober, they may not have taken me seriously. So we hatched a plan which involved me getting drunk (no problem) and phoning them up. It worked. They said that they would have me back to do some more work on me. I told them that I was drunk, they said "no problem" and to get there as soon as possible. My friend drove me there, stopping off at an off-license en-route to buy some vodka. I don't remember arriving at the clinic, I just remember waking up in a side room where they said I had slept for a couple of days. After sobering up, they informed me that I would be required to stay there for a month but I spent three weeks and left, and that was the end of rehabs for me, but not the end of booze.

CHAPTER 25

Day 5

Stage 5 - Part 2

In the distance I could see two lights heading towards us, with new found hope I excitedly pointed them out to the others. As they got closer we could hear someone shouting out, "Hallo?" the voice like us sounded desperate. Two of the volunteers appeared and greeted us with an apology. They had no explanation as to why there were no glow sticks. I had seen these volunteers (two females) at the last CP and their job was to follow on from the last runners, collecting up the markers and glow sticks and making sure that no-one was left behind. The other runners I had seen still on course at the last CP must have been picked up by the 'search and gather truck' which meant a D.N.F. for them. Paul launched into them, wanting to know why the course was not lit up but they had no explanation. He then asked them if they had a mobile phone to get in touch with the organizers. Once again they apologized and said they hadn't and agreed that they should have been supplied with some form of communication. After a while, one of the volunteers started wandering around in the distance looking for any tracks or signs of which way to go. I pointed out that what she was doing was risky and the other volunteer reminded her too. Last thing we wanted was for them to hurt themselves.

So here we were once again in the same situation but this time with two of the official volunteers. Happy days eh? At the same time (I found out later), a couple of miles up the course, there were two female runners experiencing the same thing. Ting, the female blogger, who I have mentioned earlier in the book, wrote in the official Racing the Planet blog (and I quote her):

'The glow sticks were not out yet - so I could barely see where the flags were and if I was still on course,

I COULD HAVE DIED OUT THERE! Really I was scared. As a newbie who has never done a 24 hour race, it was quite frightening. With no one around, there is no one to help, should something happen or if I got lost.'

I suppose that just about sums up what we were all feeling. The sweepers tried to reassure us and them selves that someone would have to be along shortly. We finally saw the lights of a truck in the far distance coming our way. It was not hard to see them being as we were stood in the middle of a desert at night. By the time they reached us and we had vented out our anger on a couple of the organizers, it was time to get on with the race. I'm sure you can imagine by this stage nobody was in a physical fit state to run. It must have been about 9pm by now and we still had another 10m+ to base camp. The organizers had apologized profusely over and over again as to what they explained away as a 'mix up somewhere'. They instructed us to follow their truck for a couple or so miles to the next CP and said that we would be able to sleep there for a while and to move on after we had rested. They also asked if anyone wanted to get in the truck if they felt they could no longer continue. It was said with such innocent concern I was nearly tempted, as were the other runners, but when I enquired if that meant a D.N.F. and they replied "Yes". I asked them if they thought we were fuckin' mad (jokingly) to get this far and to quit. I said I thought that because we had been left to freeze in the darkness that this was a way of them doing us a small favour (well you can but try). That statement was met with a laugh by one of the organizers, "This" he said, "is one of the toughest endurance marathons in the world. We don't do favors except to arrange to have your body flown back home." This was delivered with some good American drawl and humor.

Following the trucks tail lights, we set of once again on course. I was glad to get moving, standing still only made your legs stiffen up, plus it was much more difficult to keep warm. I was walking with Paul, who was now in complete agony. Every step he took he did slowly and limping. The two Japanese girls walked along with the sweepers and the only sound that we could hear was from the truck's stereo which was tuned to a local radio station for the benefit of the Chilean driver. I knew Paul could not go on much longer. We were moving so slow that it made it impossible for the truck to keep moving. We all tried to help Paul as best we could, but we could not take his pack as it was against the rules. Finally, Paul sank onto his knees. I could see the desperation on his face as he realized he could no longer continue. After all his efforts, the desert had beaten him and, along with his mashed up feet and legs, he could add a D.N.F.

I helped Paul off with his pack and opened the truck door for him. The heat from the truck's heaters engulfed me seductively. I so much wanted to sit down and sleep in its embrace that I quickly drew away. Paul thanked me and then apologized to me for him getting into the truck. I couldn't understand his reason to say sorry to me, but I suspected he was apologizing to everyone he knew at that time.

Following the truck was laborious and tiring. We had been moving along for a couple of hours, and every now and then someone would stick their head outside of the truck to inform us "that we're nearly there" and eventually we were.

On arriving at the CP, I noticed that there were no tents up at this camp and wondered where we were going to sleep. Well surprise, surprise, we were not going to sleep here tonight. Someone had made a mistake, we were informed, and the actual campsite (not base camp) was only another 3m up the road. By now the time was midnight and the truck that Paul had got in had disappeared. I assumed he had been whisked away for medical treatment. It has to be said that apart from the glow sticks incident, they really cared for your well being. My hat goes off to all the staff and organizers.

Yasue Fuijsaki (I named her Yoko, easier to pronounce) was the name of one of the two female Japanese runners. I didn't know it at the time but we were to become close friends and companions later on that evening and the next day. Having been informed that we had to go on another 3m to the next camp, it was decided for us to have something to eat and check out our equipment, to make sure that we had enough water, and that our spare night light worked. After watching Yoko put on extra leggings, I mentioned that my legs were numb with cold and that the only other gear I had was my shorts. The volunteers said they would have a rummage around to see if they could find something that would fit. We were invited to rest whilst we ate inside the truck. This was the second time that evening that I was to be seduced by the heat in the truck. The two Japanese girls and I got gratefully into the truck and instead of putting more clothes on to keep warm, within a minute we were for the first time that day taking them off.

The other girl who had been Yoko's running companion earlier on was speaking to her in their native tongue and you didn't need to be a linguist in order to tell something was up. Her voice was very emotional and she was quite tearful. I turned to Yoko to ask what the matter was and she informed me that her friend could not go on any longer. I joined in with Yoko trying to persuade her to continue but I'm afraid to say that once 'I can't go on attitude' takes over, it is hard to pull out of it. Let's face it, it was about 12.30am the next day and we had been on this marathon since 8am that day, nearly 16 hours and I know how she felt. The organizer was ready to move on, and said we had another 5 minutes left before he had to be on his way. None of us made a move; waiting outside for us was another 3/4m of desert road in the dark and freezing temperature. After 5 minutes, up popped his head, once again he informed us that unless we got out in the next two minutes, he would have no choice but to give us a D.N.F. Beep beep that was me out. Yoko was reluctant to leave her friend and I asked her if she wanted to go on, she said yes, but didn't want to leave her friend. It took gentle persuasion from me and one of the volunteers to get her to leave her companion behind.

Once outside again, the cold temperature greeted us in its hostile way. One of the volunteers said the only solution they had come up with to protect my legs from the cold was to bind them with some black industrial tape that they had. The cold was biting away at my legs, so anything was worth a try. So after my legs had been mummified with this black tape, I set off with Yoko walking like the tin man from out of the film 'Wizard of Oz'.

Only 3 miles we were told through the desert at midnight and to quote Ting again, in a 'SUPER COLD' temperature.

Any mere human like me will tell you the last 1m of a full marathon seems a long way away and in our physical condition, it was hard to bear. Now it wasn't only our physical condition that mattered but also our mental attitude, and that was what it would take in order to get us both through this.

Me and Yoko set off, with the volunteers taking up the rear. We moved along a pitch black dusty rocky road at a snail's pace. Both me and Yoko agreed that our packs were now becoming a burden and cutting into our shoulders. It was on this 3m section that me and Yoko got to know each other. She was 37 years old and a bit of an adventurer. Her latest conquest was climbing Kilimanjaro. She had come here with her husband (Massahi) who was somewhere in front of us (if he had not already finished this section). He had come to take part as a competitor but was also on a photographic assignment. We spoke about our families, what she watched on Japanese TV and I was surprised when she told me one of her favorite British TV series was Coronation Street. Even though we were having an interesting banter together, fatigue and cold had set in. Every now and then one of the volunteers would try to encourage us by shouting we should be near the CP. We had been assured we could camp until the next morning. At last and with great relief we made it into the camp, which was the next but last before we had completed this 50/43m day. One of the organizers was on the road to greet us but also to inform us that this campsite (which he had decided to erect) was illegal, as it was on what was regarded as a National Park.

The reason he had told us this was that someone from the authority could come along at any time and force him to take it down. I remember thinking this was highly unlikely considering it was about 3am, pitch black and bloody cold. He took us to the campfire he had built, hidden behind some rocks. Then he delivered us another blow as all the tents were occupied by other runners so there was nowhere for us to sleep. He said that we couldn't sleep next to the fire (which is what I wanted to do). The only alternative he offered us was that we could get into the back of one of the trucks.

We have a saying where I come from and that is 'I could fall asleep on a clothes line', well that's how I felt right then and so did Yoko. We had already discussed the first thing we were going to do when we reached camp and (you've guessed it) to crash out like forever. We declined the suggestion to have something hot to eat and drink, and after warming ourselves up around the camp fire, we made our way to the truck. I suggested to Yoko that she take the back seat and I climbed into the front. I could hear her rummaging around in her pack for her sleeping bag and, after several minutes climbing into it. She was, to coin a phrase, 'out like a light'. I was not so fortunate; I've never been one for being able to sleep inside vehicles.

My legs were aching and my feet, now set free from their prison, were grossly swollen. My knees were in so much pain I needed to stretch them out but there was no room in the front to do this. I tossed and turned to try and get comfortable but all in vain. There was nowhere to lay my head, or find a position to ease my aching back. I felt a right basket case. The next minute the door was opened at the driver's side and this huge Chilean man climbs into the front seat, greets me, lays his head onto the back of the seat and falls asleep. Now I'm told I can snore but if I sounded anything like this guy, then my apologies to anyone who has been on the receiving end of mine. I felt like I was next to a herd of pigs after eating a full meal. It was no good. After about half-an-hour, I knew I would get no sleep inside this truck, but the thought of stepping outside in the cold air was a daunting task.

The guy who had set up this camp site had already said that he didn't want us sleeping next to the fire, but balls to that, I needed sleep.   So, grabbing my pack and shoes, I stepped outside into the dark cold night. Climbing into my bag around the fire, I had to move myself several times into a comfortable spot; too close to the fire and I became too hot, but too far away and it became too cold.   At long last, just like father bear "this bed is just right", I'd found the right place and eventually I was 'away with the fairies'.

CHAPTER 26

You're An Alcoholic

"You're an alcoholic." I'd been to the doctor several times with trouble for my nerves but this was the first time he'd suggested I had a drink problem, but not the first time I'd heard it. I mean, of course I drank. After all, I'd been brought up with it, all my mates drank and, if you were gonna drink, you might as well get smashed. But I held a job and only had a couple of drinks in a morning just to steady my nerves. And yes, there were times when I went off sick from work 'cos I felt depressed, but an alcoholic? Come on, get real! I was informed doctors used this term if you drank more than 6 pints a night. So I was really surprised when he suggested I might like to attend AA meetings. I thought, "Okay, I'll keep him sweet," and agreed to go so long as I got my tranquilizers, and it worked.

This little charade went on for months and I made every excuse to myself as to why I drank so much. The real one being life was shit, without purpose, we were all gonna die anyway, so enjoy yourself while you can. I didn't know how to enjoy myself without booze as a result of my upbringing, I got a real enjoyable buzz out of getting drunk and stoned on drugs so, as the song goes, 'born to be wild'. Well, that was me.

Like I said, I didn't think I had a drink problem or any other problem for that matter. No, the problem was society or, to be precise, those 'conning bastards' that directed it. You know the type; if you are unemployed for any reason and you have to go with cap in hand for benefits, you are treated less than a person, you are scum. Or if you want to rent a flat and you look up the ads in the local paper, there it is: 'Flat to let, no pets and no DSS (no one on benefits). Who are these people who separate and put us into categories? To hell with them all!

There is always someone ready to kick you when you are down, so live, laugh, travel, get wrecked 'cos those are the cards you have been dealt with. Well, you have if you were born into a world of violence, poverty, and no bloody hope and if the reader is thinking this guy is so full of self-pity, I say to you correct 'cos the only pity I ever got was from myself. Even the doctors turned a blind eye at the bruises and the teachers. I knew they knew that something was wrong but they did nothing. All the signs were there when we arrived at school dressed in rags, smelly, suspicious bruises and withdrawn. For this existence we were made to feel guilty and ridiculed in front of everyone in the school. So as I said, to hell with it

As night time comes to find you
A lost wandering soul
Of pity unshaven and shaking

Your memory lays a drunken blur
Eyes that close without a care
Sleep and be happy drift in time
For tomorrow brings along your thirsty mind

Today tomorrow a month a year
A town a city how many are there
My shoes are worn destroyed by my heart
I long for a drink, to keep me apart.

With violent shakes and paranoid thoughts
You stumble through life's empty bottles and corks
Lost in a world unable to think
Kill the pain please give us a drink.

As night time comes to find you
A lost wandering soul
Of pity unshaven and shaking.

I fought frantically with the hands that pinned me down to the bed. At the cardiac unit in the hospital the doctors were fighting to inject fluid into my stomach in order to thin my blood. I was in a state of panic. Where was I? Who were these people who were holding me down? And why was I not in my flat? That's where I wanted to be, in the safety of my four walls, with my bottle. The bottle was the only thing that brought me release from the demons that tormented my head. I remember the nurse holding something next to my mouth and trying to remove the fingers I had down my throat. Didn't she know if I was sick everything would be fine, I would feel better? Then I would be able to drink again.

This was how I lived. Over the last ten years things had begun to get steadily worse. The detox clinics were becoming more frequent and when I had exhausted them, the endless visits to the hospital to dry out. Following that the consultation with various 'head' doctors who thought they could fix this Humpty Dumpty. This pattern of life was becoming the norm for me. I started to wonder what was up with everyone. I'm OK. Just need to go on benders now and then, nowt wrong with that. The delirium and tremors (DTs) were just an occupational hazard, end of. It's funny because this bender and this hospital visit, was to lead me eventually to a changing point in my life.

One, which I would not have thought possible, even in my drink-drug-fuelled mind.

I lay in a side ward with wires connecting my chest to a machine that registered my heartbeat. I was completely wasted. I don't know how long I'd been on this last bender but the doctor had been in to inform me that this time I'd been lucky.

"We nearly lost you in there, Mr Isherwood," he said. "You very nearly died". I listened, totally uninterested. "Better if I had," I thought. I was completely drained and totally paranoid. "This can't go on. We don't know what to do with you any more. You have had..."

"Have you any stronger sleeping pills? "I asked, interrupting him. "I just need to go to sleep." I heard the doctor sigh. He will go away shaking his head, I thought, just like the rest. I expected to be in here for a few days while they dried me out, then I would be discharged, my life just a drunken merry-go-round.

"Can I have a word, Billy?" The nurse (Claire Valentine) I had got to know from the cardiac ward had come down to visit me. "They are after discharging you, but I'm not going to let that happen. You are too ill to go home. I'm sending you to a psychiatric doctor for assessment. I hope you don't mind." I didn't mind. I felt too weak and disorientated to go home, plus I had no strength. I couldn't even stand up without assistance. I nodded my head in agreement with her. She smiled and left the ward. Little did I know at the time but this kind gesture by Claire was to save my life and change it in a dramatic way, I owe her much more than a thank you but thank you Claire anyway. I don't know if I was asleep or day-dreaming. Everything I saw was real and yet unreal. But I was aware of someone asking me questions. She introduced herself as a doctor.

Believe it or not, the next few weeks were a complete blur. I was in a world of my own, in my head where nobody else was allowed. I think I'd given up on life at that point. I tried to come to terms with life in the past but I found it all so boring. No matter what, any event, whatever it was, was only good if I had a drink in my hand, or should I say, down my throat.

This last visit to the hospital, which had resulted in me being admitted to the psychiatric ward, was the last straw. I had thrown in life's towel.

I'm pleased to say, God picked it up and threw it back at me and I grabbed it. I sat alone at the table eating my breakfast. The other patients had started to wander into the dining room after receiving their medication. Though I had not spoken to anyone, my eyes examined these poor unfortunate humans. I avoided any one-to-one eye contact. I felt safe inside this unit. My only desire was to be left alone. After breakfast, I retreated back into my bedroom. But this was only for a short time. The nurses did not encourage isolation. You were expected to mingle and take part in any activities they had organized for you, so they would come into our rooms at 10am and then we would have to leave because the rooms would be locked up until about 2pm.

Fourteen weeks I stayed inside that unit and it was where I met Bridget. She had walked into my room after I'd been there several weeks. The nurses had asked her to see if she could do anything with 'This Man' who had been isolating himself. She had walked into my room, introduced herself, first by name, then what her position was at the unit, an occupational

therapist.   She had asked me what my interests were.   I
remember saying I had quite a few but at that moment my only
interest was to be left alone.   She continued to press me on
various subjects and somehow I got around to telling her I like
to play (or mess around!) on a guitar.   Thus, the next morning
she re-entered my room, carrying this guitar, bless her!   My
recovery from that moment came slowly, but come it did.

CHAPTER 27

Keep on running
Keep on hiding
There's no way you can leave your past
'Cos it's right behind you

New Beginnings

I stood in the large park whilst all around me there was a hive of activity. Hundreds of competitors milled around, some doing stretch exercises, others a gentle warm-up run, whilst others rubbed ointment onto their legs. The loud-speakers were announcing the different marquees where you could get a free massage, or view the sporting accessories that were on sale. Me, I was drinking it all in. I thought, so this is what goes on before the start of a Marathon. I took another drag of my cig. I was not there just to observe; I was, in fact, a competitor! Yes, this was to be my first ever marathon, THE NOTTINGHAM MARATHON, 26.2 miles! Eighteen months after walking out of that hospital my life started to change.

And it all started by me walking through town one day and spotting an offer of 14 nights on Crete, my favorite holiday resort. "I've just been down to the travel agents in town. They're doing a deal on Crete, 14 nights for 2, only £300, I informed Bridget as she walked in from work. She smiled as she knew I'd been there back in the 70s working with me mates picking oranges. "It's at the end of May," I said excitedly. I knew like me, she liked to travel. "OK," she said, with an encouraging smile on her face. "You book it, save up, and we shall go." She was like that. She never gave anything away except for the fact that she loved me. "Right" I said, searching her face for an answer, "I will." Great! Just what I need, I thought, a purpose, a challenge. It has always been like that with me. I suppose that's why I drank a lot, I find life so boring. I had a part-time job cleaning and when I wasn't drinking, I was able to put a little by.

The first thirteen months had not been easy after being discharged from the hospital. I had moved area, got a new flat and my time was spent wandering around the town sussing out the cheap shops and also the cheap off-licenses. Though I would have weeks of sobriety, I knew the day would come when I would hit a bender and I did! I should say the pattern at the time was about six weeks, and then I would hit a bender again.

I had also enrolled in two courses at the local college, just part-time on an evening. One was sign language for the deaf the other counseling. I thought I should be good at the counseling. After all, I'd received enough over the years. All that stuff about owning your feelings, capturing your inner child, one day at a time, and powerlessness over situations, had not fallen on deaf ears and I was a good candidate. I received both my certificates in counseling but sadly, I missed my exam on sign language (I was too drunk to turn up for it). So, I signed on again for the following year, went through all the lessons, was top of the class and guess what! When the time came to take the exam, yes, I missed it. Drunk again.

"I've come to book the holiday you have advertised in the window. Two weeks in Crete," I said. "I believe the deposit is £100."

The women smiled, "Yes, this one is being booked up fast." I was not surprised. "Please take a seat." My heart was thumping. It was always like this with me; like a little child excited about getting something it wants (something I'd never known as a child). We went through the booking details until finally it was all sorted. "Right, Mr Isherwood, just bring in the balance thirteen weeks before you're due to go, and that's it. Have a nice holiday." "Oh, I will!" I smiled. I was already there in my head, snorkeling in the turquoise coral Med, dining in the local tavernas, drinking retsina, dancing with the local Greeks. I couldn't wait! The moment I came out of the travel agents, I phoned Bridget up to tell her, "Get your glad rags packed. We're off!"

As I stepped out of the bath, I caught a glimpse of myself in the mirror. I didn't look too bad really for 52. The bags under my eyes were a bit swollen but I thought my complexion looked fresh (I've always been vain!). I rolled my hand over my stomach. Beer belly, I thought. This won't do for the beach in Crete! Gonna have to do something about it. "I'm thinking of joining the gym," I announced to Bridget as she walked in from work, not even giving her time to take her coat off. "Oh, good what's brought this on?"

"Well, I gotta look good on the beach," I said. "After all, I'm representing Britain! Can't have all those so-called 'Greek gods' stealing the limelight!" She smiled and stroked my hair, like one would do to a little boy, I thought. Yet I'd never grown up, really. You're like Peter Pan someone once said of me.

"I'm really pleased," she said. I knew she meant it. Anything that took my mind off drink was a positive move.

"Right! Well, that's it sorted. There's a local gym just down the road," I said. "I shall go tomorrow. But tonight, might as well get fish and chips in, and a couple of cans of the amber nectar to oil the works, like." She never minded me having a couple of cans so long as that was it. "And then, it's goodbye, five-bellies!"

"I'm after losing a bit of weight before I go on holiday," I told Claire Fowler, a fitness trainer at the gym I'd just walked into. Claire was to become a great friend as well as a good trainer who has helped me every step of the way. She greeted me at the reception desk all smiles and definitely a bubbly personality. To describe Claire, she is about 5ft 6", slim with long blonde hair and a fresh complexion. "Have you been to a gym before?" she asked. "Yeah, well, once or twice. It was a long time ago. I'm not into body-building or owt like that," I said in my Lancashire accent. "Just want to lose a bit of this," and slapped my stomach with my hand, "and perhaps tone up a bit." "Ok. Well, I'll take you round, show you what the equipment is for and how it works on the different parts of the body. Then we'll give you a physical check-up see what's what and what will benefit you, then we can work out a training sheet for you,"

"Oh, you don't need to bother with that. I've done quite a bit with weights. It's a bit of running I fancy on one of them running machines."

"OK, well, why don't you start on the treadmill then go onto the cross-trainer?" She took me over to the treadmill. "I'll start it at a slow pace at first then you can alter the speed as you warm up." "How long do I stay on it for?" "Well, let's do twenty minutes first on this one, then twenty minutes on the cross-trainer, and see how you are."

I managed five minutes each on both and felt totally wasted!

"Never mind," Claire said encouragingly, trying to stifle a laugh as I stood red-faced and breathless, leaning on the reception desk. "This is your first time. Just keep coming back. You'll get better as you go along," I nodded, smiling in agreement with her, whilst thinking, "Are you mad? The only place I'll be going along to, after this, is for a pint." "Never again" I sighed as I stepped outside the door. I always knew people who worked out at a gym were definitely not a full shilling, and this little session proved my theory right. You see, I was the kinda bloke who, whilst out driving my car, if I came upon a jogger, I would sometimes stop to offer them a lift, just for a laugh and to get my point over.

I woke next morning hardly able to walk. Bridget had asked me the night before how the session in the gym had gone.

"Piece of cake!" I said, as was my usual reply to anything that challenged me.

"When are you going again?" she then asked,

"Oh, in a couple of day's time I'll soon get rid of this," I said, slapping my stomach. "No worries, Bruce," spoken in my best Paul Hogan Australian accent. "They told me to rest a couple of days to let my muscles relax," I lied. But I had committed myself. And that's how I ended up back in the gym a couple of days later, back on the treadmill, determined to last longer than five minutes. And I did I also stayed longer on the cross-trainer.

"Well done!" Claire said. "I told you it would get easier. We'll soon have you running a marathon." Well now, let's not get carried away, I thought.

"Yeah, right," I replied jokingly, whilst thinking: Lose stomach, go to Greece, end of. Simple. That was my plan. And for once I'm glad it turned out wrong.

Despite all my moaning and groaning, the treadmill did get easier and I was soon running 10k and feeling good about myself. One day, Claire came over to me and suggested going out running onto the road. "The treadmill is fine for getting you started," she said. "You really need to be out there, pounding the streets". I was already thinking about doing this and her suggestion was what I needed to kick-start me. My first run was about 10k (6miles). I know this because I had clocked it in the car the day before. What I didn't clock was the fact that the first half was downhill and the rest uphill. I started off quite well. It was a nice sunny day and I was feeling quite good about my new found self. I hated to admit it but I was the one with a slate short. There was something to be said about keeping yourself fit. The ancient Greeks had discovered this a long time ago about the mind and body. Keeping yourself fit, getting the old heart pumping, releases some form of chemical that stimulates the mind and, as you already know, my stimulants did the opposite.

Anyway, to get back to the run, when it came to doing the other half, the uphill bit, this was a different ball game. The old ticker was pumping all right, and a bit too much for my liking. I was totally out of breath and had to stop several times before I finally made it home. But this only served to challenge me, so the next day I was off again, and again, and *a-bloody-gain*, until I made it up that hill. I felt like *Rocky* out of them boxing movies, you know the one where he finally makes it up, then steps and does a dance with his hands in the air, well that was me, dancing on air.

I did the same run, day after day, and this time, timing myself (Yes definitely a slate short!), and I was getting faster each day, plus the run was getting easier. It was whilst I was out on one of those runs that I came upon a nurse friend who knew me from one of the many hospital admissions I had made for detox. She was running in the opposite direction to me so, when our paths crossed, she stopped and we spoke for a while. She mentioned that she had often seen me running and asked me how I was finding it. I said that I got a real buzz out of running and was getting faster. She said "When are you going to do a marathon cos there's one coming up in Nottingham shortly, will you have time to train for it?" I remember saying to her, "I don't think so," but the seed had been planted and my life was to change in a big way, eventually.

On the Sunday morning of the Nottingham Marathon, me and Bridget had risen early at about 3am in order drive to the event. I was really buzzing. I must have smoked about four cigs, waiting for her to get ready. Not because of any nerves. I was just so excited and couldn't wait to get going. My constant, obsessive running every day had paid off, and I knew I could run 30k, no worries. I had the added bonus of knowing that this was 30k training with plenty of hills. Our plan, as we set off to the event, was to stop at some services on the M1 and grab a bit off brekkie, then get there for about 9am. As we drove to the event, my mind was in a bit of turmoil, wondering what I'd let myself in for. You've done some crazy things in the past Billy, I thought, but this has got to take the cake. After all, I was 52 years old, with six months of training behind me, and here I was, ready to take on a full marathon. My biggest concern was failure.

All my life, all I'd got fed to me was *Loser!* No matter what I'd achieved or done, the only comment was, "It won't last! He's a loser, that one, just one of life's plonkers." As all these thoughts were running through my head, Bridget brought me back to earth.

"We'll pull up at the next services and get a bite to eat," she said. But I was not hungry. "Just a coffee for me," I replied. I'd already eaten some peanuts earlier. Someone told me they were good for energy. Not that I needed any. I've always been hyperactive! So I sat there smoking and drinking a cup of coffee, as Bridget tucked into a brekkie on the MI services.

I wondered what all the signs were stuck to the trees near the start line-up as I took my place, signs with 3.15, 3.50, 4.10, and 4.30 written on them. I asked a fellow-competitor what they meant. He told me it was the time you thought you would finish the marathon, so if you thought you would finish it in say 3 hours 50 minutes, you positioned yourself next to that sign on the line-up. I said jokingly something like, "Is there one for next Wednesday?"

I had a plan I had been working on during my training. It was to start off as a tortoise and finish like a hare; not to waste energy by getting out of breath. I didn't care how long it took me, so long as I finished the course and got a medal. Waiting for the 10 o'clock start bell, my heart was beating so fast, the adrenalin was pumping and my whole body was shaking. Eventually, I heard the bell go and wondered why I was still standing five minutes later. Being at the back, it took a while for our section to get moving and when we did, it was at a walk at first which kinda knocked me back. I was like a horse kicking my heels waiting to get going. Soon the runners in front of me started to speed up and I found myself jogging along with the rest of them. I remember, at some point in the race, we passed a pub. Outside there was quite a crowd cheering everyone on, all of them holding pints. I laughed inwardly at myself 'cos I wanted to be with them but I also wanted to be in this marathon. And that just about sums me up. Sometimes I'm everywhere and nowhere.

I was dressed in blue knee-length shorts, a sleeveless black top and, around my head, a black net, the ones you see the Greeks wearing. Don't know what you call them but I'd bought one when me and Bridget went there for our hols. Stuck in the top of it was a ciggie. Don't know what the other competitors made of this, but I had worn it for a laugh. The message behind it was *I don't take things seriously.*

For me, running the first seven miles is the worst. I really have to bite the bullet before I settle down. Everything inside me is screaming out for me to stop. But once I get through this barrier, I settle down and start to enjoy it. I love the feeling of running free, knowing I've already run seven miles or more and am looking good. I had overheard one competitor tell another that he had done this last year and what to watch out for was that, just before you reach the halfway mark, there was a hill and it was a bit of a bastard. I couldn't wait to get to it! That's the buzz for me, a challenge.

I completely loved it, the crowd and the cheering was magic. It was hard for me to stay focused. The warmth and encouragement was captivating. I had never felt anything like this in my life; I was hooked. My plan was working. I was going along at a steady pace and resisted the urge to speed up whenever anyone overtook me. For me this is very difficult, I took it personally, silly I know, but that's who I am. I was happy with my pace and the day was sunny and I was feeling so alive, I felt I could run forever.

Before I knew it, I was coming up to the hill. I could see in the distance the rise and fellow-competitors struggling to get up it. In fact, some had started to walk, which surprised me 'cos I thought you had to run a marathon all the way. What's the point if you didn't?

My training in Whitby on them hills had certainly paid off because, before I knew it, I was at the top and I could see the 13-mile marker in front of me. It's downhill from here, I thought (but I was wrong); just stick to this pace. I did a mental check-over on myself. I was not tired, my legs were strong, no pains in my side or feet. Yes, I was certainly enjoying this! Apart from the fact I would get a medal at the end of it, I would be able to say I had run a Marathon! A friend of mine had said to me before I started, "If you stop and walk, it doesn't count." another challenge. But it never entered my head to stop.

What happened next, as I approached the 13-mile mark, took me completely by surprise. I could see plastic cones in front of me running down the centre of the road. I wondered what they were there for as the roads had been blocked to traffic. I figured they must be there for emergency services and just dismissed them. Then I got alongside a fellow-runner and said to him something like, "Just another half to go," but he said, no way, he was only doing half a marathon; he had done the full one last year and he wouldn't do it again. Well, you can tell I've spent most of my life in bars 'cos I thought a marathon meant just that - a Marathon, all 26.2 of it. I obviously had not read the entrance form properly. So that's what the cones were there for. Those who were only doing half marathon went to the left of them and those who were doing the full went to the right.

I was the only one at that moment who turned right, but many had before me and were already miles in front. I didn't know that and thought I was pretty cool, being the only one to take on a full marathon. This thought, however, was short-lived 'cos, as I turned right, Bridget was waiting for me to cheer me on. The showman in me came out as soon as I saw her, and I gave a little dance and then a kiss on her cheek. It was then I asked her, "If there was anyone in front of me?" When she said "Loads" my heart sank a little, but there was no time to dwell on it. Another challenge, I thought and started to run with a different spring in my step.

I tried to keep my head down as I ran. I didn't want to see the markers that informed you how many miles you had to go. The only time I looked up was to see if there were any runners in front of me. Eventually, I spotted one. "A goal," I thought, "something else to concentrate on. I must overtake whoever it was." I concentrated on my breathing as I increased my speed. I'd already sussed out that for me, if I got out of breath, I would be no good for anything. I had a mental thing going on in my head, just like the numbskulls out of the *Beano*; I had the 'control centre' and I had invented all types of characters who were on my team. There was my personal trainer-cum-therapist who would tell me how to run each mile; for example, he would tell me when to speed up and when to slow down, and just munch the miles up, and also when to take a pit-stop. So, inside my head when it was time for a pit-stop, I would imagine lying down by the side of the road whilst a team of people would massage my legs and back, whilst others would give me drinks and energy bars, and so on. Crazy eh! But it worked for me.

It went something like this: *OK, Billy, you're doing good. Let's speed it up a little.* Then he would call down to the one in charge of the pedals, *OK, down on the acceleration a bit. Give us warp 4.* Then he would get on the intercom to the other departments, just like Captain Pickard in *Star Trek*, checking the ship out: *how's his legs, doing put some gas into them! Get that breathing under control! What the bloody hell are you playing at? Why is he thinking about that pain in his side? Do something about it! I want more positive thoughts.* If I was getting or feeling a little tired then it would go something like this: *OK, listen up. He's breathing too fast. Slow him down, but tell his head he could sprint this all the way if he wanted to, time for a pit-stop. Bring him in. You're doing fine, Billy. Everything is going according to plan. Relax, take it easy! Just wait until we get near the finish, then we're gonna open you up, again.* Crazy, eh But it worked for me.

The figure in the distance got nearer and nearer as I stepped on the gas. I was feeling good with all these thoughts going through my head. I was really enjoying this. Before I knew it, I had passed the 18-mile marker. I remember thinking, anything I do from here on will be a bonus. I was entering virgin territory. I had never run beyond this distance before. I wondered how I would fare. My brother Roy had come up from Newquay and was at the event with my mate Tony who lived In Nottingham. I didn't know what the time was, so I had no idea how long I had been running but I figured, by the distance I'd already run, and how long that usually took me, I'd been on the road for about three and a half hours.

As I reached the 22-mile marker, things started to take a turn for the worse. Capt. Pickard was having trouble with the ship and his team, and things started to go on meltdown. Suddenly my legs started to pack in; they felt like lead. Then I developed a stitch or two in both of my sides. My breathing was no longer smooth and flowing, but heavy and fast, and my head was crying out STOP! ENOUGH! But the figure that was in the distance was very near. In fact, it was a man and I noticed that he too, like me, was struggling. Something deep inside me would not let me stop.

I had heard other people before say the last mile is the worst. Well, for me it was sheer bloody hell. I was cursing myself for being such a geek, and for not believing my original thought that people who went running were definitely 'a slate short'. I pushed all these thoughts out of my head and concentrated on the fact that my friends were waiting for me at the finish line. I had to make it after coming this far, plus I just had to overtake this guy in front of me.

At last I saw it, the 25-mile marker, and I was just a few yards behind this guy. Capt. Pickard had somehow kicked 'ass down in the gallows' and I was finding new strength. I put all my thoughts and will-power into my plan of action and that was to beat this guy and come in on a dance and some sort of speed. As I crossed the bridge over the river Trent with just half a mile to go, I heard someone call my name out and it was my brother, Roy. He was running on the opposite side of the road from me. He was shouting out words of encouragement as he tried to keep up with me, which he managed for a short while. Then, I heard him curse and swear under his breath as he pulled up, with his words ringing in my ear: "C'mon Billy!"

My heart beat so fast on sheer, pure adrenalin; I was as high as a kite. I just don't know where I got the strength from, but suddenly I was overtaking this guy. Then I could hear Bridget, Tony and our Roy (who had taken the shortcut over the field to see me finish) shouting out my name and clapping. Yes, I did a dance. Yes, I came in sprinting and yes, I got the medal. I had completed my first ever marathon. It took me weeks to come down from it. The feeling was better then any drug I ever took and I wanted more.

The weeks went by and all I could think of was the high feeling I got from running the marathon. A high like a drug that I couldn't get out of my mind and I wanted to experience it again. Training at the gym just wasn't doing it for me and I needed a challenge. This came I believe as a divine intervention whilst watching TV one night. There was a documentary on an extreme marathon held in the Atacama Desert. I watched and taped it and then watched it over and over again. I was hooked this was my challenge. I needed that high and oh boy this would give me an extreme high. Next day the plans started and I was buzzing. Bring it on!

CHAPTER 28

Cut all the crap, the poetic word's
The illustrated scenery, the songs of the birds
The correct English literature, a poem to give strength
An inspirational message, whatever nonsense
The meaning of life, the romantic trap
Let's get real, and cut all the crap

Forget seeking answer's, the teachers to teach
The therapist, the Buddhist, the preacher's who preach
The medium's the astrologist, these flies on the wall
Their well meaning word's, we've heard them all
Set sail on life, abroad all you chancer's
The rainbow's out their, forget seeking answer's

Marsaille Madness

"Would you like to come and watch Bolton play against Middlesbrough," my friend Andrew asked? I had been living in Whitby; North Yorkshire for about a year and the millennium had come and gone. I first met Andrew whilst I was on my own watching Bolton play football on the pub telly. Bolton scored a goal. Well, me coming from Bolton area I obviously went manic with applause and so did this other guy who was stood at the side of me. The pub had been packed so I hadn't noticed him, or that he was wearing the Bolton colours' on a t-shirt.

238

He introduced himself as Andrew. I found out he came from Bolton and I was delighted, a drinking buddy at last. Andrew was a lot younger than me, somewhere in his middle 20s, with a definite, cheeky Lancashire sense of humor and we hit it off straight away. Andrew and I became firm friends and he helped me create a web page with information about myself and an appeal for sponsorship for the Atacama Desert Marathon. We have enjoyed many a good night over a beer, or three, that only drinking buddies can enjoy. When you are on your own, living in a town that you have no connection with, it can be a lonely place. So thanks a million, Andrew.

It was during these moments of sharing a beer with Andrew that my thoughts would wander back to my home town of Farnworth and to my great and life-long friend, Stan Berry. I had known Stan since I was about fourteen years old and together we did all the things and got up to all the mischief kids do at that age. For a season or two we also worked and lived together in Newquay. We had many great times it would warrant another book.

The episode I am about to tell you goes back only two years to 2005. I had gone back home to visit my mother, Mary, and to eventually meet up with Stan. My visits home now last just two days, any longer and I am on a drinking bender. Anyway, this particular visit, me and Stan went out for a Saturday session. Now Stan, being a true friend who loves me, is always trying to encourage me, to eat before we go out and not to turn out until at least three in the afternoon, and to pace my drinking. Sadly to say, it never works. To get back to what I want to tell you. This particular Saturday we had been out drinking but I had persuaded Stan to turn out at the top club for opening time at 11am. We went along and I had several drinks, chucked some darts with Stan and then we visited a few pubs. It's really good for me whenever I go home and catch up with my old mates, some of whom had worked down in Newquay for a season or two. One of the friends I always like to bump into was my old mate, Benny Davies. Every pub I went in with Stan I was knocking back the pints like they were going to go out of fashion. It was no surprise that we found ourselves back at Stan's for about five in the afternoon. I knew that would be it and Stan would not be up for going out again; he definitely has his head screwed on.

I felt fine and decided to drive back home to Whitby. Stan, of course, tried to talk me out of that one but he knew me well enough to know once my mind's was made up, that would be it.

All was going well on the journey home but, because it was winter time, the country had quite a bit of snow that year so I was taking it easy. Reaching York on the A64, I decided to give Bridget a ring to let her know I was on my way home. I had spoken to her earlier that day, whilst consuming vast quantities of beer, but when she heard my voice informing her I was on my way home and driving, she went ballistic. I couldn't understand why she was angry with me. But that's just what I'm like in drink. I expect life to be 'alcoholic rosy' in other people's heads, like mine, so when she started to 'mouth off' about me driving; I chucked the mobile onto the passenger seat.

A few seconds later it rang and for that moment, I took my eyes off the road big mistake. The next minute I was hanging upside down, strapped into my seat in an overturned car, looking at the mobile still ringing. It's at moments like this that one knows one is drunk because I couldn't think what to do; I just swung there, thinking, "Shit". A couple came along and pressed the seat belt lock and unleashed me from my prison, and then we righted the car back up. They then asked what other assistance they could offer. I was drunk and wanted them away from me like yesterday. I said I'd be fine, thanked them and sent them on their way.

The front window was smashed out, it was snowing, the car had various dents and buckles and the police could be along at any minute. I knew further up the road there was a Little Chef where I could park the car and ring Bridget, so I started up the engine. It sounded like a Sherman tank and drove like one, so at about 25 miles an hour, plus a prayer, I managed to make it to the safety of that car park and to ring Bridget who, bless her came out to me. I found the whole episode funny at the time; that's the kind of person I am, too much acid In the 70s and too much Monty Python.

February 2006, five months before the Atacama, and my brother, Roy, kindly invites me to go over to Marseilles in the south of France to watch Bolton Wanderers play Marseilles in the European play-offs. Would I go if he paid, he asked? I willingly said yes. A full week in the south of France, a chance to rest my knees and watch my favourite team, Bolton, play! What more could you ask? So off I set. I caught the plane at London city airport, waited there for three hours before boarding, and didn't take one alcoholic drink!

My changeover connection to Marseilles was at Amsterdam. Now, I don't know which glue-sniffing planner thought I could get off that plane, arriving at 7pm, and be able to connect with the 7.20pm flight to Marseilles. How on earth can you exit a plane, go through customs, find your terminal connection, board your connecting flight all in 20 minutes? Well, the simple answer is, you can't! And neither could I. So the result of this was that they kindly offered to put me up in a hotel in Amsterdam 'till the next day when I was to check back in at the airport at 4.50am.

As you can imagine, I was pretty pissed off by now, knowing that my brother was waiting for me at a bar opposite the hotel in Marseilles that evening. So I did the obvious thing - for me. I ended up getting pissed-up in the hotel, just to even the balance. I didn't get to bed until 1.30am, so I asked a porter for a 4am wake-up call. Still hung-over the next morning, I managed to make the flight to Marseilles.

I had a great time when I finally arrived in France. I met up with my brother and continued on my diet of liquid gold. "What on earth is bloody wrong with me?" I thought, as I carried on drinking. This is something I'd been trying to figure out for years. I'm just never satisfied with what I've got, or not got. The only answer I came up with was that I was deprived of being allowed to be a kid as I grew up and lack of love. To be starved of love is a big wound to heal.

Any addiction or mental fight that's hard to take on can be burnt into your innermost being with a vision to be victorious no matter what life throws you. You then have to personalize it, own it yourself, then this attitude will see you through any ordeal. Or that's the theory! Remember enjoy your little victories, and don't allow anyone to put you down. I used to sing Elton Johns song 'I'm Still Standing' it kept me going through thick and thin.

I arrived at Marseilles airport at midday to be greeted by torrential rain. I caught a bus to the city centre and found the hotel. My brother said he'd booked me a room and I just had to go to the reception, giving my name and room number, and he'd catch me later. He was going to the ground to buy the tickets for the match.

Having checked in at the hotel and received my room key, I went upstairs to the third floor, where my room was. On entering, I quickly discovered Roy had forgotten to inform me that we were sharing. Nothing wrong in this, I thought. There were two single beds. But when I went inside the wardrobe to hang up my stuff, I noticed he'd claimed all the coat hangers! I remember just smiling, throwing my stuff on the bed, taking a shower, putting on fresh duds, rubbing my hands and feeling excited. "OK," I said, "let's go say hello to Marseilles."

I felt good walking around the city. The rain had stopped and I was here for a week with our kid. It would be only the second time in ten years I had seen Bolton play live, and never had I seen them play abroad. I wandered around the city for a while taking in the sights. My brother had said he would be back at the hotel around 2pm so I had a couple of hours to burn.

Now, it doesn't take a brain surgeon to work out what I would end up doing. And yes, I eventually found myself in a bar. I have to point out, by this time the rain had kicked off again. It was a good excuse to go and shelter and have a beer or two. I found a bar called (well, it was something to do with a villain). I thought, this sounds my kind of bar: you know where you're at with your own crowd! Not that I considered myself a villain, just a friendly 'Del boy', you know, a kind of modern-day wheeler-dealer.

I walked in and greeted the barman with the customary "Bonjour" and then ordered a beer. What the heck! I was in the south of France and these kinda opportunities only come once in a while. After several beers and a chat with the barman, it was time to go back to the hotel to meet my brother.

As I entered the hotel, I was just about to ask the receptionist if she had seen my brother when I heard someone shouting from above me, "Now then, slack arse!" Yes, it was my brother coming down the hotel steps. He informed me we were off to meet up with a French female artist for a few beers, then on for a meal. Was I up for it? Well, can a duck swim? I was on holiday and anything connected with a few beers I was up for. It felt so right to be here with our kid, just the tonic I needed, to get away from the worries of trying to raise the £1600, essential for the Atacama.

We set off to meet this female artist, with our Roy trying to convince me that there was nothing sexual in it. I believed him. He was sincere in his marriage, this I knew. But let's get real! When you're in the south of France, holidaying for a week, going to watch your favourite footie team, drinking beer, and with a French women to boot... You should not put yourself in this position to start with, innocent or not! As it turned out, he was sincere. Like me, he's a friendly guy, just out to have a good time.

It turned out this French female was an artist, but more a piss-artist and out for what she could get. She was also a bit of a nutter. When we met up with her, our Roy went through the formal introductions. Then we settled down to a few beers and a laugh. To cut a long afternoon story short, we went walkabout, frequently stopping to check out the bars.

Eventually we decided to have one more beer stop, and then go for a meal. This is when things started to go wrong.

We walked into this restaurant. As the artist (can't remember her name) went to walk through the door, the waiter, who was stood behind it to let someone out, slammed it shut, straight in her face! She was not amused. In fact, she was furious, and let rip in her French tongue at this poor waiter. No amount of apologies by the waiter calmed her down. The manager was called. By this time she had definitely lost the plot, and turned her venom on me and Roy as we tried to get her to see it was an accident and not to let it spoil our evening. Suddenly, she swiped all the drinks off our table. We were then asked to leave by the manager who threatened to phone the police. Surprise, surprise!

Our fellowship together lasted about another hour. Our Roy calmly tried to persuade her not to let this incident spoil the evening, and to go for our planned meal. As for me, the 'die was cast'. I couldn't verbally relate to her and just wanted to get away. Looking back, this event must have been an omen for the coming evening.

She continued to argue throughout the meal, calling us both English pigs, and screaming that her face hurt, and that she should sue the restaurant, and we should be her witnesses. She was like a woman possessed. I eventually stood up, said "C'mon, Roy, let's go," and told her to fuck off.

Without the artist, we went on to the bar that I had first called in that day, where I was also on first-name terms with the owner. We told him about this girl and the incident and he said that we should be careful who we met up with in this city as it was full of con-artists. I laughed and said that was another name she could put in front of her title.

I left our kid still drinking at about 2.30am. I was all in after the flight and needed some sleep, plus I was legless. That night our Roy got his mobile phone lifted by some French youths who surrounded him in a friendly way while one of them 'dipped his pocket'. Also, the next day Bolton lost to Marseilles by an own goal. See what I mean about an omen?

The night after the match had been played, we had a couple more beers, drowning our sorrows along with the Bolton fans, and then I went back to the hotel at about 12.30am. I had to be at the airport for 4am the next morning for the flight to Heathrow.

Having arrived at Heathrow, I caught a train to King's Cross, and one from there to York. The train at King's Cross was so full I was forced to stand in a corridor with other fellow-passengers. Next to me were a group of lads. I got talking to them, telling them about my adventures in Marseilles and the reason for going. Half-an-hour into the journey the beers started to be passed around. I had brought some with me - I was, after all, still on a bender - and we shared them out together. The train eventually pulled up at York station and I got off somewhat pissed. It was only after I caught my connecting train to Scarborough that I realised I'd left my holdall on the last train. Inside it was my driving licence, passport and wallet, plus a digital camera with all the photos I had taken in Marseilles. I was pissed up and pissed off.

A few days later, back home, I got a phone call from a porter on that train. He had found my hold all and wallet (minus money) and my phone number. We arranged to meet a few days later at York station where he would be passing through on his duties to London. I enquired about the camera but, sadly, it was not in my bag.

Despite it all, I really did have a good time in Marseilles and so did our kid. Life is built up of memories, good or bad. As the saying goes in Lancashire, whatever life dishes out for you, "Tha mon learn ta get on wi' it".

CHAPTER 29

The pain gets worse and worse it strangles me inside
My hearts bled all it can so it's working on my mind
I'm running thru a corridor with its walls painted black
Looking for the sign exit but the demons pull me back

Arrows of pain and torment fired from every side
I'm holding on to a bottle who desires me to come inside
I take a look thru the windows tainted with all its lies
See people smiling back at me
Holding chains surprise, surprise

My heart is pounding loudly there's sweat on my brow
Fe fi fo fum I have to escape somehow
The clock is ticking madly time is running out
My brain might just explode
Fuck that help, get me out, get me out

The corridor got longer may as well lie down and die
There's a door in the corner with a signpost pointing why
I open it with uncertainty take a little step outside
Fuck me I'm back at the beginning
Running with nowhere to hide

Snake Bite

Two very close friends of mine who I worked with at the Beresford Hotel, Brian and Irene Townsend, kindly agree me to come down to Newquay to stay with them for a short while and rest. On the train journey down I got completely pissed and got off at Plymouth station and ended up walking around the city till I found a bar. After a couple of drinks I somehow managed to make it back to the station and catch a train into Newquay. I found myself in the Great Western bar drinking with another of my mates Bodge. He was working in their as the barman. Brian came to collect me and take me back to his house. One could not wish for better friends. Brian is a quiet, placid, friendly guy and Irene so sweet and helpful and I love them both very much. I'm sorry and ashamed to say I carried on drinking in their home and though I isolated myself in one of the bedrooms I was causing them great concern. After a few days of me getting worse for wear due to the drink I ask Brian if he would take me to the doctors, he kindly agreed and took me the next day. It was whilst we were both sitting in the waiting room that I had an alcoholic fit and don't really remember much after that except I was taken by ambulance to Truro Hospital to dry out. I was in there for two weeks and upon discharge Brian and Irene kindly invite me to stay once again. Bless them.

Both full and empty bottles of cider lay cluttered all over the living room floor, alongside the videos I always got out whenever I went on a bender. Judging by the vast number of bottles, I guess I'd been on this one for about four days. After the Nottingham marathon, I was flying on a high tide of emotion, completely buzzed out. It took my legs a few days to recover, but my head was still up there. I was constantly looking at the medal I had hung on the wall, plus my mate Tony had taken a video of me coming in at the finish and I kept popping it on just to re-live the moment on screen. How or why I ended up on this bender is a question I cannot answer. I am an alcoholic who likes to have a drink now and then, no matter how ill it makes me. Sometimes I can drink socially and not go on a bender, but these times are few.

Running was certainly helping me stay sober for longer than 6 weeks and the more I ran and battled against this disease the stronger I got but it was a slow long journey. I knew if I was gonna beat the boozer I had to find a purpose to replace it but the biggest thing was to find myself. The periods of my drinking days, whenever I went on a bender, were getting shorter. In the past, when I went on a bender, it could last between five and six weeks. Now I could only manage about four days. When I had sobered up completely, which usually takes anything from three to four days with medication; I went back inside the gym and on the treadmill. Claire was there as always ready to talk and give me encouragement I never found her to be judgmental. I had to build the miles up again, but slowly. I am no spring chicken, and each bender takes its toll of me, but I was eager to get back onto the roads. I was finding out slowly that I just loved running, especially early in the mornings, listening to my music on the I Pod. I felt so in control of my self with no-one around to give me grief, whether they intended to or not. Any situation, at times, can upset me. I don't seem to have the usual coping mechanisms that most people have but then I've never been taught. I'm better off on my own most times. Don't get me wrong. I love socializing, and have a good sense of humour. It's just that I can relax more in my own company.

I knew as I took another drink from the bottle of White Lightning cider and lay on the sofa that I had to get back to the gym. It took me a while to compose myself and walk to the doctors for the medication that helped me slowly withdraw from alcohol. The doctor is only a quarter of a mile from where I live. Now you would think it would be no problem for me to walk there having just completed a marathon, but I'd been drinking for several days and hobbled up the road like an old man, leaning against walls as I went along. My doctor was very patient with me and as he wrote out the prescription he congratulated me on my new-found ability to run.

The headline about me in the local paper, written by journalist Alex Fredman read 'Billy Facing Biggest Battle Yet'. Then it went on to say how I was attempting to run the Atacama Marathon and how I was also battling against the booze. What I had failed to tell Alex was that I was losing this battle with just sixteen weeks to go before I flew out to Chile to take part in the desert marathon.

I decided to enter the Redcar half marathon in preparation for the desert. I had run this one before the previous year, as well as The Great North Run. The course is mostly flat and also it's a half marathon. I decided I would run it carrying a backpack weighing in at 14 pounds. It usually takes me about 1 hour 55 minutes to complete a half marathon but I didn't have a clue how long it would take whilst carrying this added weight. This was not my first concern; having the stamina to run it and finish was my main target. I have to have my music when running as it completely takes my mind off what I'm doing and also gives me the lift I need. When Claire at the gym, asked me if another member of the gym could run it with me, I was a bit pissed off even though I said yes. I was not mad with Claire or the man she was suggesting I run with. It's just that I like running on my own. On the day of the event I met this bloke, who introduced himself as Robin and we set off in my car towards Redcar. The day was bright and sunny and apart from my companion I was looking forward to the run. This would be my real first attempt at distance running carrying a backpack. I had taken it out with me on my short runs and was finding it not too hard. Inside I had stuffed loads of thick hardback books but this wasn't the pack I was taking with me; this was an old one and the straps kept sliding down which meant every now and then I had to keep yanking them up as my pack slipped down onto my lower back.

On our way to Redcar we engaged in chit chat, mostly with Robin asking me what the Redcar run was like and if the run was hilly with any rough roads to run along. I assured him the roads were flat and fine except for about two miles on a cinder-like path. I told him that I would be listening to my music and that I don't really engage in talking as I need to stay focused. I explained that I would be running with a back pack and if at any point in the race I was holding him back, he was welcome to run on ahead without me. He just smiled and said it would probably be me that ran on ahead. I must admit I harbored these thoughts myself but as you shall see, it didn't turn out that way for me. We parked the car with about half-an-hour to spare and slowly made our way to the start line. I was keeping an eye out for the toilet. I always seemed to want to pee loads before the start; I know it's just nerves. We positioned ourselves at the back of the field and I put on the pack. I had a sort of poster on the back of my pack with the words *Whitby on Tour 2006 Atacama Marathon*. The run got underway and we both started off at a slow pace. After a couple of miles, I decided to 'up the pace' a little. I was feeling strong both physically and mentally but I was also aware that this was Robin's first ever competitive run and I knew he would be feeling nervous wondering whether he would make it. Added to this was the fact that his wife was driving out to watch him (she hadn't travelled with us 'cos we had set off early in the morning).

Every now and then words were exchanged between us - the usual stuff like, how's it going, you OK? But mostly we ran in silence. The course was mainly on the main road but we also cut through some streets. After about four miles the runners had pretty much spread out, and me and Robin were definitely taking up the rear. Robin looked in fine fettle with an even pace and though I had speeded up a little, he matched mine. After the first watering hole, which was about 4 miles from the start I noticed that he was pulling in front and I was dropping back a little. The shoulder straps on my pack were really annoying me. I was forever yanking them back up tightly and this simple action started to affect my concentration. Having passed the 9 mile marker, which was the longest I had ever run carrying a 14 pound weight, the backs of my legs were starting to ache, and my lower back was giving me some gyp. Robin asked me if I was OK and I said yeah then invited him to run on ahead as I knew I was struggling. It was only a few weeks ago that I had been recovering from a drinking session and added to this it was hot, but he refused and said that we would finish it together. I started to give myself a right bollocking; cursing myself for continuing to drink (even though I didn't seem to have the power to stop), *how the fuck*, I challenged myself, *how are you ever gonna run a fuckin' desert marathon when ya struggling to run just 13 miles and only carrying half the weight?* I'd already read from the official *Racing The Planet* web page that the average pack weighed between 25 to 31 pounds. After the self-bollocking, I reminded myself that I was a Lancashire lad and a Farnworth one at that, so I adopted the 'fuck you, bring it on' attitude.

With just two miles to go (always the longest), every part of my body was screaming for me to stop and Robin even suggested it. I knew I was in deep shit. With the training programme I had taken on still waiting for me and only a few weeks to go, I suddenly felt like throwing up when I thought of the Atacama marathon. But I gritted my teeth, told Robin I was OK to carry on, turned up the volume from my iPod and got my head down. After what felt like forever, we were running along the sea front with just half a mile to go. I always like to save a bit of strength for the run in as I like to come in with a bit of a sprint but, on this occasion, I just about made it. We collected our t-shirts with the Redcar half marathon logo on, shook hands and went our separate ways; Robin off to meet his wife and me off to the pub. Well, that's what I felt like doing. I was really pissed off as it had taken me about 2hours 20mins to complete this half marathon and it had been a struggle.

Driving back to Whitby I gave myself a really good talking to and also to God 'cos, no matter what, I just had to get myself together. I not only had to, I wanted to. I wasn't happy with drinking; certainly not drinking the way I was as I knew it was destroying me. I also knew that I was getting a better buzz from running as it made me feel so alive. It also gave me self-worth, which was something I rarely ever felt about myself. A course of action was needed to 'up my training' and to stay away from the booze. I hadn't a problem with the first part, but the second was a different ball game. I decided I would just have to 'bite the bullet'. However, as you shall see once again, instead of 'biting the bullet', I 'shot' myself with it instead.

Claire from the gym was going the extra mile to help and encourage me. She wrote me a training program, and also worked out the right food to eat in preparation for the desert. I was able to follow the training bit but the food part I failed miserably. I just love my fish and chips and all stuff that's supposed to be what is called junk food. I knew I caused her worry and pain whenever I went on a bender, but she was always there to pick me up when I appeared in the gym. I knew she was putting herself out for me. She to was always entering marathons, she is a very competitive lady having also run the London Marathon several times as well as her parents Cedric and Ann. For me it goes without saying she was an inspiration.

I had decided to go and stay with our Roy who lived in Cornwall and get some serious training in, so I turned up there on a Saturday. At that time England were in the World Cup and there was a match on that Sunday, so I decided to go to the pub, see some of my mates, and enjoy the game over a few beers. Not a good idea, I know, but I thought, as it was getting nearer to the Atacama, I wouldn't go on a bender. Wrong! I did, for a few days, much to the disappointment of our Roy who didn't know what to do with me. However, I didn't go on my usual long drinking session and after a few days I was ready to get some serious training in. My brother had taken me all around the Cornish coastline near to where he lived. Pointed out the different paths I could run on and showed me all the high sand dunes. Ideal training, I thought, and I couldn't wait to run along them.

On the first day I decided to go for a run along the headland. I got up about 4am, put on my running gear and drove off at about 5am towards the headland. After parking my car, I reached into the back for my backpack for my water bottle and set off at a slow run to warm up. The Cornish coast is beautiful; and the blue Atlantic surf washing the golden beaches is a sight to behold.

Our Roy had worked out the route distance of the 10 miles I wanted to run and as he had lived down there for about thirty years, I trusted his judgment. All was going well as I ran across the rough, marshy areas and was heading towards the beaches and sand dunes. I had been running for about an hour and a half and I figured I'd done about 8 miles, based on knowing that I can run about three miles in half an hour. I had just run up and back down the first sand dune and was half way up the second, when what felt like an electric shock shot through the back of my right leg and brought me crashing to the ground. I had never had an injury so I didn't know what damage I had done to my leg. I lay on the floor for a while, my mind confused as to what had happened. When I attempted to stand, the pain in the back of my leg was excruciating.

It was still only about six o'clock in the morning and there was nobody in sight. I couldn't stay lying around - it's not in my nature to hang around for anything! So I started to crawl. After about thirty minutes of crawling, I stumbled across an old bloke walking his dog. I must have looked like one of those foreign legion soldiers, crawling out of a desert with a backpack on, gagging for water. Looking up at him from my crawling position, I told him I'd been out running and must have pulled a muscle in the back of my leg. His reply was typical Cornish (by the way I love the Cornish), "Bugger innit" he said, and continued on his way. I eventually made it by crawling and hobbling back to my car and drove to our Roy's cottage.

That was my running sessions over with in Cornwall and my drinking sessions took over. Roy eventually drove me back to Whitby, leaving my car back in Cornwall because he couldn't cope with me. I continued to drink for a few days - don't know how many - until I eventually sobered up. My leg was still painful and it was difficult to put any weight on it. I eventually 'got it together' to go to the gym and see Ian, the sports physiotherapist. I lay on the bed as Ian applied oil and began to massage my painful legs. I asked him what I had done. At first he reckoned that I may have pulled a muscle. Then on careful examination, he laughed and said surprisingly, I'd been bitten by a snake and pointed out to me two pronged, tiny holes on the muscle of my calf.

Running was certainly helping me stay sober for longer periods. In the past I could only manage about 3 weeks. The periods of drinking, whenever I went on a bender, were also getting shorter. When I went on a bender in the past, it could last between four and five weeks: now I could only manage about four days, which, on reflection, wasn't too bad for my health and my bank balance let alone all the other things in life that drink can wreak havoc with.

When I had sobered up completely, which usually takes anything from four to five days with medication; I went back inside the gym and onto the treadmill. I had to build the miles up again, but slowly. I am no spring chicken and each bender takes its toll on me. I was eager to get back onto the roads as the Atacama Desert Marathon was approaching fast.

CHAPTER 30

Bender In The Med

Bridget and I did go to Crete in May 2005 and had a great time plus I stayed sober. Little did I know, a year later in May 2006, I would be back training in the Mediterranean just a few months away from the Atacama

I had decided to go over there for a month, staying on a campsite I had found on the internet. The plan was to take my son, Billy Roy (named after me and my brother), who was nineteen at the time and was courting a girl called Lisa. I'd made up my mind to have a bit of a holiday with my son and a couple of beers, before I took up any training. With only twelve weeks to go before my run in the sun began I knew I had to be careful regarding the booze.

The goods on the campsite were grossly overpriced, especially the booze. So me and my son ventured further than the beaches and bars and stumbled across a Lidl supermarket. An oasis! Cheap food and cheap, cheap booze! Happy days! We had some laughs and I enjoyed his company, like me, he has a good sense of humor. Sadly, like most teenagers who find themselves in love, he was missing Lisa and she was missing him. He didn't stay the full month and returned home to be with Lisa. I carried on drinking and got pissed. I phoned Bridget to ask if she would come over and spend the last couple of weeks with me. Little did she know I was drinking heavily. I couldn't stand, let alone walk properly. I stumbled each morning drunkenly to Lidl to buy my day's supply of booze, staggered back to my tent, sat outside in the sun, listened to music on my I Pod, and got drunk.

Finally, the day came when I was to meet Bridget at the airport, just outside Chania (pronounced Hania). How I 'got it together' to catch a bus there, I will never know, but get there I did and carried on drinking in a taverna just outside the airport. Bridget found me wandering drunkenly around the airport with blood all down my front looking filthy and unshaven. She burst into tears when she saw me and just stood and cried, I drunkenly laughed, 'what's up cock, your in the Med, you should be happy' We took a taxi back to the campsite and I ended up arguing with the driver over the price. The driver ended up pulling over and asking us to get out until Bridget calmed the situation. Back at the campsite, Bridget took one look and decided she was not going to stay there. The tent was full of cans and empty bottles, spilt booze on the bedding, dirty clothes some reeking of urine and a great pile of vomit just in the doorway of the tent. She walked off she didn't want to be around that. Bridget came back after a while and took me into Chania where she rented a room. Eventually I sobered up but it took me a week where she spent most of the time watching over me in the room. I did manage to get a small amount of training in and the first day I went for a run on the beach carrying my fourteen-pound backpack, I managed fifteen minutes. I had drunk all my water and threw up in the sand. But I persisted and by the end of the holidays I managed to run seven miles.

Most of my training was spent running around the countryside of Whitby. The terrain around this part of the country has everything to offer the runner, rough tracks, hills, the beach, but above all the scenery. I would get up in summer time around 4am, put on my gear and headphones, and within minutes I would be out in the open country. I felt so alive running through the countryside, passing the farm animals, all lazily munching away and offering me inquisitive looks. Now and then a fox would step out in front of my path, pure joy; you can't beat nature for beauty and peace. It's the towns and cities that screw us up. That's the reason I have to get away and have a holiday. Recharge my brain, unless you're one of them people who enjoy the *'rat race' shit.*

I had entered as many marathons in the run up to the Atacama that I could afford, which is not easy when you're still an active alcoholic. One run that I entered was the Brass Monkey Run over a distance of 13 miles. The course started off in York next to the racecourse. Once again I was recovering from drink and had only been sober for about three weeks. It usually takes me about a week or so after a bender to get my fitness back to some sort of running order, but my head takes a bit longer. I knew I had about two weeks to prepare for the York run. I don't know what Bridget or the P.T instructors at the gym thought of me, knowing that I was still going on drink binges but if they felt/thought anything, they had the wisdom to keep it to themselves. I only ever received encouragement from them, as well as from others who cared for me.

By the time the York half marathon came around, I had built up my fitness level and was running 12 miles whilst carrying 14 pounds in my pack. I remember the day was pretty miserable weather-wise, as we all lined up at the start. I had the same paper advert strapped to the back of my pack which read:

'Whitby on Tour
June 2006
The Atacama Marathon

Any form of advertising was needed in order to get sponsorship. As the race got under way, I had positioned myself as usual at the back of the pack. It had started to drizzle, and I was feeling miserable, the worst of it was I didn't know why. I suppose on reflection raising the money for the Atacama was mentally taking its toll on me and Bridget. My running plan in preparation for the Atacama was to run little steps to munch up the miles, but this was difficult to keep up, especially when you are running along with a group. I had to discipline myself, which sounds rich coming from someone who had no resolves when it comes to the booze.

I was six miles into the run, the straps on my pack were hurting my shoulders, and my lower back was painful. I couldn't see any runners in front of me, but I knew there were a few behind. I was getting more pissed off by the mile. Once again Capt Pikard took over and kicked me into gear with positive/negative thoughts. Try to imagine: he put into my head that *this is the Atacama and there will be times when you will feel like giving up with all kinda complaints, 'what yah gonna do then eh?' You can withdraw at any time, come home, "you're no spring chicken", people will say at least you tried.* Bollocks to that I said inside my head whilst I was running. I remember thinking, it's a good job people can't read our thoughts. Pickard would positively encourage me with *c'mon Billy you can this, it's time to rip the labels off especially the one 'a leopard never changes its spots'.*

I gritted my teeth, pumped up the volume on my headphones and thought *'let's burn some rubber'*. I eventually saw a female runner about three hundred yards in front of me. She was running uphill across a bridge. *OK,* I thought, *a challenge 'lets get her'.* Focus, focus, focus. Like a lioness eyeing up a gazelle, I increased my speed slightly, got my head down and went for her. Soon I was passing her and eyeing up another runner, and another; the hunt was on.

I'm sure you've figured out by now I'm no super fit runner, but I am a 'let's kick arse bastard'. I don't mean anything personal; it's just for the demons inside my head.

Once a positive attitude is taken up in anything, you should get positive results. I believe we need to look at these two words ('positive' and 'attitude') separately. This is not a lesson in philosophy and I'm no expert, just a drunk. Even when sober I have the mind of a drunk, but I also have my thoughts, so read on. I have had a lot of 'head' experts giving me all sorts of philosophy crap, so this is my 'crap' or maybe not, you choose. First, positive: for me this is about my capabilities. I am not disabled in my legs, I have no serious illness so there is no reason whatsoever why I shouldn't be able to run if I choose to. That, for me, is positive thinking.

Attitude, on the other hand, is a bit more difficult to train. There are some poor unfortunates who have a *'I give in, that's all I can do'* attitude', and only go so far in anything which is challenging. This I believe is a barrier to them in life 'this far and no further' is a comfort zone and for some that's all they want "thank you very much". So why did I liken these people to 'poor unfortunates' because I feel they already know deep inside themselves that there is something missing in their lives. They might not admit it to themselves but they sure as hell feel it. Remember Capt Kirk's words (Star Trek), "To Boldly Go Where No Man Has Been Before". That, for me, is a challenging attitude. Submit to the positive, accept the challenge, put the two together and there you have it, positive attitude.

With this new found zeal I overtook two others; I have to admit I get a buzz whenever I overtake someone. I had passed the 11 mile marker and, as always for me, the last couple of miles be it a half or full marathon is always the hardest to finish. I passed by other competitors who had already finished the race and received an applause which is the usual custom. By this time my shoulders and lower back were causing me a lot of pain. We runners owe a lot to the spectators, with their cheering and applause, they carry you through the last couple of miles, not forgetting the bands that sometimes play along the course. Half a mile to go and this is when I open up (or Capt Pickard) my speed. By this time I just wanted to finish but I also wanted to come in running at some sort of good speed. It's nice to know if you still have that strength left in you. I finished this half marathon with 14 pound on my back in a time of 2h 20m and I was pleased with the timing. I felt my fitness preparation for the Atacama was going well, but not so the staying off the drink; that was a separate battle, one which I hoped and prayed I would one day conquer. But with only a few months left before the Atacama, I hit another bender.

CHAPTER 31

Day 5

Friday July 27th
Stage 5 - Part 3

Morning came too quick, my head was pounding and I awoke feeling I'd done a couple of rounds with Amir Khan, the great Bolton boxing champion. I was woken by the voices of the other competitors who were sat around the fire eating their breakfast. We greeted each other with the usual formalities, enquiring about each other's injuries, how they felt; stuff like that. But my first thought was for Yoko as I climbed out of my sleeping bag and made my way towards the truck she was sleeping in. Yoko had been sad last night having to leave her friend behind; I was concerned for her mental well being and didn't want her to feel deflated in any way. My anxious thoughts were unfounded; Yoko was up and about, dressing herself for our last remaining 3 miles. The mood around the camp was once again festive; as far as everyone was concerned it was nearly over, and today was Saturday. We were informed that we should reach base camp by lunchtime and that we would have the rest of the day off 'till Sunday, when we'd do the final stage of this 150 mile marathon and go on to the finish line in the town of San Pedro.

No early morning briefing this morning with Pierre, just words of encouragement and a "well done everyone, see you later" from an official. We could be on our way at anytime, but we all more or less decided that we would start off at 8am. Looking around at the other competitors' faces, they all bore the tired strains of this grueling event, but their spirits remained strong. I felt so bloody tired, I was bordering on hallucinations. It all seemed like the last few days had been a bad dream and I so much wanted to wake up from it. At 8am, me and Yoko set off with the other competitors. There was no official line up, no count down, everyone just set off at a walk, apart from one or two who still had a bit of running left in them. The sun was beginning to rise in the clear blue sky bringing with it its welcoming warm rays. With the thought of 'it's nearly all over' in our minds and the rest of the day off at base camp, we had new springs in our steps.

We had officially till 3pm today to reach base camp so we were not in that much of a hurry, which is just as well really as both me and Yoko hobbled along with our mashed worn out feet, legs and backs. All around us, the view was spectacular as we had entered into a pass that had sliced its way into a mountain. The sides of the mountain and the ground were covered with some sort of white substance, and it was like we were entering Santa's grotto; in fact I could hear a competitor in the distance singing a Christmas carol. This atmosphere just added to lifting our spirits up that bit more. The walls of the mountain seemed to reach up to the sky; at times you could see the sun shining down on us, at others the walls would close in blotting out the sun and once again the temperature would drop, but all in all just being in it was exhilarating to the spirit. One or two of the competitors began yodeling, and I started singing, '*The hills are alive with the sound of music...*' Unfortunately, after being inside this pass for a time, following the red markers, there seemed no end to it. The pass just went on and on and on. Warm one minute the next cold. In the distance I noticed that the path was coming to an end and I could see the rocky ledges barring the pass. As we got nearer I heard the familiar French voice of my friend, Pierre, in the distance, and I saw him stood in the middle of these rocks helping our fellow competitors over them.

Apparently he had stayed there all night to assist each runner safely over these sharp rocky ledges. We had to scale them carefully for there was a sheer drop of about 10ft that fell onto more rocks on the other side. I approached him with a smile and a greeting of, 'I would like to strangle you' delivered humorously, and he told me I'd have to get in the queue. With careful steps me and Yoko made it over the rocks and with a wave and 'I'll see you in hell' from me to Pierre, we were on our way again back inside Santa's grotto. A seven-person U.K team (who else?) were running for the charity *Save the Rhino* and took it in turns to carry this bloody great rhino suit - complete with head and horn - over the entire course, and I applaud them. I did suggest to one of the runners they could run for 'Save Billy' next time. I asked Yoko how she was feeling. Bless her, I knew that like me she was in pain, but she smilingly said 'OK'.

We had been in this pass for about three hours, when we came upon the rhino team who were sat down and swapping over the suit. We took time out to sit with them and have a bite to eat. I really wanted to take my shoes off as my feet were throbbing but I resisted the urge to just rip them off.

On the next stretch, me and Yoko decided to do a little running, as we so desperately wanted to get to base camp. This proved to be unsuccessful as our feet and legs were all in, still it was worth a try. Winston Churchill said in the Second World

War "give us the tools and we will do the job"; me and Yoko needed new legs, feet and backs to finish this job but none were coming. Would you believe it? We came to another ledge with a volunteer there to help us over it. This time we had to climb down a very rocky part, and I informed him that I could no longer feel my feet so took the descent slowly, assisting Yoko down once I had got to the bottom. "Only another 1.5km to base camp," he said. I didn't believe him and to quote Ting again:

"We were told we were only 1.5km from base camp - the longest 1.5km ever! Sometimes I really think their distances are off somewhat".

In the distance we could see the *Racing the Planet* banner strung over the day's finish line along with the international flags. Me and Yoko stopped to compose ourselves. We had to come in running and with a smile on our faces, so I turned to Yoko, gave her a high five and said, "No fuckin' surrender, eh?" We had made it! We ran into the camp holding hands to the applause of several competitors and volunteers, and Yoko's husband was there to greet her. I felt envious and wished that my children and Bridget had been there to greet me. The official time for both me and Yoko was 27:43:15, which included the five-hour rest we had at the last camp the night before.

The atmosphere inside the camp was festive. The Chilean volunteers had brought along musical instruments and were putting on a show for everyone, and competitors were either sleeping in their bags outside their tents or just relaxing in the sun. I left Yoko and her husband with a hug and made my way to my tent. Inside it was empty and I was glad as I needed time and space on my own to collect my thoughts. I just couldn't take it in that I had done the 50 mile and once inside the tent, I broke down and wept.

Sleep evaded me, my head was buzzing with so many thoughts racing through it. I needed to get my shoes off and my feet treated so I made my way to the medical tent. Inside were two members, a male and a female, of the *Save the Rhino* team (don't remember their names)? The man was having his dressing removed from his feet and I felt sorry for him as he let loose a loud scream; I knew the pain. The girl declined the offer from the American doctor to remove hers and I couldn't blame her. Paul, the runner I had spent some time with the previous night, was laid out on a bed having his feet treated and also had an I.V. drip inside him. Soon it was my turn. I told the doctor I just didn't know how I was going to get these shoes off as my feet and ankles had become so swollen in the shoes that I couldn't move my toes. On inspection, he told me that he couldn't cut them anymore, as they would most certainly fall apart, and there was still 10k/6m of the race to finish tomorrow. We both sat looking at my feet then, with complete insanity and no regard of the consequences, I untied both laces and ripped them off. Fortunately the shoes remained intact. "That was the easy bit," said the doc, "next comes the dressings." I didn't care. My feet began to be soothed having been released from their vice-like prison, but they were indeed both badly swollen.

I was determined not to scream out when he began to take off the plasters covering the blisters. Gripping the sides of the chair, I said, through gritted teeth, "Let's do it". So, with Bob Marley jamming in the background, the doc set to the task. It was bloody painful and I did let out a yelp now. Finally the dressings were off and where my blisters had been, more had formed. The doc decided to take some photos of my feet "for future reference", he said. Looking down at my brand new shoes, it was hard to believe the state they were in. I'd only ran in them a few times in preparation for *the Atacama* to break them in, yet here they were, cut up, tattered and torn. I wondered whether they would hold out for tomorrow's final run in. Having got my feet photographed and treated, I slipped on my cozy slippers to walk (hobble) around the camp and have a 'chin wag' with friends I had made. On my way over here, when I was at Heathrow airport, I met three young lads from London who were flying out to take part and I had become a somewhat 'father figure' to them; boring them, I suspect (but they didn't agree), with my philosophy on life. I would check them out each morning and would quote to them a Capt Mannering's phrase from Dad's Army, "there's a war on you know" to encourage them for the hardships we were to face each day. That phrase became popular among our little group. One morning a young American guy we had befriended came up to me, smiled and said, "Hi Billy" in that lovely friendly American way, then asked whether I was ready for today. I replied, "No" and, with a huge grin, he said, "there's a war on you know"

Tomorrow was the official day of rest day, yet instead of being full of excitement that it would soon be all over and hopefully I would collect the medal. I was shattered both physically and mentally and so were my shoes. I felt there was nothing more I had left in me to give, and yet I still had another grueling run through the desert in front of me. Did I have enough left to go that extra mile or, in this case, 6 miles? I wearily lay down in the sand and allowed the warmth of the sun to send me to sleep. The last part of the race could wait.

CHAPTER 32

R.N.L.I

As part of my efforts to advertise myself and my challenge, I got in touch with the RNLI (Royal National Lifeboat Institution). I offered to run a full marathon around Whitby to raise funds for them and also advertise for sponsorship for myself. The run was to begin at 10am at the band stand and a friend who works the boats called John agreed to host the show for me by telling the crowd through his microphone why I was running. He played records throughout the day plus kept the crowd informed as to how many miles I'd run. The run started at the foot of a hill known as The Khyber Pass it was fairly steep and got steeper each time I ran up it. I had planned the course to run around the outskirts of town but each circuit would take me through the town and each circuit was 2 and half mile long so I ran 11 circuits.

The mayor Rob Broadley was to join me on the start and also Denise Taylor and her daughter Hannah also ran a couple of circuits with me. Denise in fact the night before had been on a girlie night and was suffering from a Bacardi breezer hangover, but despite this she completed 3 laps with me. Claire was away in the Alps somewhere but she kept on phoning to find out how I was doing. Her mum and dad, Cedric and Ann Fowler, Rebecca Hunt and Dr Rory Newman also joined in the run to give me some support. On the last lap I was really feeling the pain helped on by the hill of the Khyber Pass. It was on this that I was joined by Nurse Freda Verrill from Whitby hospital who had helped me in the past when I was admitted for Alcohol detoxification. She joined me for the last run round and was a great encouragement in getting me round this final lap. Ian Carr from the gym stayed there all day keeping my time and shouting out words of encouragement. I completed it in 4hrs 15mins not bad for me and a personnel best. Hilary and Doug Townsend plus their children Megan and Sam also recorded the event, cheered me on throughout the day. I owe these people a lot.

Harry Kidger the owner of The Fitness Machine never judged me when I slipped back on the drink. On the contrary he would invite me down to the gym to talk things over with him " you know where we are " were his kind words to me. My daughter Bethany used to come to the gym to watch me train and she would set tasks as to how many miles I had to do on the tread mill plus time me bless her. My other daughter Hayley would phone me with offering encouragement with the words "you can do it dad I know you can" bless her too, also my son Billy would try to keep me on the straight and narrow reminding me of the task in front of me, I love them all so much.

I had only a few months left to train and I was on another bender. I do have some good reasons for this one which I choose not to go into, except to say some very nasty lies were told about me to the Whitby Gazette. I believe these lies were designed through jealousy and bitterness and were to thwart my plans also to send me over the top.

This time I was scared drinking so close to the event. Bridget bless her never ear bashed me she was so supportive she had the good sense to know that this was my battle; she would however remind me what I had to lose. I didn't want to go to the doctors I didn't want anyone to know I was back on the bottle too many people had seen me running around the town training for the desert marathon so I drove out of town to buy my supply of booze then locked myself away to do battle with the demons. Drinking was not the same anymore I knew and felt it. The old me was disappearing I loved my new found self worth and that I wasn't a loser and yes," a leopard can change its fuckin spots. Well this human leopard was having a bloody good try. This was my last bender it was full on training for the Atacama with only 6 weeks left to go.

CHAPTER 33

The final stage
Day 7

29th July 2006
Distance 10k (6 miles)

Dead man running. This thought entered my head as I lay curled up in my sleeping bag trying to keep warm. It didn't matter that today was the last day of the grueling marathon, it brought me no joy. I was at the end of my tether both physically and mentally - as the saying goes, totally wasted. In fact I was quoted in the official report as saying, "I would only be happy once the medal is around my neck". Once again I struggled to get to sleep the night before because of the cold. My only comfort at that moment was the fact that despite whatever happens today tonight I shall be lying in a bed.

I struggled out of my bag and habitually put on my socks and shorts; all the rest of my running gear including my jacket was already on. Just like the other nights, I had slept in them and couldn't give a toss on how I looked or smelt; animalistic nature had taken over. People had told me that I had lost weight; not surprising really as I hadn't eaten much of the dried food muck I had brought with me to feed me through the marathon. My stomach was aching for some proper food, you know, fish and chips, pie and chips, egg and chips, and top of the list, steak and chips. I was definitely gonna binge on this plus loads of ice cold coke, and a couple of fags when I got home.

I made my way over to the fire and, not surprisingly after yesterday's carnival atmosphere there were more of the competitors sat around, just chilling out. Most had caught up with their sleep and were eager for the day to begin. This was the last 10k to run and then it was party time in the square of San Pedro. We had been promised lots of beer and pizza. The race was to be staggered in three groups. The first group to which I belonged, set off at 10am, then the next bunch at 11am, and finally the elite runners three hours later at 12 o'clock. The reason behind this was to get all runners back at the square around the same time; it goes without saying really that some of the elite finished well before others who had set off at 10am.

The sun was high above our heads and the temperature in its 90's as we lined up for the 10k start. The bell rang and we were off on our final run of this marathon cheered on by the elite runners who had to endure waiting for their time to start. Our group set off to lots of screaming and well wishes ringing in our ears. To start with, the ground was flat and sandy and once again I had not bothered to listen to the briefing about the terrain we would cross. No point really, I had thought. I'd not listened the other days "bring it on" was my attitude, plus sometimes it's better not knowing what to expect. Just as well really cos very quickly everything changed. I saw my friend Pierre helping competitors to negotiate another rocky ledge, with a nasty drop, should you put a foot wrong.

By this time I had gone passed caring; in fact I actually shared a joke with him which included the line that "I would gladly pull the trap door". I limped my way over it and continued limping on the route. I passed one poor competitor who was having trouble with both his legs. He told me they had been given him morphine for the past couple of days for the pain but they had now run out. He never told me what was up with his legs. I didn't ask, I was shattered myself. It was too hot and six miles on any road, let alone in the desert after already covering 142m is bloody purgatory. Well it was for me.

As I ran I thought about what I had to do when I got back, I had to go to my hotel to pick some mementos. I was gonna get a photo with me holding 'me up at the finish flag should I manage to complete the course and with me wearing the medal. This was causing me stress for I knew that when I eventually got back to my hotel room, I was gonna make love to the bed but I had to push these thoughts out of my head. First I had to finish but if you could have seen me I'm sure you would have phoned for an ambulance, or maybe the undertakers.

The run through the town of San Pedro is one I shall never forget. I passed little shack-like buildings which had families stood outside with the little children waving every kind of national flag and I remember passing a little smiling Mexican girl who was waving one with the union jack; I felt like a national hero. At last there was the banner proclaiming *Atacama Racing The Planet 2006* in the distance. There was a Chilean band banging out the local music, people were dancing in the street, and competitors who had already finished and were wearing their medals were shouting out words of encouragement to me. I could see Mary, the organizer, standing next to the town's president and his wife holding a medal in her hand. I was shuffling along at what resembled some kind of run and then I passed under the banner. Mary handed the medal to the president's wife and she hung it around my neck. I kissed her on each cheek, shook hands with the president and then received the hugs and well wishes from the other competitors and volunteers. The three lads from England who I'd met at Heathrow were there to congratulate me and also take the photos I promised to take back, including one with me holding up the Bolton Wanderers' scarf.

After all this rigmarole had finished, the first thing I did was to go and get a beer. Some things never change. With beer in hand, I limped to a shop where I knew I could phone up Bridget to tell her I had done it. The conversation went like this, "Bridget, Hallo, me, "Houston mission accomplished, permission to come home". Bridget, I believe, cried with joy whilst saying "yes" the tears for me were to come later; in fact 10 weeks later. I hobbled back to the square where other competitors were still finishing and ate about three pizzas and drank some more beer.

There was to be an award ceremony at a hotel around 4pm that afternoon; by this time it was about 2pm. I hobbled back to my hotel, took off the clothes I had ran and slept in for the past six days and took a shower. It seemed to take ages for me to clean the desert filth I had accumulated over the past six days before I felt reasonably clean. Coming out of the shower I went into the bag I had brought along to get the clothes to change into. As I was getting dressed my eye caught the medal I had so casually slung onto the bed. It occurred to me then that I had not looked at it properly; in fact I hadn't even given it a second thought. I picked it up and whilst looking at it the memories of the last six days and nights in the desert came flooding back: getting lost, bloody cold, all alone, tired, sometimes hallucinating, sleepless nights, not being able to eat, the salt flats, the heat, the bloody mountainous sand dunes, the cold fast-flowing rivers, having my toes injected to cut the blisters, the pain in my legs, shoulders and back, through 150 miles. I smiled, kissed the medal and said "yes Roy, 4,4,2, no fuckin' surrender.

The flight back to England was horrendous for me. I just wanted a bed and some good old fish and chips but I had another 15 hours or more of a flight journey in front of me. Worst of all, I had bought a train ticket from Kings Cross to York which I could only use at a certain time and day which was going to be tight to meet this deadline. I couldn't sleep at all throughout the whole journey. Once we touched down in Madrid, I had a 3 hour wait and with no money left, I hobbled around the airport mostly back and forth to the toilet.

The plane left on time from Madrid so if all went well I would quite easily make my train connection. But sod's law, things didn't go according to plan and once the plane was flying over London the pilot announced that there was heavy fog over the airport and that we were in a queue. We would have to circle to wait our turn to land. I knew straight away I would not be able to make the train but I was passed caring and decided that I would get my head down at Heathrow and hitch it back home tomorrow.

The plane landed and I arose wearily from my seat. At least I was back home. I thought 'Sod it'. I'd been through bloody hell for the last six days so one more day won't make any difference. Reaching for my bag, I exited the plane and turned my mobile phone on. Instantly I got a message from Bridget asking me where I was and before I had time to reply she rang. "Where are you?" she asked. "I'm at Heathrow airport," I replied. "So am I," she said. Do you know that feeling when your blood rushes through your entire body? Well mine was on the move, I could have cried. What a sight for tired eyes she was, when I saw her.

Bless her. We hugged and kissed then she told me she had booked us a room at a travel lodge.

When we arrived at the lodge, I was starving so we asked if there were any restaurants around which were open. By this time it was past midnight and yes, there was. Thank god for Burger King and Big Macs; I ate two burgers with a large coke and I nearly made myself sick. Once back in the lodge, Bridget took several photos of me with my medal and also my heavily plastered feet then I fell into the bed and slept.

In the weeks after the event I was kept busy with an interview on Radio Cleveland and guest speaker at a local business group (which my friend Andrew had organized). Bridget threw a bit of a get together for me with some of our friends. People were congratulating me. My friends Claire, Denise, Harry and Ian were full of praise but I felt totally unaffected by it all. It just reminded me of when I had come off tripping... did it really happen?

Before the Atacama I would wander down to the seafront in Whitby. There is a little breakfast bar on the front and I would buy a coffee and sit on the pier looking out towards the sea. I would watch the fishermen unload their catch and listen to their tales and jokes and, despite all my worries about the event that lay in front of me, watching these hard men sharing comradeship left me with a wonderful sense of peace.

Several weeks after I had completed the marathon, I was sat once again drinking a coffee looking out to sea when it suddenly hit me, everything I had endured in the desert came flooding back. I had done it and had got the medal and, as the fishermen jokingly unloaded their catch, I looked away and wept.

CHAPTER 34

The Epilogue

After thirty years of alcohol and drug abuse, with rehabilitation clinics, counselling, A.A. meetings and reading every self-help book I could get my hands on, I had still carried on abusing alcohol/drugs. So what brought about the change? How can a man at the age of 54, who doctors had informed would be dead from abusing alcohol/drugs, if not by suicide - inside of three years suddenly rise from his death bed? In this next chapter I hope I will be able to explain exactly what happened to me, for let's remember here is a man who enjoyed getting drunk, getting stoned, partying, an ex-football hooligan, ex-skinhead, ex-mod in fact an 'ex' everything but a person who wasn't remotely interested in running in any shape or form. What brought about such a change that he would find himself running a desert marathon?

The year was around 1993, and once again I found myself in hospital in Scarborough. The hospital was called St Mary's and it's where those unfortunate people who have some form of mental illness or, like myself, addicts are taken to.

I had been inside this hospital several times over the years. The nurses had got used to me so it came to the point where they would just medicate me, dry me out, leave me to myself, then kick me out (they call it discharge). I lay in my bed sweating, shaking, my heart pounding and totally paranoid, just staring at the ceiling. Beside my bed was a bowl for me to throw up in which I did quite regularly. When I wanted to go to the toilet, it was a slow unsteady job as I held on to the walls and anything else within reach to steady me. I can't remember how I ended up in that hospital; I know I was admitted through being on an alcohol bender but for how long and where I just don't know.

I do however remember the day that was to change my life forever even if it was 13yrs in coming. I was laid in my bed when I heard "Hallo Billy". Looking up I noticed a lady who went to the church I used to attend when my kids were little. She asked me how I was. I remember thinking, *piss off and leave me alone.* How do you explain paranoia, that feeling of hopelessness, confusion, and no bloody hope for life? I figured she must have felt my irritation of her presence so she waved me goodbye and left.

"Hallo Billy". I opened my eyes to see the same lady who spotted me yesterday stood at the side of my bed. "Don't worry, I'm not staying," she said.

"Good," I thought.

"I've just fetched you a book I thought you might like to read. It's about a farmer called Jim Wilkinson who lives in Yorkshire and who has had a calling from God. He's turned his farm into a place where people can come and worship God and also receive prayer for healing and invite God into their lives. The books called 'Miracle Valley'." I smiled back at her sarcastically and said something like, "I'm a bit busy at the moment". "I'll just leave the book at the side of your bed then shall I?" she said. "Yeah, I'll give it a gander later," I sighed, closing my eyes hoping she would get the message. She did and left.

That book lay on my bedside cabinet for a few days. I was so heavily drugged on the detox medicine I didn't know what day it was. Eventually and slowly I started to come back onto the planet. I wasn't there yet but I could just about make it to the toilet without clinging to the walls. It was on one of these return visits back to my bed that I noticed the book. Having no-one to talk to as I always made sure people were not welcome at my bedside and that included the nursing staff and with nothing better to do, I picked up the book and started reading about this Yorkshire farmer.

I recalled the lady who gave it to me saying about God and how he can change life. I suppose I just wanted the chapter about that bit 'cos mine certainly needed changing. Unfortunately there was no index stating 'God will change your life, Chapter 7, so I had to start at the beginning. Jim wasted no time in his chapters 'cos it was all there how God loves you and that meant BILLY and if you were to invite him into your life he would definitely come and set about changing you.

I was desperate for some kinda answer to who I was and why I drank. It was no good just saying you're an alcoholic 'cos that's not the reason why. It didn't matter whether it was the abuse I suffered as a child, or whether I like drink so much and that's what turned me into an alcoholic. Whatever the reason I needed changing. I couldn't do it myself, already tried that but the pain and demons were too strong inside of me …*Humpty Dumpty* you know, *all the king's horses and all the king's men couldn't put him back together again.* Well in my case neither could the doctors, psychiatrists or counselling put this egg back to any kind of shape or form.

So for no other reason than that, I delved into the book. What the heck, I thought, it can't do any harm. Anyroad there was no television room so I had nowt better to do. They say God moves in mysterious ways and without me knowing it, he was on the move inside of me and when God moves nothing can stop him. So, like a fish caught securely on the end of a line, I was being ever so gently reeled in.

I just couldn't put that bloody book down. Nearly every page had some kind of story of God's love and power and how Jesus wanted me, Billy Isherwood, to have a relationship with him. But did I want it? My head said no but my heart cried out for love and a sense of belonging. Halfway through the book I had made up my mind I needed to get in touch with this Jim Wilkinson and just like the old days, 'score off' him, but this time I wanted a deal off Jesus. Right, I thought, I'll phone him up (Jim not Jesus, I would have phoned Jesus up if I could have). Reaching for some change inside my locker, I made my way to the hospital phone and this is how it went.

OK, dial 192, get number.

"Hallo, directory enquires? I want the number of a farm called Miracle Valley."

Operator: "One moment please, sorry I have nothing listed under that name."

"Well it's in Yorkshire and I'm just reading a book about it". Whilst standing there still sweating and shaking, I wondered whether I was losing the plot but what the heck I'd already done that.

Operator: "Just one moment. I can't find anything, I'll get a supervisor." Now even in my confused drugged-up state of mind, this had never happened to me before; usually you had to have a surname as well as an address. I stood leaning against the wall aware of the nursing staff watching me. It's was the first time they had seen me in any place different inside the hospital except coming and going to the toilet. I reckon they thought I was ordering a *Joey baxi* (Taxi) as I'd done that before on previous admissions and discharged myself.

The supervisor came onto the phone.

"Hallo, this is the supervisor. How may I help you?" God I thought, here we go again. "Look." I said, "I'm reading this book called *Miracle Valley* and I just want the phone number…

"One moment please." By this time I wanted to crawl back under my bedclothes and block the world out. I held my ground, looking around crazily at everyone as my paranoid brain thought everyone was watching me. Suddenly she came back on the line talking like someone who had just won the lottery.

"I've got it," she said, "the number is..."

"Hang on a moment. I need to get some paper and a pen." Running up to one of the nursing staff, I asked her if she had any. She asked me what I wanted them for. "It's a phone number I want to write down."

"Who are you ringing?" she enquired.

"The Cask Inn" I replied sarcastically, "Gonna see if I can order a carry out".

"Wait a moment and I'll fetch you some." Then smiling, she said, "Get a drink for me too". I reckon putting up with us misfits she needed one. Returning to the phone I shakily wrote down the number the supervisor had given me. If I thought that the little ordeal I'd had with the operator was a bit strange, when I rang the number it blew my head away. Let me explain again.

I dialed the number and waited, holding on to the walls. I was beginning to shake again and I remember thinking it must be nearly time for my pills to calm me down. It seemed ages before I heard a male voice on the other end of the phone say "hallo" and this is how this conversation went.

"Hallo, my name is Billy and I am a patient at St Mary's Hospital in Scarborough. I am an alcoholic and also a drug user and have been for thirty years. I'm reading a book called *Miracle Valley...*"

"Praise The Lord," the voice interrupted.

"...by someone called Jim Wilkinson".

The voice replied, "That's me".

"Well," I said, "I want to meet this Jesus you're writing about".

"Hallelujah," cried Jim.

"I want to discharge myself from the hospital and come to your place."

"Amen," said Jim, "we have a meeting on Friday".

"OK, see you then."

Leaving the phone, I went straight up to the nurses' desk and said, "I'm discharging myself". "What for?" enquired the nurse, "you are not fit yet to leave the hospital. Let me fetch the doctor". My mind was already made up so as she went to fetch the doc; I was already at my bed packing my stuff. The doctor came and I explained to him I was leaving and going to give my heart to Jesus. Maybe he too thought I had lost the plot but he just smiled, said, "OK," and added, "I hope you do find God," then he added, "you need him". He didn't need to tell me that. I knew I had no other answers. I'd been searching long enough and for me there was nothing left in this world available to help me. I'd been round enough and had exhausted all the professional help.

Jim sent someone to visit me at the hospital. His name was David Nellist and he lived in the Scarborough area, and he turned up within a few hours of me ringing Jim. It was arranged for me to go to the Friday meeting and to stay there for three days.

I stood in a large barn full of people all smiling and greeting each other. The barn was decorated with banners all declaring God's love for us. There was a large stage at the front with musicians happily dancing around and playing away. The evening started off singing songs to God. It was so different to a church where everything is done in whispers. I was captivated by the enthusiasm of the congregation who were dancing around and waving flags about. Had not been a church I could have been at a rock concert. I had been primed as to how the evening went. We would sing a few songs, listen to a sermon then there would be an altar call. This meant anyone who wanted prayer for anything or, like me, wanted to give their life to God and invite Jesus into their hearts, went forward. Well that was me and I couldn't wait for it to come. Despite the atmosphere in the place, I was still withdrawing and shaking badly.

Finally the time came for the altar call and I was the first one up. Soon there was a long line of people stood there and I was stood in the middle. Jim and some of the elders started at the end of the line and stood around the person they were praying for, putting their hands on their head and shoulders. I noticed as I stood there that some people were falling down. This had been explained to me earlier and it was what they called 'being slain by the spirit', in other words the Holy Spirit had entered their bodies with such an impact that it floored them. Well. I thought. That ain't happening to me. Sod that

I'm not falling anywhere, done enough of that when I was drunk. So I put my right foot behind me and leaned on it. Before long Jim was facing me with some geezer who had preached the sermon. He was smiling at me and he asked what I had come forward for. I told him I wanted this Jesus in my life. He then asked me if I wanted to repent for my past sins, I said yeah but that could take all night and I wanted Jesus now. He smiled and asked, "Are you sorry for any hurt or wrong doing you have done in your life?" I said "Yes," and meant it.

He led me into what they call 'a sinner's prayer' and asked me to invite Jesus into my life. Having done this, he went to move away, but I didn't feel any different so I pulled him back and said, "Is that it? Am I in? Is there nothing else?" He replied, "Have you been anointed with oil?" I asked him if that was part of the deal. He replied, "You should be anointed". He then went and picked up a bottle that was next to the altar and coming back to me, he poured a drop on his finger and went to make the sign of the cross on my forehead. But before he had finished doing this I was flat out on the floor, filled with so much peace, love and power which was washing through my body. I have never felt anything like it before, no drug or drink I had taken had lifted me up into this realm. I stood on a mountain with the wind blowing through me, but not just any kind of wind this was indescribable, this was the Holy Spirit, so I'm told, full of power, love and peace washing me clean. I don't know how long I remained on that floor but I would have been happy to have stayed there all night. Eventually I got up and the first thing I realized was I had stopped shaking and I no longer had any paranoid thoughts inside my head. I was totally at peace. That night I slept in the cottage on the farm and was told the next day that I was laughing all night in my sleep.

I am going to write another book of how God took over my life and began to heal me, it was not an instant healing and I have had many falls but not once would I let go of neither God, nor him of me and slowly he led me from Alcohol to The Atacama.

I started this book with a quote from one of my hero's Fred Dibnah so it's only right and fitting to finish with another quote from Fred:

"Did you like that?"

Atacama Ahhh

The desert was long
Filled with joy, pain, and tear's
Along with my backpack I carried my fears
I wished it over before it had begun
And John Lennon sang 'here come's the sun'

The desert was long
I ran on with my past
Alcohol and drug binge's where coming up fast
The demon's in my head came out to taunt
You useless bastard they'd laugh and point

The desert was long
But I made it to day three
I smiled at the memory's that haunted me
The rehabs and hospital's barely able to walk
Friend's I'd buried I ran on thru the dark

The desert was long
My eyes took in the sights
Those mountainous sand dunes
Reminded me of my life's plight
The poverty and violence the belt lashed around my neck
But I was still standing yet not holding a full deck

The desert was long
Those salt flats a hard slog
I remember the cobbled streets
I walked as a boy wearing clogs
The fast flowing rivers
So cold and deep
And I was a kid
With no socks on my feet

The desert was long
But I had to run to time
I was raised a slave
So I bought the will to mind
No fuckin surrender said my brother Roy
I ran on as a man but inside a boy

The desert was over
The medal won
But I was empty and drained
No light in me son
I've been called many names
And done things I aint oughta
But I walked from alcohol
And ran the Atacama

Lightning Source UK Ltd.
Milton Keynes UK
UKOW04f2254111213

222869UK00001B/33/P